Adva

"When Jewish histo_____ _____ _____ _____ __ ___ _____
eth through the early decades of the twenty-first century
are written, there will be particularly dark chapters concerning the moral and Jewish demise of American Jewry.
In the 1960s, virtually every non-Orthodox synagogue
along with secular Jewish organizations began abandoning both Jewish and liberal moral values and replacing
them with the left-wing values of the universities and the
mainstream media. If academia and the *New York Times*
said there were more than two sexes, or that America
was a fundamentally racist country, that is what most
American Jews said. Even American Jewry's legendary
support for Zionism and Israel began to dissipate. By
the turn of the twenty-first century, the most pro-Israel
Americans were evangelical Christians, not Jews. To
cite one example of far too many, the Anti-Defamation
League, founded to combat antisemitism, now foments
more antisemitism than it combats. If you want to know
why and how this happened, this is the book to read. It is
also the book future historians will study to comprehend
the almost incomprehensible: how the Jews of the freest,
most opportunity-giving, and most pro-Jewish country in history came to align themselves with forces that
embraced anti-American values."

> —**Dennis Prager,** co-founder of Prager University
> (PragerU), the most viewed conservative video site
> in the world, and author of ten bestselling books,
> including three of a projected five-volume com-
> mentary on the Torah, *The Rational Bible*

"The authors of this courageous twenty-two essay collection show that the U.S. Jewish establishment consists of weak, politicized bureaucrats who 'seem more loyal to a progressive ideology than to the safety of Jews.' Covering topics ranging from theory (history and psychology) to gritty detail (Virginia and North Carolina case studies), *Betrayal* loudly rings the alarm for a somnolent American Jewry. Read it and wake others."

—**Daniel Pipes**, president of the Middle East Forum

"Today's America is scarred by ever-increasing anti-Semitism. It befouls the nation's colleges and universities, now seeps widely into K–12 education, has established an ugly foothold in our political institutions including the halls of Congress, permeates virtually all of social media, once more defiles our workplaces, and inexorably redounds in attacks, including physical assaults, on Jews and Jewish institutions. The glaring failure of most major Jewish organizations, particularly legacy bodies, to confront the assault and the threats, to mount a forceful campaign to fight the bigotry, is a scandal. That organizations and their leaders too often even embrace the Jew-haters, cultivating agendas that consign protection of the community to a low priority, amplifies the disgrace. The essays of the present volume offer vivid evidence of those failures and their dire ramifications for American Jews not only in threats unchecked but in threats intensified by the dereliction of feckless leaders.

It is a wake-up call that must be heard, internalized and acted on by American Jews if they hope to turn back the hate-mongering sweeping over them."

—**Kenneth Levin**, psychiatrist, historian, and author of *The Oslo Syndrome: Delusions of a People Under Siege*

"If you want to believe that all is well in the Jewish world…don't read this book. If you want to keep your faith in the Jewish legacy organizations and establishment leaders…don't read this book. If you want to bury your head in the sand and decide that America—and especially Woke America, which most Jews worship—is not changing and turning anti-Jewish and anti-Zionist, don't read this book. If, however, you think it's time for the American Jewish community, its organizations, and its leadership, to have an honest, challenging, vigorous debate about where we are going—and what mistakes we have made—then, indeed, read this important, illuminating, sometimes depressing, but ultimately inspiring, book."

—**Gil Troy**, distinguished scholar of North American history at McGill University and editor of the three-volume set *Theodor Herzl: Zionist Writings*

"With anti-Semitism on the rise and violence simmering, American Jews are frantically looking for leadership. Tragically, all too often they find muddled minds and moral cowardice, ossified institutions, and partisan affinities winning the day. Dr. Charles Jacobs and Avi Goldwasser have given us not only a maddening, stirring, and absolutely necessary record of this colossal communal failure, but also just the hopeful catalyst we need to start rebuilding amid the wreckage."

—**Liel Leibovitz**, editor-at-large
for *Tablet Magazine*

BETRAYAL

BETRAYAL

THE FAILURE OF AMERICAN JEWISH LEADERSHIP

Edited and Compiled by

CHARLES JACOBS
AND AVI GOLDWASSER

WICKED SON

A WICKED SON BOOK
An Imprint of Post Hill Press
ISBN: 978-1-63758-878-9
ISBN (eBook): 978-1-63758-879-6

Betrayal:
The Failure of American Jewish Leadership
© 2023 by Charles Jacobs and Avi Goldwasser
All Rights Reserved

Cover Design by Jim Villaflores

Post Hill Press
New York • Nashville
posthillpress.com

Published in the United States of America
1 2 3 4 5 6 7 8 9 10

DEDICATION

To Dr. Robert J. (Bob) Shillman who, with unmatched generosity, provides the needed ammunition (funding) to those who fight to defend and protect the Jewish people.

And to our dear friend and board member William R. (Bill) Sapers (*z"l*) who refused to remain silent when he discovered that the Jew-hating Muslim Brotherhood was constructing a mega-mosque in Boston, even when Boston's Jewish leaders preferred to ignore the growing threat.

ESSAYS

ACKNOWLEDGMENTS

This book is long overdue. The failure of the American Jewish establishment to counter the growing hostility toward the Jewish community is endangering Jews across the country.

This failure is scandalous. It is due to a lack of understanding of why Jews are hated and face growing hostility, along with the leaders' obvious lack of courage. At this time, when strong leadership is urgently needed, we have weak, politicized bureaucrats too often more concerned with their social status, the perks of power, and their organizations' financial success than with their responsibility to defend the community. As can be seen in their priorities, staffing, and programs, they seem more loyal to a progressive ideology than to the safety of Jews. Refusing to acknowledge the current ugly realities, they double down on failed strategies, hoping foolishly that increased effort will result in success.

Twelve of the twenty-two essays in this book first appeared in the remarkable online magazine the *White Rose*, published by veteran writer, cultural critic, and art curator Karen Lehrman Bloch. The magazine is named in honor of the anti-Nazi White Rose resistance movement, which published and distributed pamphlets calling for active opposition to the Nazi regime. The *White Rose* is an invaluable trumpet for inspiring classical liberalism and for exposing disguised illiberalism. This collection owes its existence to Karen's vision.

I want to thank Avi Goldwasser, my tireless partner in Jewish activism, for co-writing our essay which appears at the beginning of the book and frames the book's perspective. Our essay outlines the American Jewish predicament, which is the basis for our new organization, the Jewish Leadership Project.

We also wish to thank David Bernstein of Bombardier Books, of which Wicked Son is an imprint, for his guidance and for publishing this collection.

We wish to express our gratitude to each and every one of the authors who appear in this collection. Our essayists provide insightful answers to questions which must be addressed if we are to prevail against the cancerous growth of Jew-hatred in our time: Where and why did Jewish leadership go wrong? And, what is to be done? The Jewish community urgently needs to understand the magnitude of its leaders' failures. For too long, wealthy Jewish elites have successfully obscured and even censored the harsh truth.

We want to thank Ben Poser for his hours of careful work in proof-reading, researching, editing each essay (as well as providing the necessary citations), and co-authoring the book's epilogue.

Finally, I wish to thank my wife Jean, whose love and patience sustains me.

Charles Jacobs
December 20, 2022

INTRODUCTION

CHARLES JACOBS AND AVI GOLDWASSER

American Jewry is under siege, ideologically and physically. In the media, on college campuses, in the streets of major cities, even in high schools and in Congress, Jews and the Jewish state are smeared, hated, and attacked. Celebrities spew anti-Jewish ravings, including praise of Hitler and denial of the Holocaust, to tens of millions of followers. This is a new time for Jews in America.

Jews cannot control the forces arrayed against us, but one thing we should be able to do is influence our own leadership. It is clear that the establishment Jewish organizations—the Anti-Defamation League (ADL), the American Jewish Committee, the Conference of Presidents of Major American Jewish Organizations, regional Federations, Jewish Community Relations Councils across the country, Union for Reform Judaism, the Jewish Council for Public Affairs, and most rabbis—have failed to respond effectively to these mounting assaults.

The essays in this book explore the nature and extent of this failure by American Jewish leaders, including specific examples and an analysis of why Jewish leaders are failing in their mission to protect their communities.

This collection of essays is intended to publicly critique a failing Jewish establishment with the full understanding that many Jews view such rebuke as divisive and prefer to show unity. As a vulnerable minority, Jews have usually made public criticism of their leaders a near taboo. In recent decades, though, criticizing Jewish leaders has been acceptable, even common, when the target is "right-wing" Jews. Ironically, for too many American Jews, the democratically elected leaders of the Jewish state can be pilloried time and again, but the undemocratically, donor-selected leaders here may not be questioned as this would "break Jewish unity."

We believe that we have a duty to tell the Jewish community what we know from our decades' long experience witnessing the dangerous consequences of the Jewish establishment's policies, thinking, and actions. We know that many American Jews think as we do, and many of them are working hard to counteract the failures of our leaders.

We have spent the past decades fighting Jew-haters, but we no longer believe that the American Jewish community can prevail against a surge of anti-Semitism without the full resources of the Jewish community.

Many of these essays originally appeared in the May 2022 issue of the *White Rose* magazine.* With the expanded collection in this book, we hope to inspire many others to join us in challenging the current Jewish leadership to change course, and to encourage new leaders to muster the courage to defend American Jews.

Part I: Analysis

This book's first section describes the current predicament of America's Jews. We describe today's state of affairs and show how we got here. The liberalism of the past, which made long-standing Jewish communal policies sensible, has been replaced by a radical and insidious "progressive" ideology that has seduced most mainstream Jewish leaders (who are oblivious, too conflict-averse, or just cowardly) to think their way out of this trap.

In the opening essay we, **Charles Jacobs** and **Avi Goldwasser** (having spent more than two decades advocating for Israel and the American Jewish community), lay out our perspective on the enormity of Jewish leadership's failure. We describe from personal experience how, presented with irrefutable facts about vicious lies attacking Israel in the national media, the abuse of Jewish college students at Columbia University, terrorist-linked Muslim Brotherhood mosques in Boston, and anti-Semitic indoctrination in high school classrooms, Jewish leaders consistently responded by characterizing our concerns as exaggerated, or by explaining that they had other more important priorities, or by promising that this or that concern is something they would "handle" privately. The result: Problems, small at their beginnings, which were left unaddressed by the most powerful and well-funded Jewish establishment organizations, have metastasized and have brought us to the dangerous situation in which we now find ourselves.

We did not just criticize; we also set out a ten-point program which all serious Jewish leaders should adopt. The first step requires declaring a state of emergency (and includes forming coalitions with true friends), prioritizing Jewish communal resources for the protection of the community, and, most importantly, fighting back. "Not for the first time in Jewish history," we say, "are we at a watershed moment. But we are an accomplished community, with very talented individuals. We can and must find proud, brave, and competent leadership to secure a better Jewish future."

Jonathan S. Tobin explains how the ADL, the "Jewish Defense Department," politicized by its CEO, has utterly failed to protect the community. "Are donors to the Anti-Defamation League," he asks, "aware of what they are funding? Do they know that the organization created to fight prejudice and attacks against Jews is on the record supporting an ideology that grants a permission slip to anti-Semitism?"

Richard A. Landes analyzes the historical and psychosocial dynamics of failed leadership, highlighting how "universalist utopianism" and a "malignant moral narcissism" have blinded Jewish leadership. "For Jewish leaders," he writes, "the problem of how to deal with radical Muslims was particularly difficult since one of the most distinctive elements of the radicals' global jihadi wing was a virulent anti-Semitism." In many ways, this Islamic Jew-hatred is far more virulent than that of the Nazis, yet this massive, genocidal threat seems beyond the comprehension of our morally preening leaders.

Joshua Block pinpoints the specific moment in which American Jews were abandoned by the party they had called their home. After Representative Ilhan Omar (D-MN) and Representative Rashida Tlaib (D-MI) spewed anti-Semitic barbs at America's Jews, Democratic Party leader Nancy Pelosi was asked to specifically condemn them and their bigotry. Instead, the "Squad" was able to persuade Democrats in the House of Representatives to issue a resolution against "hate" in general, and "Islamophobia" in particular, which absolved Omar of any culpability. Block explains why this should be remembered as "American Jews' political Kristallnacht."

Rebecca Sugar, noting how Jewish leaders flee from the problem and manifestations of leftist anti-Semitism, asks if Jews are simply getting the leaders they deserve. "What most American Jews are really shocked by, but couldn't see until it became inescapably obvious, is the fast-growing, unabashed anti-Semitism of the American political left, where they themselves reside."

Caroline B. Glick posits that the concept of the "two-state solution" gutted and destroyed American Zionism. Having now replaced the Jewish people's right to a state as Israel's *raison d'être*, such a "solution" is both immoral and impossible, for it is based upon the lie that the ultimate responsibility for the Arab–Israeli conflict lies with Israel. While the facts on the ground have time and again exposed this thirty-year-old plan as delusional, its feel-good intentions have—to Israel's infinite detriment—led diaspora Jewish leadership to effectively re-define Zionism itself as support for this ultimately anti-Jewish fantasy.

Naya Lekht, Ph.D., an educator and activist, dives into de-Judaized, "woke" Jewish education's now-forgotten Stalinist roots. As Lekht demonstrates, corrupted Hebrew schools now churning out legions of anti-Israel socialists have not derived their educational philosophy from Judaism but, in fact, from *anti*-Jewish Soviet policy. Thinly clothing Marxist indoctrination in Jewish-sounding ideals of "social justice," these failed institutions knowingly or unknowingly subscribe to Stalin's concept of "socialist in content, national in form." By replacing Judaism with "social justice," leftist Jewish leaders have imported Stalin's policy of destroying Jewish peoplehood to America, and left brainwashed Jewish youngsters feeling that "Zionism," at best, "has fulfilled its purpose."

Richard L. Kronenfeld, Ph.D., shows how our leaders, blinded by feel-good altruism and addicted to virtue signaling, are siding with minorities whose hostility toward Jews and Israel they ignore or excuse. All done by "invoking a 16th century Kabbalistic concept, *tikkun olam*, literally 'healing/repairing the world,' thereby affording them a convenient way to escape the burden of being a Jew." Falsely equating Judaism with socialism, secular Jewish leaders embraced utopian ideologies and positions which made it impossible for them to tell friend from foe, and hijacked their heritage for partisan purposes.

Bruce D. Abramson, Ph.D., documents how American Jewish leadership institutions have failed because their priorities are antithetical to Jewish interests. Unmoored from the centering force of Judaism and Jewish particularism, leadership institutions—the ADL in particular—have instead invested their moral clout into fighting the enemies of the left, as opposed to the enemies of the Jews. "A Jewish community that assigns communal safety a low priority and Jewish distinctiveness an even lower one," he writes, "lacks self-respect. Perhaps, as a community that disrespects so much of our own distinctive traditions, we have the leadership we deserve."

Thane Rosenbaum writes that cowardice and comfort explain much of the failure. Holocaust-era leaders like Rabbi Stephen Wise were so ensconced in their quasi-aristocratic position as loyal New Deal Democrats that they valued their friendship with President Roosevelt over fighting to save Jews from the Nazis. "Leadership without exercising moral courage, without undertaking risks and performing selfless acts," he says, "is not leadership.... The grogger that is so grating on Purim is reserved, one night, for Haman, but never for Hamas."

Part II: Proof Points

The second part of this book presents on-the-ground descriptions of how American Jewish leadership has failed. Responding to anti-Semitic campus activism, delusional and utopian rabbinic dogma, and morally confused, cowering community "leaders," both experts and activists alike document the *tangible* cost of Jewish leadership's failure. They also suggest a way forward, and even, perhaps, hope for a new crop of Jewish leaders who will fight, and know how to fight, for the Jewish community.

Morton A. Klein, president of the Zionist Organization of America (ZOA), documents how America's mainstream Jewish organizations failed to arm or inoculate Jews with the simple, basic facts to counter the demonization of Israel. Israel does not occupy "Palestinian" land; the Palestinian Authority rewards the murderers of Jews with cash payments; the Palestinians opted for *jihad* rather than generous Israeli peace offers. This failure to teach and insist on such simple truths has brought American Jews nothing but contempt. Klein then exposes the ADL's failed strategy of relying on the most liberal Jewish groups to engage "soft critics" of Israel.

Alan M. Dershowitz, once one of the Jewish liberal establishment's most beloved speakers, explains how his former friends and political allies have used false charges against him and his legal defense of President Donald Trump to smear his name and discard one of the Jewish people's most masterful defenders. In fact, they have preferred *anti*-Zionists over "tainted" Zionists like Dershowitz. "Jewish leaders' first priority is to defend the community," he says. "This dark time of rising anti-Semitism and anti-Zionism must be a time of unity and fortitude, not petty partisanship or skittish kowtowing to the kangaroo court of public opinion."

Rabbi Cary Kozberg describes how he was forced to leave Reform Judaism, as it abandoned its own principles. He notes that today's Reform leaders have increasingly embraced the values and worldview of contemporary progressivism. The "big tent" which once accommodated diverse beliefs and approaches has morphed into a confining cement bunker of theological and political progressive orthodoxy. That orthodoxy has one objective: the promotion of "social justice," which no one seems able to define, rather than Judaism.

M. Zuhdi Jasser, a Reform Muslim leader, explains how the ADL and other leading Jewish institutions minimize or whitewash Islamist anti-Semitism and abandon legitimate Muslim reformers. "...[G]roups like the ADL," he writes, "have sat on the sidelines as American Islamist groups born out of the Muslim Brotherhood have radicalized American Muslims and poisoned the discourse against reformist groups like the Muslim Reform Movement."

William A. Jacobson and **Johanna E. Markind** show how defense-only strategies have lost the campuses. After taking over as ADL leader in 2015, Obama acolyte Jonathan Greenblatt doubled down on the ADL's leftist, universalist identity, while his condemnations of anti-Semitism on campus and off-campus have been mostly tepid. Under his stewardship, the organization largely ignored anti-Semitism from Black Lives Matter and other "politically incorrect" sources. By contrast, he has turned the ADL's ire on Jews and Jewish organizations which work to expose the anti-Semitism on campus, which it minimizes or ignores.

Rebecca G. Schgallis gives first-hand insight into the failure of the Jewish Community Relations Council (JCRC) of Fairfax County, Virginia. Faced with rampant anti-Israel indoctrination from the local school board—which included a Muslim Brotherhood-linked terrorism supporter—the JCRC prioritized its "relationships" with "victim groups" over its duty to protect its own community. Even worse, the JCRC urged the Jewish community to fall in line behind the teaching of critical race theory in the schools, which inevitably portrays Jews in a negative light—as aligned with and benefitting from "white privilege."

Karen D. Hurvitz reveals how the lame Boston JCRC strategy to shield the community from the K–12 anti-Semitic critical race theory movement is bound to fail. She points to the example of California, where the group responsible for the first radical, anti-Israel version of ethnic studies curriculum has bypassed the so-called guard rails that naïve Jewish organizations established. This group did so by forming relationships with many California school districts and have managed to persuade schools to use its original radical curriculum instead of the approved one.

Joanne Bregman shows that the JCRCs' national umbrella—the Jewish Council for Public Affairs (JCPA)—undermines the Jewish community by promoting "progressive" theology. In reality, it has become just another "woke" organization whose local branches' self-selected members abet its political activism.

Lauri B. Regan grants us an inside look into the leftist hijacking of the American Zionist Movement (AZM). Regan describes how her efforts to build an AZM committed to "fight[ing] the growing scourge of antisemitism, anti-Zionism, and Holocaust denial" were blocked by leftist groups, which eventually forced her out of the organization. "Cancel culture has arrived at the AZM," she writes. "I'm out. They're in."

Amy Rosenthal, M.D., and **Josh Ravitch** describe how, in the face of their local JCRC's cowardice, they fought and continue to fight against the anti-Israel Boycott, Divestment, and Sanctions (BDS) movement in North Carolina. The lesson is: "Where leadership is lacking, step up and lead. Our 'leaders' might actually follow."

Henry Srebrnik sketches the Jewish situation in Canada, which parallels that of American Jewry. In a nation that has been called the most socially welcoming, economically secure, pro-Israel, and religiously tolerant for diaspora Jews, past or present, the "progressive" revolution, plus mass immigration from anti-Jewish cultures, has turned things upside down. Jewish leaders there have also failed. Like their American counterparts during the Holocaust, Canadian Jewish leaders mostly cower in silence while their supposed allies in the Liberal government continuously betray them.

Charles Jacobs and **Ben Poser** focus the book's epilogue on the surging threat of black anti-Semitism. Louis Farrakhan's Jew-hatred has now spread to his celebrity acolytes like Kanye West and Kyrie Irving, and black Jew-hatred has caught fire, both online and in the streets. Yet, through it all, American Jewish leaders seem bewildered and paralyzed. The ADL, for political reasons, has for years chosen to mostly ignore Jew-hatred from non-white sources. The authors suggest why this is so, and why the ADL refuses to employ a unique and likely effective strategy to fight back.

The purpose of this book is to be a wake-up call for the American Jewish community to take action and hold our failing Jewish leaders and their patron donors accountable. At a time when Jews are under siege, the need for effective Jewish leadership is more urgent than ever.

---

* *White Rose Magazine*, Issue VIII (May 2022). https://whiterosemagazine. com/issue-008/.

PART I

ANALYSIS

1

THE JEWISH COMMUNITY CANNOT SURVIVE BETRAYAL BY ITS LEADERSHIP

CHARLES JACOBS AND AVI GOLDWASSER

"…[W]hat physicians say about consumptive illnesses is applicable here: that at the beginning, such an illness is easy to cure but difficult to diagnose; but as time passes, not having been recognized or treated at the outset, it becomes easy to diagnose but difficult to cure."[1]
—Niccolò Machiavelli, *The Prince*

This is not the country we grew up in. The Jewish community is under siege. According to the FBI, Jews are the primary targets of hate crimes in America. An analysis of FBI reports reveals that a Jewish person is twice as likely to be a victim of a hate crime as a black person or a Muslim, ten times more likely than an Asian or a Latino, and twenty times more likely than a non-Hispanic white person.[2]

Jews are being beaten in the streets of New York City, murdered in Pittsburgh, San Diego, and Jersey City, stabbed in Boston, taken hostage in Texas, and harassed and bullied on college campuses across the country. In more than a few places, Jews live with rising anxiety. Most Jewish community buildings require security. Israel, the Jewish state, is defamed and demonized by the mainstream media, and maligned in both the U.S. Congress and the United Nations, as anti-Zionism becomes the new anti-Semitism.

Hostility toward American Jews continues to grow. In March of 2022, the NYPD reported that anti-Semitic hate crimes in New York City were up 409 percent.[3] A recent American Jewish Committee (AJC) poll found that four in ten Jews avoid making themselves identifiable as Jews, avoid going to Jewish events, or refrain from posting Jewish-related content online.[4] Ninety percent of Jews think anti-Semitism is a problem in America.[5]

In what seems like a perfect storm, Jews face assaults simultaneously from four major ideological camps: (1) Lethal white nationalists attack Jews in the name of white supremacy, blaming them for supporting multiculturalism and rising Third World immigration. (2) Radical black nationalists—including Farrakhan-following celebrities,[6] academics, and politicians—attack Jews in the name of black liberation and "equity." (3) Radical progressives and segments of the Democratic Party promote the genocide-enabling Boycott, Divestment, and Sanctions (BDS) movement and anti-Jewish critical race theory, inciting an ideological assault on Israel and Jews in the name of "social justice" and Palestinian nationalism. This new assault is a kind of "virtuous Jew-hatred," socially acceptable and even fashionable, not easily countered by facts, logic, or reason. (4) Finally, far too many Muslims, many from anti-Semitic cultures, embody an ancient religious hatred (the Jews rejected Muhammad) and are further inflamed by their tribal support of Palestinians. Islamic anti-Israel movements are funded by petrodollars mostly from Qatar and Saudi Arabia. Dozens of imams in American mosques can be seen in videos preaching incitement and hatred of Jews.[7] Muslims have attacked Jews on America's streets.[8]

The ongoing demonization of Jews in the media, on college campuses, in Congress, and (most recently) in K–12 education, is ominous, reminiscent of the Nazis' initial measures to render Jews less than human. History does not offer many examples where rising anti-Semitism resolved itself peacefully. Rabbi Abraham Joshua Heschel, as his daughter Susannah remembered, often taught that the Holocaust "did not begin with the building of the crematoria," but with the "defamation" of the Jews.[9]

The animus behind these tribal, theological, and ideological assaults did not suddenly appear but has been openly building over decades. The resulting crescendo of hate was predictable, but the "red flags" were mostly rationalized away, minimized, or ignored by most mainstream Jewish leaders. Based on their actions and priorities, Jewish leaders seem to prefer to devote precious Jewish resources to virtue-signaling activities for mostly non-Jewish causes.[10] Within the establishment Jewish leadership, the Zionist Organization of America (ZOA) has been the lone, unfaltering exception.

The abolitionist leader Frederick Douglass understood the consequences of failed leadership. He said: "Find out just what any people will quietly submit to and you have found out the exact measure of injustice and wrong which will be imposed upon them…."[11]

There are many reasons for the current Jewish predicament. Many are not within our control, but one thing truly ought to be: Jewish leadership.

The simple truth is that those Jewish establishment organizations whose mission is the defense and well-being of the Jewish community—the ADL, the AJC, the Federations, and the networks of JCRCs—are failing to protect American Jewry. The leadership seems both ideologically conflicted and conflict-averse. Most significantly, our leaders and their major donors are not being held accountable for these failures. After decades of Jewish success in American society, Jewish leaders have grown complacent—or perhaps corrupted by our good fortune. Today, most of our Jewish leaders and their major donors are part of the economic elite and are not directly affected by the rising hatred and violence. Self-indulgent and sometimes arrogant, they suppress dissenting voices and diverse opinions. They often seem more occupied by their social standing than demonstrating real concern for the Jewish community.

In a nutshell, Jewish establishment leaders are stuck in a comfortable, older strategic paradigm. For decades, they promoted policies that allied Jews with blacks, and then with other disadvantaged minorities, in their struggles for civil and equal rights. They justified these policies, and the resulting outlay of precious Jewish resources, not only as consistent with Jewish values but also as protective of the community. The assumption was that our compassion and magnanimity toward others would reveal our goodness to all, and thus engender reciprocity and solidarity from these groups. Ignoring tribal self-interest and projecting their Jewish values onto their "allies," Jewish leaders pursued a naïve and simplistic strategy: "We will help them and they will support us." Predictably, they were wrong.

Not surprisingly, there was no reciprocity and no solidarity. With very few exceptions, physical and ideological attacks on Jews did not elicit the expected condemnations of anti-Semitism from their alleged allies. Our leaders seem to have missed the dramatic shift in America's cultural and political landscape, which has taken place over the past several decades. The liberalism of the past that made long-standing Jewish policies sensible has been replaced by a radical and insidious ideology, one that resembles a theology.[12] "Post-modernism" and "progressivism," whose adherents are called "woke," label Jews as "privileged white oppressors." This ideology has captured and energized the progressive Left. It has also infected too many Jews seeking mainstream acceptance and an escape from the burden of being Jewish.

Not only do Jewish leaders seem willfully blind to this mass cultural change, they seem oblivious to the damage they cause by their stubborn refusal to be "mugged by reality." One shameful consequence: They fail to react with passion against attacks on Jews from their imagined ideological partners. Like "generals fighting the last war," they cling to a more comfortable misunderstanding of the threat by focusing mainly on the extremist right, the small gangs of violent thugs who have minimal support compared to the vast influence of major media, college campuses, Islamists, and "progressive" politicians. So, they simply see Nazis everywhere. They have painted themselves, and us, into a corner. Even more ominous in the long term is the failure of Jewish leaders to stop the drift of Jewish youth, educators, and even our rabbis away from Judaism to progressive ideologies, which are most often anti-Zionist. Young Jews are not educated to understand Jewish peoplehood and that being Jewish means more than being observant. It's being part of the long history of the Judean people with a unique and amazing culture.

When challenged about this new reality—in which the reigning ideology of their "allies" divides America into oppressors and oppressed and consigns Jews to the former class—Jewish leaders often seem to be in outright denial. Some will grudgingly acknowledge the problem, but we have seen none who show a willingness to consider the need for a serious rethink, a new strategy. Mostly, Jewish leaders are doubling down on their failed policies or going through the motions of "rethinking" by organizing taskforces and committees. Most important, there is little evidence that our leaders or donors are being held accountable for their massive negligence and failure.

Several strategic leadership failures have severe long-term consequences for the community. These must be addressed immediately.

Failing to Stop Demonization of Jews in the Media When the Problem Was Still Limited

This failure to address the demonization of Israel in the media, which now extends to most of the mainstream media, meant that Jewish leaders, especially the ADL—the so-called Jewish Defense Department—failed to understand that the ideological assault on the Jewish state was the "new anti-Semitism." Anti-Zionism made Jew-hatred culturally and socially acceptable under the guise of human rights and free speech. Every major Jewish legacy organization, except for the ZOA, failed to see the long-term consequences, and thus refused to expose and combat it.

In 1989, as *The Boston Globe* was bashing the Jewish state on practically a daily basis,[13] Andrea Levin and Charles Jacobs contemplated forming a media watchdog group to expose and combat media bias against Israel. As they were forming the Boston branch of the Committee for Accuracy in Middle East Reporting and Analysis (CAMERA), they were asked by New England's ADL representative, Lenny Zakim (of blessed memory), and by the former leader of the American Israel Public Affairs Committee (AIPAC), Steve Grossman, to let the ADL undertake this task instead. Zakim and Grossman argued that since the ADL spoke with the voice of the Jewish people, if Abe Foxman, the ADL's legendary head at the time, explained to the public that the media was lying about the Jewish people, it would be more powerful than if a new start-up did so. But Foxman declined without any explanation. What was lost on him, and on the Jewish establishment, was the strategic significance of how the media and other key public and cultural institutions influence our political leaders and the general public. This was an historic blunder.

Failing to Stop Demonization, Harassment, Intimidation, and Exclusion of Jews on Campus When the Problem Was Still Limited

In 2003, we were asked by Jewish students at Columbia University to help them to deal with anti-Israel professors who were harassing and intimidating Jewish pro-Israel students. Nobody in leadership positions in New York City, the most populous Jewish city in the world, would help the students: not the Jewish professors, not Hillel, not the ADL, not the Federation, not the AJC.

Our 2004 documentary, *Columbia Unbecoming*, recorded the abuse of Jewish students and the failure of the university to stop the abuse.[14] The documentary received major press coverage, including TV news reports.[15] For the first time, many in the Jewish community learned about the hostility that Jewish students face. Sadly, the events at Columbia failed to mobilize the Jewish establishment. They told us the problem was not so bad and that bringing attention to it would only make it worse. They preferred to handle the situation quietly, with the university administration, behind closed doors. They told us to go away, and let them handle the matter, implying that we were intruding on their turf. David Harris told us that his AJC only does diplomacy and would not get involved on campus. Now, twenty years later, many of the anti-Israel diplomats and politicians the AJC must confront have been "Palestinianized" on campus. The vacuum created by failed Jewish leadership resulted in grassroots campaigns to support Jewish students, including by the David Project, the ZOA, StandWithUs, CAMERA on Campus, Aish ha-Torah, Students Supporting Israel, and others.

We hoped that *Columbia Unbecoming* would awaken Jewish leadership and the public to anti-Semitism masked as anti-Zionism. It mostly failed to accomplish this goal. Only in 2021 did the ADL finally acknowledge the campus problem.[16] Failing to deal effectively with Columbia University's egregious behavior emboldened the Jew-hating radicals. There are now dozens of "unbecoming" (that is, hostile) universities. As with an untreated infection, the poison has spread aggressively.[17]

Lack of action by Jewish leadership has contributed to the fact that 50 percent of Jews on American college campuses now feel that "they must hide who they are out of fear," according to a recent AJC poll.[18] This failure to address the hostility on campus has allowed the metastasis of a malignant academic culture that has led to the takeover of departments of Middle East Studies by radical anti-Semites, the growth of Students for Justice in Palestine promoting the BDS movement, the infiltration and corruption of Jewish Studies programs, and the exclusion of Jewish students from fully participating in campus activities.

Failing to Stop anti-Israel Education in High Schools Now Exploding Across the Nation via Ethnic Studies Curricula and Critical Race Theory

Leveraging their campus successes, anti-Zionists then extended their efforts to K–12 education with funding from Saudi Arabia, Qatar, and progressive U.S. think tanks. In 2011, informed by parents, we discovered that a Saudi-funded text—*The Arab World Studies Notebook*—was being used as a history text in high schools in Newton, Massachusetts.[19] The *Notebook* was part of a curriculum taught to teachers across America by an anti-Israel Arab organization. Newton teachers were trained at an event sponsored by the anti-Israel Harvard Center for Middle Eastern Studies. The Center's director, Paul Beran, an anti-Israel activist for several years, was an organizer of BDS campaigns against Israel.[20] One "lesson" used the Hamas Charter as a primary source, but the Newton version of the Charter was doctored.[21] It erased the original language that called for the murder of every Jew on the planet, by substituting the word "Zionists" for Jews. The teachers' guide explained that the unit's purpose was to show the conflict as a resolvable land and border dispute and not a complicated religious conflict. A grassroots effort to find out what else was being taught in the schools was stymied when school administrators rejected transparency and refused to make their teaching materials public. None of the established Jewish organizations in Boston would help us. In fact, they supported the school committee, claiming that we were exaggerating.[22] To date, the curriculum is still not public.[23] More recently, with the introduction of California's "ethnic studies" curriculum, the assault on Jews and Israel has become turbo-charged. Most of Boston's Jewish establishment leaders are being co-opted with vague promises of phantom "guardrails" to prevent anti-Jewish or anti-Israel indoctrination.[24] Again, gullible or delusional Jewish leadership is failing to protect the community as the next generation of Americans is being groomed for hostility toward Jews. This situation is being made far worse with the widespread introduction of critical race theory and "ethnic studies," which reject merit in favor of tribal quotas and identity politics.[25] Historically, Jewish success was based on merit while Jewish exclusion was based on quotas. Many Jewish leaders feel trapped by the conflict between their universalist and utopian impulses and their fiduciary responsibility to the Jewish community.

Failing to Recognize the Long-Term Threat of the Growing Radicalization of the American Muslim Community

Jewish leaders enamored of, and relieved by, simplistic feel-good solutions to complex social problems preached the gospel of interfaith dialogue as the magic formula for resolving tribal conflicts. In 2003, *The Boston Herald* reported that Muslims tied to terrorism were planning to build a mega-mosque in the Boston suburb of Roxbury.[26] Included on the mosque's board was the late "spiritual leader" of the terrorist Muslim Brotherhood,[27] Yusuf al-Qaradhawi,[28] whose preaching—easily accessed online—calls for the murder of Jews[29] and gays[30] worldwide. Based on internal mosque documents we obtained, it was clear that the goal of the mosque's owners was to radicalize the historically moderate Boston Muslim community, as well as proselytize in Boston's black community where the mosque was to be located. Concerned with these developments, we organized a meeting of Boston Jewish leaders, including executives of Boston's Federation, the Combined Jewish Philanthropies (CJP), the ADL, the AJC, and the local JCRC. We presented evidence on the ownership and control of the mosque, its hateful ideology, and its connections to terror groups. The Jewish leaders, displaying a significant deficit of imagination and courage, believed that the only proper response was to engage more intensely in interfaith dialogue.

"What else can we do?" they asked. They refused to consider educating the Jews and the public about the threat posed by radical

Islam. We urged them to share what they knew about the funders and officials of the mosque with Boston's well-intentioned but naïve mayor or with Massachusetts' governor. They refused. They refused to use their political capital on this matter. By 2015, more than a dozen congregants of both of the Islamic Society of Boston's mosques—one in Roxbury, one in Cambridge—were in jail, deported, on the run, or dead from their connections to terrorism.[31] This includes the Boston Marathon bombers, who were part-time congregants at the Cambridge mosque.

The Jewish leaders were not influenced by hard evidence, such as copies of checks from terror groups to the mosques or from the mosques to the terror groups.[32] We showed them anti-Semitic writings, sermons, and videos of anti-Semitic harangues. We showed them instructions on the mosque's website on how husbands, displeased by their wives' conduct, should beat them.[33] Nothing, it seemed, would cause them to deviate from their comforting dogmatic beliefs that "mutual understanding" and dialogue would mitigate any threat. They also refused to learn the lessons of Muslim migration to Europe and its resulting violence against Jews. They were more concerned with offending a "vulnerable minority" than with the long-term safety of their own community. Their mantra was, "If we are nice to them, they will be nice to us." Facts be damned.

What Is to Be Done?

Most mainstream Jewish leaders are promoting universalist fantasies—but to bring "kumbaya" to the arena of identity politics is to unilaterally disarm.[34]

On these matters, our leaders prefer not to "follow the evolutionary science," which teaches that tribes are more likely to seek dominance than equality. Tribes are formed to provide protection to their members, and depend on strong leaders for survival. Tribes are not guided by global moral principles and ethics, such as compassion or reciprocity. Instead, they are motivated by concrete tribal interests. Our Jewish leaders have projected their own values and ethics onto other groups, ignoring the reality that politics and warfare have always been about tribal power conflict. Many European Jews hoped that the "international community" would save them from the Nazis. Today, many American Jewish leaders place their bets on "allies" whom they mistake for partners.[35] They failed to learn the clearest lesson of history: No one will fight to protect the Jews but the Jews.

For decades, we have been fighting our external enemies: the biased media, the professoriate, the weak-kneed college administrators, leftist anti-Zionists, high schools with poisoned lesson plans, Muslim anti-Semites, and followers of Louis Farrakhan. We have finally concluded that the Jewish community cannot prevail against this organized rolling tsunami of hatred with the existing misguided establishment leaders who lack courage and imagination and are beholden to a progressive ideology that limits their range of effective actions.

It's well known that Jewish leaders are not elected but are anointed by wealthy donors, who are often part of the country's ruling elites. They are conflicted between their fiduciary responsibilities to the community, their progressive ideology, and how their actions may negatively affect their social standing. They are often forced to rationalize why their efforts to maintain the status quo and their personal power are actually good-faith attempts to live up to their responsibilities to fellow Jews.[36]

It's irrational to continue with the current policies and leaders and to expect different results. For the benefit of the community, Jewish leaders must acknowledge their failure—and not just privately. Many Jewish leaders—however morally confused, delusional, utopian, or in denial of the painful realities—believe that they are well-intentioned people. Given the recent upsurge in anti-Semitism, however, and the rebranding of Jews as adjacent white oppressors, one can only hope that they are (internally at least) going through a reassessment of the root causes of their failures, without which new strategies cannot be developed. Forming committees is not the answer. Leadership is about having a vision as well as the ability to inspire people to act on that vision. It is possible but unlikely that the same leaders who got us into this crisis are capable of getting us out of it.

Jewish leaders need fresh ideas. The Jewish community needs to engage in open discussions by encouraging broad community participation in addressing the crisis Jews are facing.

To help to promote this process we are forming a national network of Jewish community activists, many of whom have been generally ignored, canceled, or suppressed by the Jewish establishment. These activists are interested in promoting creative new strategies for their communities by challenging local Jewish leadership—their rabbis, local Federations, the ADL, AJC, and the JCRCs—to break out of their failed ideological straitjackets and explore new thinking. To help to organize such a network, we have created a new initiative: the Jewish Leadership Project.[37]

Given today's realities, we urge Jewish leadership to take the following ten actions:

1. Immediately declare a state of emergency and mobilize the community.
2. Increase physical security to protect Jews, not just Jewish institutions.

3. Prioritize Jewish communal resources for the protection of the community.

4. Educate the public about the nature of today's anti-Semitism, and deconstruct poisonous academic and social theories which demonize and marginalize Jews.

5. Rethink Holocaust education and make it relevant to contemporary Jew-hatred.

6. Educate Jewish youth about the threat to their future.

7. Make Jewish religious education affordable.

8. Build alliances based on mutual interests and honest reciprocity.

9. Experiment with alternative solutions to find out what is effective.

10. Develop a new leadership class which is willing to fight for the community.

Not for the first time in Jewish history are we at a watershed moment. But we are an accomplished community with very talented individuals. We can and must find proud, brave, and competent leadership to secure a Jewish future.

Charles Jacobs has, over four decades, founded, co-founded, and led several Jewish and human rights organizations, including the American Anti-Slavery Group, the David Project, Americans for Peace and Tolerance, and the Boston branch of the Committee for Accuracy in Middle East Reporting and Analysis (CAMERA). In 2000, he received Boston's Freedom Award from Coretta Scott King for his work in helping to liberate thousands of black slaves in Sudan.[38] In 2007, The Forward named him as among America's top fifty Jewish leaders.[39] He holds a doctorate in Education from Harvard University. Today, Charles and Avi Goldwasser lead the Jewish Leadership Project.

Avi Goldwasser is a social activist and film producer. He is a co-founder of the David Project, which was established to support Jewish students on campuses. He has served on the board of directors of several Jewish organizations including the Boston branch of the American Jewish Committee (AJC), the Boston Jewish Community Relations Council (JCRC), and Bureau of Jewish Education (BJE). *Goldwasser has produced several acclaimed films, including the award-winning documentary* The Forgotten Refugees *(2004),*[40] The J Street Challenge: The Seductive Allure of Peace in Our Time *(2014),*[41] *and several campus-related films including* Columbia Unbecoming *(2004)*[42] *and* Hate Spaces: The Politics of Intolerance on Campus *(2016).*[43]

---

[1] Niccolò Machiavelli, *The Prince*, ed. and trans. Peter Bondanella (Oxford: Oxford World Classics, 2005), p. 12.

[2] See George Flesh, "Anti-Semitism: The numbers don't lie," *JNS*, January 21, 2022. https://bit.ly/3DCafoF.

[3] David Israel, "NYPD: Hate Crimes Against Jews Up 409%," *The Jewish Press*, March 9, 2022. https://bit.ly/3dpIyEO.

[4] "The State of Antisemitism in America 2021: AJC's Survey of American Jews," *American Jewish Committee*. https://bit.ly/3DCcd8s.

[5] Aaron Bandler, "New AJC Survey: Rise in Fear Among American Jews," *The Jewish Journal*, October 26, 2021. https://bit.ly/3qSYnXY.

[6] See Epilogue.

[7] Mohammed al-Adzee, "Antisemitism In Sermons In U.S. Mosques," *Middle East Media Research Institute*, November 8, 2021. https://bit.ly/3Lvrkm3.

[8] Ryan Saavedra, "Jews Attacked On Streets Of New York City, In Restaurant By Alleged Pro-Palestinian Extremists: Reports," *The Daily Wire*, May 21, 2021. https://bit.ly/3RYoWXk.

[9] Susannah Heschel, ed., introduction to Rabbi Abraham Joshua Heschel, *Moral Grandeur and Spiritual Audacity* (New York, NY: Noonday Press, 1997), p. viii.

[10] See "Criminal Justice Reform Principles," *Jewish Community Relations Council of Boston*, September 12, 2020. https://bit.ly/3SjXS4W.

[11] "'The Significance of Emancipation in the West Indies' (1857)," in *The Portable Frederick Douglass*, ed. John Stauffer and Henry Louis Gates, Jr. (London: Penguin Books, 2016), p. 288.

[12] See Dennis Prager, "Explaining the Left, Part III: Leftism as Secular Religion," *DennisPrager.com*, August 28, 2018. https://bit.ly/3C2FUyB.

[13] See, for example, the Associated Press, "Israelis convict blind Palestinian," *The Boston Globe*, October 28, 1986. https://bit.ly/3FqYSR2. "LOD, Israel—A blind Palestinian who had been freed from prison in a 1985 prisoner exchange was sentenced to life imprisonment yesterday after being convicted of masterminding several terrorist attacks in Jerusalem. The man, Allah Eldin Bazian, was sentenced by an Israeli military court. The prosecutor said Bazian was the leader of a seven-man guerrilla group that killed an Israeli woman and a British tourist in April and wounded a visitor from Germany earlier this year. Bazian, 22, of Jerusalem *was blinded while preparing a bomb in 1979.* (AP)" [Emphasis added]

[14] See apeacet. "Columbia Unbecoming (2004)." Filmed 2004. YouTube video, 37:00. Posted July 19, 2020. https://bit.ly/37te7bB.

[15] See apeacet. "Columbia University in the News." Filmed 2004. YouTube video, 4:21. Posted October 4, 2018. https://bit.ly/3xyoPKc.

[16] "One-Third of Jewish Students Experienced Antisemitism on College Campuses in Last School Year, New Survey Finds," *Anti-Defamation League*, October 25, 2021. https://bit.ly/3dyFR3M.

[17] Tal Fortgang, "To the Antisemites Who Sit Next to Me at School," *Common Sense*, April 24, 2022. https://bit.ly/3DCSuFC.

[18] "AJC Policy: Countering Antisemitism and Confronting Hatred at Home and Abroad," *American Jewish Committee*, January 2022. https://bit.ly/3Slgy4h.

[19] Dr. Richard L. Cravatts, "High School History Stacked Against Israel—in the USA," *Israel National News*, November 28, 2011. https://bit.ly/3SioJxY.

[20] Steven Stotsky, "Harvard's Middle East Outreach Center Headed by BDS Supporter," *Committee for Accuracy in Middle East Reporting and Analysis*, December 13, 2011. https://bit.ly/3BUhbMP.

[21] See apeacet. "Anti-Israel Indoctrination @ Newton High." Filmed 2016. YouTube video, 20:12. Posted April 7, 2016. https://bit.ly/3QUCLoE. The relevant portion begins at 9:15.

[22] Jacob Kamaras, "ADL downplays controversy over anti-Israel texts in curriculum of Newton, Mass.," *JNS*, April 15, 2013. https://bit.ly/3BtVzFB.

[23] See Stotsky, *Indoctrinating Our Youth: How a U.S. Public School Curriculum Skews the Arab-Israeli Conflict and Islam* (Boston, MA: Committee

for Accuracy in Middle East Reporting in America, 2017). https://bit.ly/3BxBYV3.

24 Karen D. Hurvitz, "US Jewish leaders asleep in the face of anti-Israel school curricula," *JNS*, February 28, 2022. https://bit.ly/3dyGXwq.

25 Pamela Paresky and Lee Jussim, "Why No One Should Accept a 'Critical Ethnic Studies' Curriculum. Least of All, Jews," *The Jewish Journal*, January 27, 2021. https://bit.ly/3RYTGHP.

26 Jonathan Wells, Jack Meyers, Maggie Mulvihill, and Kevin Wisniewski, "Radical Islam: Outspoken cleric, jailed activist tied to new Hub mosque," *The Boston Herald*, October 28, 2003. https://bit.ly/3LoV6cl.

27 See Discover the Networks, "Muslim Brotherhood (MB)," *The David Horowitz Freedom Center*. http://bit.ly/34waTS6. See also Tony Duheaume, "ANALYSIS: The Nazi roots of Muslim Brotherhood," *Al-Arabiyah*, June 27, 2018. http://bit.ly/2WsNlt6.

28 See Discover the Networks, "Sheikh Yusuf Al-Qaradawi," *The David Horowitz Freedom Center*. http://bit.ly/3VaEIzM.

29 "Sheik Yousuf Al-Qaradhawi: Allah Imposed Hitler upon the Jews to Punish Them—'Allah Willing, the Next Time Will Be at the Hand of the Believers,'" *Middle East Media Research Institute*, January 28, 2009. https://bit.ly/3Brtz5u.

30 "Sheik Yousuf Al-Qaradhawi: Homosexuals Should Be Punished Like Fornicators But Their Harm Is Less When Not Done in Public," *Middle East Media Research Institute*, June 5, 2006. https://bit.ly/3SizdNS.

31 See Americans for Peace and Tolerance, *The Case Against the Islamic Society of Boston* (Boston, MA: Americans for Peace and Tolerance, April 2016), pp. 23–25. https://bit.ly/3R1wqrf.

32 *Ibid.*, pp. 26–30.

33 *Ibid.*, p. 34.

34 See https://www.noplaceforhate.org/.

35 See Brooke Singman, "Controversial Islamic center hosts interfaith call for peace, despite terror ties," *Fox News*, December 10, 2016. https://bit.ly/3QW28WY.

36 See Jonathan S. Tobin, "For Jewish Federations, is there such a thing as a Jewish priority?", *JNS*, February 22, 2022. https://bit.ly/3UriAlg.

37 For more information, go to www.jewishleadershipproject.org.

38 See American Anti-Slavery Group. "CBS WBZ 4 News New England: Dr. Charles Jacobs (September 24, 2000)." Filmed September 24, 2000. YouTube video, 6:55. Posted June 28, 2019. https://bit.ly/3D8VWXZ.

39 "*Forward* 50, 2007," *The Forward*, November 2007. Archived January 8, 2009. https://bit.ly/3CLR3UA.

40 See Israel's Voice. "The Forgotten Refugees Full Documentary Movie." Filmed 2004. YouTube video, 49:01. Posted December 19, 2014. https://bit.ly/3Sbb5w7.

41 See apeacet. "The J Street Challenge (Full Film in HD)." Filmed 2014. YouTube video, 1:04:27. Posted March 23, 2015. http://bit.ly/41clAnR.

42 See apeacet. "Columbia Unbecoming (2004)."

43 See apeacet. "Hate Spaces: The Politics of Intolerance on Campus (45-Minute Version)." Filmed 2016. YouTube video, 46:35. Posted July 30, 2018. https://bit.ly/3VCJDdN.

2

THE ADL IS UNDERMINING THE BATTLE AGAINST ANTI-SEMITISM

JONATHAN S. TOBIN

A re donors to the ADL aware of what they are funding?

Do they know that the organization created to fight prejudice and attacks against Jews is on the record supporting an ideology that grants a permission slip to anti-Semitism?

Do they know that the group still considered to be the gold standard for monitoring hate crimes is promoting the notion that Jews should be divided along racial lines—an explicit acceptance of radical theories that categorize Jews and the State of Israel as a function of "white privilege"?

Do they know that the organization committed to support Israel has, in recent years, often joined with those sniping at it and hired vicious critics of the Jewish state as staff members, such as Tema Smith?[1]

Do they know that a group that prided itself on nonpartisanship and building bipartisan coalitions against anti-Semitism has cast those principles to the winds and become part of America's political tribal wars?

Do they know that the organization that always considered defense of civil liberties essential to its mission has now joined hands with Big Tech companies to promote censorship of ideas and organizations?

Perhaps many of those still pouring money into the ADL's coffers are aware of all this and are supportive of the sea change in the organization. The abandonment of core principles and its job of defending Jews places the ADL on the same side of those it is pledged to fight. This is one more casualty of the shift in culture that has produced toxic divisions tearing apart the fabric of American society.

Most of the many American Jewish organizations and institutions founded in the early twentieth century have long since become obsolete. The Jewish hospitals created to find places for unhired Jewish doctors and the Jewish country clubs established to compete with the exclusionary non-Jewish facilities have long since become secular once those barriers evaporated.

Many national organizations that once were considered essential platforms for speaking up for a beleaguered community are now mere shadows of themselves as they struggle to find a purpose as their constituencies changed or disappeared altogether.

But there is one national Jewish institution that not only still has a job but arguably is faced with an even more daunting task and bigger responsibilities than it did when it first opened its doors: the ADL.

Outraged over the anti-Semitic hate that fueled both the wrongful murder conviction of Atlanta businessman Leo Frank and his subsequent lynching in 1915, the B'nai B'rith organization established the ADL to deal specifically with the plague of anti-Semitism. The daunting challenges of a century ago—in the form of hate sponsored by auto magnate Henry Ford or populist preachers directly invoking age-old stereotypes about Jewish "aliens" and "power brokers"— have evolved to reach even wider audiences on the Internet. The delegitimization of the Jews and the Jewish state is louder than ever and has now become a feature of the increasingly influential left wing of the Democratic Party, which has embraced radical notions, such as "intersectionality" and critical race theory, opening the door to anti-Semitism.

That makes the ADL, which has become not only independent of its initial sponsor, but an organizational powerhouse with a massive fundraising machine, more important than ever. Its infrastructure of regional offices and large staff perform the task of monitoring acts of anti-Semitism at a time when attacks on Jews are not only on the rise but essentially mainstreamed under the guise of "criticism" of Israel. As open calls for Israel's destruction and the stigmatizing of its supporters as racists and oppressors have become commonplace, an effective Jewish defense organization with the clout of the ADL ought to be a vital tool in combating this problem.

But the ADL is failing.

That failure can't be measured financially, since the ADL is raising more money than ever before. Nor is it a communication problem, as the ADL retains its status as a go-to source for comments about Jewish issues as well as the ultimate arbiter in determining what constitutes anti-Semitism.

Yet, its failure is palpable.

Ever since its current CEO, Jonathan Greenblatt, succeeded longtime head Abe Foxman in 2015, the former Clinton and Obama administration staffer has largely discarded the group's non-partisan stance. Greenblatt has effectively turned it into just one more partisan advocacy group supporting Democratic Party talking points on a variety of issues, including those that have little or nothing to do with the defense of Jewish interests. As his grip on the organization solidified, the ADL also became an ally of ideologically driven Big Tech firms seeking to enforce Internet censorship. In this way, the ADL has fallen far short of the needs of an increasingly embattled Jewish community.

As worrisome as those actions are, the problem has grown even worse in recent years. The ADL's prioritization of its ties with left-wing allies has also led to decisions that not only undermine its core mission, such as the sanctioning of partisan weaponizing of the issue of anti-Semitism, but its willingness to endorse ideas that enable anti-Semitism and the delegitimization of Jews and Israel has, incredibly, placed it in the position of aiding and abetting the very forces it was created to oppose. As a result, it is not simply an example of failing Jewish leadership, it is a group that now must be considered increasingly part of the problem rather than the solution to the dilemmas faced by American Jewry.

The organization that Greenblatt inherited from Foxman (the ADL's venerable leader who worked for the group for fifty years and led it for twenty-eight) was politically liberal on many issues, but scrupulously non-partisan. Although the ADL had long since branched out into the business of educating communities on the dangers of all sorts of prejudice, it was still focused on its primary mission of combating anti-Semitism, including that which is directed at the Jewish state.

Greenblatt immediately began re-orienting the organization to be more directly in line with his own partisan instincts. He had previously been a staff member of the Barack Obama White House, which was itself embroiled in a number of disputes with Israel and the Jewish community. President Obama's determination to pursue a policy of appeasement toward Iran and its nuclear ambitions placed him in conflict with Israel—which viewed Tehran as an existential threat—and put him at odds with American Jews and certain members of Congress, who agreed with former Israeli Prime Minister Benjamin Netanyahu's opinion about the disastrous nature of the nuclear deal. In seeking to dismiss those arguments, Obama and his staff—including those who were orchestrating what former national security advisor Ben Rhodes called their media "echo chamber"[2]—were at pains to spin the debate as one between a president pursuing his nation's interests and a powerful lobby that was buying support in Congress, a trope of traditional anti-Semitism.

But far from seeking to confront his former colleagues, Greenblatt was more interested in using the ADL to critique Netanyahu. He went out of his way in 2016 to publicly oppose Netanyahu's claim that the Palestinians' desire to push Jews out of West Bank communities would amount to "ethnic cleansing."[3] According to Greenblatt, that was a wrongful use of Holocaust terminology. Yet he was guilty himself of using a similar analogy to criticize enforcement of American laws against illegal immigration.[4]

There is, however, more at play here than mere hypocrisy. Though Greenblatt will occasionally criticize a Democrat for an anti-Semitic utterance or inappropriate Holocaust analogy, under his leadership, the ADL became focused on aiding the "resistance" to the administration of President Donald Trump, constantly accusing him of inciting or inspiring a rise in anti-Semitism on the far right. Indeed, the ADL became a prop for branding Trump an anti-Semite and a Nazi.

While Trump's intemperate and vulgar tone—as well as his willingness to attack opponents and critics—was unorthodox, Greenblatt's repeated attempts to connect the dots between his comments and far right extremists was rooted primarily in partisanship, not a defense of the Jews. That was apparent when it came to seemingly blaming the president for acts of violence against Jews, such as the attacks on synagogues in Pittsburgh and Poway.[5] But it was also the case with respect to Greenblatt's willingness to lend the ADL's prestige to the false claim that President Trump had somehow endorsed or expressed moral indifference to the neo-Nazis who marched in Charlottesville, Virginia, on August 11, 2017, because of his comment taken out of context about "very fine people" being on both sides of the barricades there.[6] Trump had been referring to people who disagreed about the need to clear public squares of all memorials to Confederates and those killed in the Civil War, not those in the confrontation with neo-Nazis.[7]

In doing so, the ADL aligned itself with the political views of most of its donors. But in addition to committing itself to a misleading partisan narrative about Trump, Greenblatt also pushed the group into a confrontation with the Trump administration over issues that had nothing to do with anti-Semitism. For example, the ADL announced its opposition to the nomination of Brett Kavanaugh to the Supreme Court within seconds of the announcement,[8] signaling that the ADL would oppose any conservative.

The ADL condemned former Secretary of State Mike Pompeo,[9] a man who was not only a friend to the Jewish community during his time in Congress and as director of the CIA but also helped to make historic breakthroughs for pro-Israel policies at the State Department. During his confirmation hearings, the ADL attacked him for his "bigotry" in denouncing anti-Semitic Islamist radicals.[10] That could be seen in the same context as Greenblatt's reversal of Foxman's opposition to the building of a Muslim community center and mosque near the 9/11 Ground Zero of lower Manhattan.[11] The ADL's stance promoted the false narrative in which the real victims of the attacks were American Muslims, suffering from a mythical backlash by the rest of American society.

The ADL also found itself closely aligned with Big Tech companies that it previously criticized for allowing anti-Semitism on social media. Though some of those firms, such as Facebook, initially refused to go along with the ADL's push for censoring hateful opinions, they soon found that the ADL was a willing partner when it came to justifying Silicon Valley's shift toward censoring conservative opinions. The ADL's efforts to steer those who logged on to hate websites to better sources of information led to another hate website that was spreading anti-Semitism. And its alliance with PayPal, intended to help to weed out alleged radical groups, put it in the position of endorsing censorship more than fighting hate.[12]

Despite the group's claims to the contrary, the ADL's leftist tilt caused it to be perceived as having shifted its priorities away from strictly Jewish issues. This led to even more dangerous problems than the disintegration of its gold-standard status as the ultimate authority on anti-Semitism. The spread of intersectional ideology—which lumps together all groups and peoples who claim to be oppressed because of their color or indigenous background and similarly views all their opponents as linked by "white privilege"—has convinced many on the American left that the Palestinian war against Israel is somehow analogous to the struggle for civil rights in the U.S. in the 1960s.

This has led not only to attacks on Israel as a beneficiary of "white privilege"—the irony that a majority of Israeli Jews trace their origins to the Middle East or North Africa and are therefore "people of color" under the definition accepted by the left is lost on the Jewish state's critics—but it has also provided fuel for a rising tide of anti-Semitism in which assertions of Israel's illegitimacy are the primary line of attack.

This has proved troublesome for the ADL because of the way Greenblatt has helped to steer it into a position where it is an important ally for a party whose left wing—including its young rock stars of the congressional "Squad"—are not only anti-Israel, but, in the case of Representatives Ilhan Omar (D-MN) and Rashida Tlaib (D-MI), are open supporters of the anti-Semitic BDS movement, which seeks Israel's elimination. The group's defense of Omar and Tlaib against criticisms from Trump about their anti-Semitism undermined its credibility in speaking up against the BDS movement while simultaneously earning it brickbats from the left.

Just as important, when the Black Lives Matter (BLM) movement rose once again to prominence in the summer of 2020 after the death of George Floyd, the ADL was swept along with the rest of the country's leftists into supporting its demands. The anti-Semitic connections of the radicals behind BLM and the vicious attacks on Israel in its platform[13] should have placed the ADL first among the movement's critics. But in the moral panic about race that has infected America's leftist elites, the ADL felt compelled to endorse the movement,[14] defend it against its critics, and, crucially, take a supportive position concerning the CRT indoctrination that was linked to the protests.

Throughout 2022, Greenblatt felt compelled to note that anti-Semitism is a problem on the left as well as on the far right, especially once incitement against Israel during the conflict with Hamas terrorists in May 2021 led to an outbreak of violent attacks against Jews in the U.S. This incitement was led by left-wing Democrats like Omar, Tlaib, and their popular colleague Representative Alexandria Ocasio-Cortez (D-NY), who were appealing to intersectional ideology to justify their stance, libeling Israel and letting Hamas off the hook for firing thousands of rockets and missiles. The ADL was put in an awkward position and was forced to push back against the delegitimizing smears heard on the floor of Congress, as well as from far-left and Islamist-friendly groups, such as the Council on American-Islamic Relations (CAIR).[15]

Yet that didn't cause Greenblatt or his group to rethink their endorsement of CRT. To the contrary, as was revealed after Greenblatt intervened to provide cover for *The View* host Whoopi Goldberg after she spouted racialist nonsense about the Holocaust in which she claimed it was merely a case of whites attacking other whites.[16]

A definition of racism had been posted on the ADL website (in which racism was limited to prejudice against persons "of color") that was similar to the gross comments for which Goldberg had to apologize with Greenblatt's assistance. After the rise of BLM, the ADL altered its definition of racism from "the belief that a particular race is superior or inferior to another" and that "a person's social and moral traits are predetermined by his or her inborn biological characteristics." The new definition held that: "The marginalization and/or oppression of people of color based on a socially constructed racial hierarchy that privileges white people."[17]

As soon as the Goldberg controversy occurred, the ADL scrubbed the intersectional definition from its website and restored the old entry, although appending to it a lengthy note reportedly by Greenblatt, claiming that the group's focus on the racism of whites was "true," but "not the whole truth."[18]

This Orwellian turn on the part of the ADL is noteworthy. Yet it's also an element of another controversy in which it became embroiled at the same time when it hired activist Tema Smith as its new director of Jewish outreach and partnerships.[19] Smith has a long history as a bitter critic of Israel and left-wing Twitter troll.[20] In an earlier time, it would have been unimaginable for a group that was as solidly pro-Israel and reflexively centrist as the ADL to hire such a person, but she was the perfect job candidate for the Greenblatt era.

The most serious problem with the hire is not what she might have posted on Twitter in the past but her current assignment. While outreach is important for the entire Jewish world in a time of rising assimilation and a Jewish population that is largely disconnected from the community and a sense of Jewish peoplehood, Smith's brief is focused on "Jews of color." That Jews who are not white sometimes face discrimination within the community is deplorable and should be condemned. Jews come in all different colors and from many places of origin (something that the non-Jewish Whoopi Goldberg doesn't seem to understand). The idea of dividing Jews by skin color can never be accepted any more than bias against converts should be tolerated.

In its eagerness to get in on the fashion of racialist rhetoric on the left and in the Democratic Party, the ADL is embracing the cause of "Jews of color." In doing so, it and others on the left have lumped in a variety of communities, including Jews from Middle Eastern, Mediterranean, and North African countries, most of whom do not identify with the term. As such, the ADL is not only undermining a basic concept of Jewish unity, it is also utilizing the same intersectional playbook used by Israel-haters to brand the Jewish state and its supporters as possessing "white privilege."

Jews should not be defined by skin color; no one should. The point of the civil rights movement was to discard the obsession with race that fueled segregation. America should aspire to a colorblind society, and yet CRT and intersectionality demand that race be treated as the most important element in defining any person. Joining with its left-wing allies to apply this idea to Jews across the board, the ADL is again undermining the cause for which it was founded and providing useful cover to those who are seeking to harm the Jewish people, here and in Israel.

At a time when both the statistics that the ADL compiles about hate and the tenor of the national conversation confirm that anti-Semitism is on the rise, the need for an effective Jewish defense agency focused on anti-Semitism is real and urgent.

The ADL now finds itself a rare Jewish organization with a mission that is at least as relevant to Jewish life today as when it was founded in 1913. That should make it a group whose continued efforts are not only necessary but deserving of support from the broadest cross-section of Jewish life.

Far more important is the way the ADL's embrace of BLM extremists and CRT gives a boost to the very forces on the left, who, because of their influence in Washington and among a younger generation of Democrats, now pose the most important threat to Jewish life in America. That is not merely a setback for the ADL. It is an abandonment of the very purpose of its existence.

It is ironic that this is happening at a time when the ADL's influence and financial clout are greater than ever. But it is also a paradigm of how Jewish leadership is failing American Jewry's best interests all the while claiming to be defending them.

Jonathan S. Tobin is editor-in-chief of JNS.org, a senior contributor to The Federalist, *and a columnist for the* New York Post *and* Newsweek. *He can be followed on Twitter at @jonathans_tobin.*

1. Debbie Hall, "Tema Smith and the ADL: Controversy Explained," *Scholars for Peace in the Middle East*, February 25, 2022. https://bit.ly/3yRPQIX.

2. "Obama aide Rhodes claims they built 'echo chamber' to sell Iran deal," *Fox News*, May 6, 2016. https://fxn.ws/3eJvFGq.

3. Jonathan Greenblatt, "The Palestinians Are Not 'Ethnic Cleansing' Jewish Settlers," *Anti-Defamation League*, September 13, 2016. https://bit.ly/3TA4j46.

4. Greenblatt, "Closing the Borders to Refugees: Wrong in the 1930s, and Wrong Today," *Anti-Defamation League*, November 19, 2015. Archived September 20, 2021. https://bit.ly/3CGVZZL. The post has since been deleted.

5. For partisan dilution of message, see "Poway Attack Illustrates Danger Right-Wing Extremists Pose to Jews, Muslims," *Anti-Defamation League*, May 2, 2019. https://bit.ly/3ScuOM0. See also Matthew Chapman, "'Very perilous moment': ADL leader says MAGA 'terror attack' portends worse to come," *Raw Story*, January 5, 2022. https://bit.ly/3VPa2VY.

6. Daniel Sugarman, "ADL condemns Trump's comments on Charlottesville rally," *The Jewish Chronicle*, August 16, 2017. https://bit.ly/3TysHmY.

7. See "What Happened in Charlottesville?", *Prager University*, August 5, 2019. https://bit.ly/3s6w34N.

8. "ADL Response to the President's Nomination of Judge Brett Kavanaugh to Serve as an Associate Justice of the United States Supreme Court," *Anti-Defamation League*, July 9, 2018. https://bit.ly/3yB0Vhv.

9. See Jane Eisner, "Mike Pompeo Is An Anti-Muslim Bigot. Shouldn't Jewish Leaders Condemn Him, Too?", *The Forward*, March 20, 2018. https://bit.ly/3EXNCMh. Greenblatt told *The Forward* that "Mike Pompeo's own statements and record of close associations with organizations that have frequently expressed hostility to Muslims and have trafficked in anti-Muslim conspiracy theories raise serious concerns about his fitness to serve as secretary of state. We are reviewing the record and statements of Pompeo and will offer questions for the upcoming confirmation hearings, as we have done frequently with key Cabinet nominees, and urge senators to closely examine his record."

10   Greenblatt and Marvin D. Nathan, "ADL Letter to Senate Foreign Relations Committee on the Nomination of Mike Pompeo as Secretary of State," *Anti-Defamation League*, April 10, 2018. https://bit.ly/3s8NphE.

11   Greenblatt, "It's Time to Admit It: The Left Has an Antisemitism Problem," *Newsweek*, July 9, 2021. https://bit.ly/3MqAPUb.

12   See "PayPal Partners with ADL to Fight Extremism and Protect Marginalized Communities," *Anti-Defamation League*, July 26, 2021. https://bit.ly/3ESoLcn.

13   See "A Cut in US Military Expenditures and A Reallocation of those Funds to Invest in Domestic Infrastructure and Community Wellbeing," *Movement 4 Black Lives*. https://bit.ly/3TfVQ63. See p. 3.

14   Daniel Greenfield, "ADL Signs Black Lives Matter Letter Alongside Anti-Israel Groups," *FrontPage Magazine*, September 1, 2020. https://bit.ly/3eCKM4x.

15   "Head of ADL Blasts Muslim Advocacy Org CAIR for 'Blatant Antisemitism,'" *The Algemeiner*, December 13, 2021. https://bit.ly/3CJYAlD.

16   Ian Haworth, "ADL CEO Rejects Whoopi Goldberg's Holocaust Claims, But Did He Contradict ADL's New Definition Of Racism?", *The Daily Wire*, February 1, 2022. https://bit.ly/3Tw71aV.

17   Ashe Schow, "ADL Changes Its Definition Of Racism Again, Calls It An 'Interim Definition,'" *The Daily Wire*, February 3, 2022. https://bit.ly/3EULwNa.

18   Greenblatt, "Getting it Right in Defining Racism," *Medium*, February 2, 2022. https://bit.ly/3spuIq9.

19   See Hall, "Tema Smith and the ADL: Controversy Explained."

20   Greenfield, "ADL Hires Director for Jewish Outreach Who Hates Jews," *FrontPage Magazine*, January 31, 2022. https://bit.ly/3RUm2C8.

3

MORAL NARCISSISM AND THE PSYCHOLOGY OF FAILURE

RICHARD A. LANDES

C urrently, Western elites are enamored of a discourse best described as "utopian universalism," a vision of a peaceful world, rid of oppression and discrimination—a world with no borders and with freedom and human rights for all. Certain dominant memes carry the message: "violence never solved anything," "war is not the answer,"[1] "who are we to judge?" and "all cultures are equal," along with their despised opposites: tribalism, racism, nationalism, us/ them thinking, and any kind of phobia ("homo-," "trans-," "xeno-," "Islamo-"). The list is ever growing.

These sentiments have trapped many Jews, especially most of their leaders, in a rhetorical cage with few venues for escape because defending specifically Jewish interests now is, by definition, parochial and anti-universalist. Trying to square the circle of defending Jews and their traditions—yet being in synch with the wider, now anti-traditionalist society—is nearly impossible.

This universalist utopianism has been around for a long time, with its first powerful assertions during the Enlightenment and the creation of democracies. Since the mid-twentieth century, the outlook has become institutionalized in global systems—the U.N., Geneva Conventions, universal human rights—that were increasingly demanding, even as the real world proved recalcitrant. In the twenty-first century, a utopian discourse that deconstructs power and prejudice and detects their workings everywhere has spread from radical pockets of academia to become the coin of the realm. Many share the vision of bending the "arc of the moral universe... toward justice."[2] Anyone who contests this high moral discourse is stigmatized with this epoch's most loathsome epithet: racist.

Jews are particularly susceptible to accusations of failing to live up to messianic expectations. In its religious form, this utopianism lies behind the messianic dreams from the prophets to the present; in its secular forms, it inspires world-perfecting movements from communism to globalism to critical (race) theory. Currently its most passionate Jewish adherents, both religious and secular, invoke *tikkun olam*—"repairing the world"[3]—as a messianic vocation. For Jews, especially in diaspora, signaling to the dominant gentile culture that Jews accept and are eager to contribute to the larger society has often been a key strategy to survival. In modern times, when the surrounding culture has adopted many (originally) Jewish utopian ideals in the process of forging democratic, civil societies, Jewish leaders have tended to publicly promote these utopian ideals as proof of their good will.

For most people, being seen as virtuous has a social and psychosocial motivation. It is almost a necessary life skill to encourage others to think one is a person of principle. The problem arises when one's own (or one's people's) values differ from the larger collective, and one faces a choice between signaling one's virtue according to the consensus while betraying one's true values on the one hand or staying faithful to one's values and enduring the disapproval, even rejection, that such defiance inevitably brings, on the other.

Some observers have characterized the choice of public "honor" over private integrity as a form of "moral narcissism," namely, adopting what are seen by most as moral positions because they make you look and feel good about yourself, regardless of the consequences for others.[4] For moral narcissists, signaling virtue trumps acting virtuously. At their most noxious, they become "luxury beliefs" by which people signal their high status by embracing ideas that aspire to help but actually hinder the objects of their "concern"—such as defunding police, open borders, and gender fluidity.[5]

The Oslo Syndrome and the Crisis of Jewish Leadership

Jewish leaders (including official heads of Jewish organizations dedicated to protecting the Jewish communities they serve, and prominent spiritual and academic figures) faced a dilemma at the beginning of the new millennium. In 2000 and 2001, global events occurred that put Western moral narcissists in a position to do terrible harm to the very democracies that made their pleasant utopian dreams seem so close to realization.

The 1990s were, in the eyes of many hopefuls, the "happy years" when one could (with some justification) look forward to an end of history, even to a global civil society, a realization of Kant's enlightenment dream of "perpetual peace." This was particularly true of Jews and Israelis because the so-called Oslo Peace Process promised an end to that long, terrible war of survival that Israel had been fighting since birth. Finally, we could come to a positive-sum outcome for Israelis and Palestinians, "land for peace." And it all depended on a somewhat utopian projection, that the Palestinians were ready to leave behind their sworn desire for vengeance and join global civil society. So powerful had this dream gripped Jews around the world that when Yasser Arafat made it clear, in Arabic, that this was "land for war,"[6] even the Israeli intelligence community ignored the evidence and forged forward with the pleasant dream.[7]

Israeli and Jewish leaders, enthralled by the prospects of peace, accused any who pointed out the problems of projecting a liberal psychology and culture onto the Palestinians as suffering from "a post-Holocaust syndrome," an inability to let go of the fears of the past. In a fine illustration of the role of a malignant moral narcissism, they considered that "resistance to the Oslo process constituted a greater offense than Palestinian violations of the Accord."[8] In other words, those Jews who expressed concern got in the way of peace. Psychiatrist Ken Levin called this mindset the "Oslo syndrome."[9]

This aggressively hopeful posture had particular appeal for American Jewish leaders who had pursued and were deeply committed to the positive-sum values of the civil societies in which they lived. Organizations like the AJC and the ADL carried on extensive activities with other minorities, defending their "human rights," protecting them from prejudice, helping to strengthen their communities, and extending the hand of friendship. It was at once a great "optic" and—as these leaders assured anyone who wondered why so much effort went into making friends rather than helping the Jewish community—when the time came that Jews needed support, their friends would reciprocate. Win-win.

Then, in late 2000, Arafat let the soldiers out of the Trojan horse he had long touted as his Oslo strategy, and a bloody suicide-terror Jihad ensued in which more than 1,000 Israelis (percentagewise, the U.S. equivalent of 50,000),[10] mostly civilians, were killed and many more maimed by bombs carefully assembled with ball bearings, to spread the damage as far and wide as possible. Astonishingly, the "good people"—the progressives, the "post-Zionists," the post-colonialists—sided with the Palestinians and blamed Israel, the stronger party, for not doing enough, for not giving enough for peace. Since nothing in the utopian worldview could allow evidence that the gamble over the Palestinians' intentions had failed—it would be "racist" to say the Palestinian leadership *wanted* war—it could only be that Israel was responsible. As French President Jacques Chirac said to Israeli Prime Minister Ehud Barak: "We cannot make anyone believe that the Palestinians are the aggressors."[11]

As a result, quite the contrary to what the Jewish leadership's twentieth-century strategy anticipated, in a massive shift of the Overton Window, the Palestinian cause became a litmus test of liberal credentials.[12] No matter how violently and despicably Palestinians behaved, with their unprecedented war of suicide terror and genocidal hate speech, Jewish leaders looked to their allies for a defense that never came. On the contrary, as Paul Berman put it: "Palestinian terror" had become "the measure of Israeli guilt."[13] Rather than get help from its liberal and minority friends so carefully cultivated during the "happy '90s," Jewish leadership got the cold shoulder and worse. Many expected allies joined the campaign against Israel and told the Jews that the Palestinians' murderous hatred of the Jews had nothing to do with anti-Semitism and that any Jewish objections were just abusing accusations of anti-Semitism in order to silence "any criticism" of Israel.[14]

Faced with the evidence that their effort to make peace had failed and that those with "Holocaust syndrome" (who had warned of malevolent Palestinian intentions) were correct, many of these good folks doubled down: We were so close; if only Israel had given more, *then* Arafat would have said yes. Jews were tempted to believe that after the Holocaust, in the West and now even in "Palestine," the siege was over. They refused to look at counterevidence. Indeed, what had been a risky gamble in the '90s—Palestinians are ready for peace and deserve a state of their own—became dogma in the '00s precisely as the gamble failed spectacularly. Anyone opposed was a heartless racist.

9/11 recapitulated this dynamic and made things even worse. Here was a declaration of war on the West every bit as vicious as the Intifada—suicidal jihadis targeting civilians—but now on a global scale, outside Dar al-Islam. Many thought-leaders—academics, journalists, pundits, politicians—found themselves, just like the Israeli and Jewish "peace camp," in an impossible situation. According to democratic principles, American Muslims could and should enjoy the religious freedoms (basic civil rights) that everyone else in a democracy did, and accordingly there was great concern over the rights of "ordinary Muslims" who are not part of this apocalyptic jihad waged by a Saudi from the caves of Afghanistan. By democratic standards, any move to constrain Muslims *qua* Muslims was out of the question. It also was an extremely bad optic: In order to live up to our liberal and progressive standards, some reasoned, we must not even "appear" to "take sides."[15] The West, by its own utopian virtues, rhetorically and unilaterally disarmed.

And when confronted with the evidence that some Muslims, enjoying the rights of democratic citizens (which they did not have in Muslim-majority countries), found jihadi goals attractive—imposing

Shariah law in Dar al-Harb,[16] death penalty for apostates and blasphemers, supporting terrorist groups,[17] calling for the overthrow of the democratic governments,[18] preaching paranoid conspiracy theories[19] and exterminationist anti-Semitism,[20] and protecting shame-murders[21]—the tolerant response did not waver. On the contrary, our presidents assured us that "Islam is peace"[22] and "99.9% of Muslims" reject this "medieval" religious war.[23]

Anyone who tried to point out the problem (that there was indeed a civilizational culture that promoted jihadi values) was accused of Islamophobia. In a parody of the Oslo syndrome, Western progressives considered criticism of Muslims and Islam a greater offense than the terror of those fighting to establish a global caliphate. Progressives fetishized Muslim "otherness,"[24] making their embrace a sign of moral rectitude,[25] and any resistance to such a suicidal alliance an indicator of xenophobia, Islamophobia, or "right-wing" fascism.[26] The utopians insisted on a politically correct set of beliefs and imposed them on everyone else:

- Islam is a religion of peace.
- The jihadis attacking the West have "hijacked" the religion and have nothing to do with true Islam.
- Efforts to link Islam to terror, including the expression "radical Islam," are Islamophobic.
- Islamophobia is the early twenty-first-century equivalent to anti-Semitism in the early twentieth century (that is, the rise of the Nazis) and a vile form of racism.
- The Palestinians are freedom fighters trying to end an imperialist-colonialist occupation that denies them their inalienable human rights.
- Palestinian freedom fighters must not be called terrorists.

Jewish Leadership in the Twenty-First Century

For Jewish leaders, the problem of how to deal with radical Muslims was particularly difficult since one of the most distinctive elements of the radicals' global jihadi wing was a virulent anti-Semitism[27] as bad as that of the Nazis (at least German priests and ministers didn't generally preach genocide from the pulpit).[28] This exterminationist Judeophobia permeates the Muslim world both in Muslim-majority countries and among diaspora Muslims.[29] The overwhelming support of progressives for the politically correct narrative, including its obscuring of this genocidal anti-Semitism, made Muslim hatred of Israel somehow legitimate. Progressives who had no problem "oppos[ing] Jewish ethno-nationalism without being a bigot"[30] banned those who opposed triumphalist Muslim terror-imperialism as deplorable Islamophobes from the public sphere.[31] Jewish leaders had to choose between looking good to their fellow progressives or defending Jews from a sudden and growing "new anti-Semitism,"[32] thereby alienating their "allies."

Given the choice between public honor (virtuous progressives) and private guilt (abandoning their constituency) or public shame (stigmatized as Islamophobic) and private integrity (doing their job), Jewish leaders chose the former. In so doing they joined their fellow progressives in standing down before Islamic triumphalist aggression. And like their colleagues, they expressed outrage when critics called their judgment into question. It became a parody of "human rights" and "anti-racism" that enabled those who would destroy those values to prevail.

But moral narcissism is not mere hypocrisy. Hypocrites know that they are insincere; moral narcissists believe in their virtue. They fervently insist to themselves and anyone who will listen on their sincerity (the cheapest of virtues). They are filled with passionate intensity. They think of themselves as the avatars of the biblical prophets, proudly and indignantly denouncing the sins of their own people.[33] They see themselves as "good Jews" and moral paragons. They soar high above the deplorables whose primitive values they disdain. And the larger the gap between pretense and reality, between hypocrisy and integrity, the more vehement their protestations.

This insistence on their sincerity is nowhere more evident than in the moral narcissist's response to opposition. Rather than engage in a dialogue with those Jews, equally concerned for the fate of their people (bringing relevant observations to the discussion of "what to do"), they responded with indignation and anger. Having been warned repeatedly by Dr. Charles Jacobs, for example, that the massive mosque being built in Roxbury, Massachusetts, was in fact a Muslim Brotherhood-backed, Wahhabi-funded initiative with profound anti-Semitic and anti-democratic tendencies, the local Jewish leadership persisted in its warm support.

When all "private means" had been exhausted, Jacobs named one of the culprits in an op-ed in the Boston *Jewish Advocate*.[34] The response, signed by eighty-three rabbis and rabbinical students who were "shocked and appalled," excoriated Jacobs for his "vicious personal attack" and "destructive campaign against Boston's Muslim community based on innuendo, half-truths, and unproven conspiracy theories." And then they proclaimed their virtue:

> During these difficult times, Rabbi [Eric] Gurvis [then rabbi of Temple Shalom in Newton, Massachusetts], along with other courageous religious leaders are attempting to foster a different kind

of politics. We support his commitment to interfaith dialogue and cooperation. We stand together in our commitment to a community in which neighbors seek to know one another and join together for the common good.[35]

All of this occurred three years before two young Muslims, products of the jihadi ideology propounded at that mosque and its affiliate in Cambridge,[36] carried out the bombing of the Boston Marathon on April 15, 2013. Had these rabbis heeded rather than censured these warnings—had they been as self-critical as they were ready to criticize their own people—many people, Jewish and gentile, might have been spared much suffering.

The tale of this process and its consequences is long and painful, filled with catastrophic errors peppered occasionally with the signs of a backbone, of a commitment to why Jewish leaders exist—to protect their communities. Overall, however, the past two decades have witnessed catastrophes for Jews around the world:

- The spread of BDS and its lethal narratives.
- The increasing dis-ease with Jewish students on campus.
- The ability for vicious accusations to stymie major politicians.[37]
- The catastrophic wedge driven between leftist Jews, especially youth, and the most progressive state (by light years) in the Middle East.
- The increasing street violence against Jews, part of the largest wave of Jew-hatred in the West since the Holocaust's ecumenical wave of exterminationist anti-Semitism in Europe.

The disastrous course of the first decades of the twenty-first century—the spread of BDS and its lethal narratives, the increasing hostility toward and marginalization of Jewish students on campus, the growing demonization of Israel by congressional Democrats, the increasing street violence against Jews—weighs heavily on the shoulders of Jewish leaders, if not for enabling and inciting it, then in failing to oppose it. They could afford to atone next Yom Kippur for:

- The sin of pretending to be moral and preening as a "good, self-critical Jew," even as they betrayed their people's interest, even as they submitted to lethal narratives.
- The sin of justifying hatred of their people in order to gain approval of their gentile peers.
- The sin of hearing someone speak hateful words about their people and remaining silent.
- The sin of denouncing "right-wing" anti-Semitism and downplaying "left-wing" and Muslim anti-Semitism.
- The sin of attacking a fellow Jew in order to appear to outsiders as a "good Jew."

The defense of the Jewish people and their only state in the twenty-first century is, ironically, also the defense of a global civil society in which people can live free, can prosper, and can live at peace with their neighbors. In betraying their own people, Jewish leaders have let down democracies and progressive values the world over.

Richard A. Landes, *an historian living in Jerusalem, is former professor of history at Boston University. His work focuses on apocalyptic and millennial beliefs at the turn of the first and second millennia, 1000 and 2000 C.E. His books include* The Apocalyptic Year 1000 *(2003)* *and* Heaven on Earth: The Varieties of the Millennial Experience *(2011). He coined the term "Pallywood" in 2003 while investigating the Muhammad al-Durah affair and maintains a blog critical of Western journalism,* The Augean Stables. *His latest book is* Can "The Whole World" Be Wrong? Lethal Journalism, Antisemitism, and Global Jihad *(Academic Studies Press, 2022).*

---

[1] See Alexandra Ocasio-Cortez (@RepAOC). Twitter post. January 27, 2022. 4:05 P.M. Archived January 28, 2022. https://bit.ly/3MDG96N. "The conflict between Ukraine and Russia is profoundly concerning, but military conflict is not the solution. We must seek a diplomatic resolution rather than escalate tensions—and avoid sanctions that hurt the Ukrainian people."

[2] See John Nichols, "Barack Obama Charts an Arc of History That Bends Toward Justice," *The Nation*, January 21, 2013. Archived July 17, 2015. https://bit.ly/3EPKCBg.

[3] See Jonathan Neumann, *To Heal the World: How the Jewish Left Corrupts Judaism and Endangers Israel* (New York, NY: All Points Books, 2018).

[4] See Peter Berkowitz, "The Perils of Moral Narcissism," *RealClearPolitics*, July 12, 2016. https://bit.ly/3MED8Dg.

[5] See Rob Henderson, "Thorstein Veblen's Theory of the Leisure Class—A Status Update," *Quillette*, November 16, 2019. https://bit.ly/3MIklqD.

[6] See Richard A. Landes, "Oslo's Misreading of an Honor-Shame Culture," *Israel Journal of Foreign Affairs*, Vol. 13, No. 2 (2019): 189–205. https://bit.ly/3TAX8ZP.

[7] Yossi Melman, "Don't Confuse Us With Facts," *Haaretz*, August 16, 2002. https://bit.ly/3s1A7U5.

[8] Jennifer Roskies, "Oslo's Betrayal," *Tablet*, September 13, 2018. https://bit.ly/3yQq0Fb.

[9] See Kenneth Levin, *The Oslo Syndrome: Delusions of a People Under Siege* (Hanover, NH: Smith & Kraus Global, 2005). See also https://oslosyndrome.blogspot.com/.

[10] Dan Radlauer, "An Engineered Tragedy Statistical Analysis of Casualties in the Palestinian-Israeli Conflict: September 2000–September 2002," *EretzYisroel.org*. https://bit.ly/3TzuQ1t.

[11] Quoted in Gilead Sher, *The Israeli-Palestinian Negotiations, 1999–2001: Within Reach* (London: Routledge, 2006), p. 162. See also Charles Enderlin, *Shattered Dreams: The Failure of the Peace Process in the Middle East, 1995–2002*, trans. Susan Fairfield (New York, NY: Other Press, 2003), p. 304. Enderlin renders the quotation, "No one can believe that the Palestinians are to blame for this chain of violence."

[12] See Ian Buruma, "How to Talk About Israel," *The New York Times*, August 31, 2003. https://nyti.ms/3D9ruwM.

[13] Paul L. Berman, *Terror and Liberalism* (New York, NY: W. W. Norton & Company, 2003), p. 134.

[14] Tariq Ali, "Notes on Anti-Semitism, Zionism and Palestine," *Counterpunch*, March 4, 2004. https://bit.ly/3EOydxt. Quoted in David Hirsh, "Accusations of malicious intent in debates about the Palestine-Israel conflict and about antisemitism: The Livingstone Formulation, 'playing the antisemitism card' and contesting the boundaries of antiracist discourse," *Transversal*, Vol. 1 (2010): 47–77. https://bit.ly/3yLX555.

[15] Christine Chinlund, "Who should wear the 'terrorist' label?", *The Boston Globe*, September 8, 2003. https://bit.ly/3D7JPKG. See also Stephen M. Walt, "Why They Hate Us (I): on military occupation," *Foreign Policy*, November 23, 2009. https://bit.ly/3MW8tl7. See also Walt, "Why they hate us (II): How many Muslims has the U.S. killed in the past 30 years?", *Foreign Policy*, November 30, 2009. https://bit.ly/3yRb2yL.

[16] "Poll of U.S. Muslims Reveals Ominous Levels Of Support For Islamic Supremacists' Doctrine of Shariah, Jihad," *Center for Security Policy*, June 23, 2015. https://bit.ly/3CMho3E.

[17] See "Islam in the UK," *MarkHumphrys.com*. https://markhumphrys.com/islam.uk.html.

[18] See Andrew C. McCarthy, *The Grand Jihad: How Islam and the Left Sabotage America* (New York, NY: Encounter Books, 2010).

[19] Robert Philpot, "44% of UK Muslims back anti-Semitic conspiracy theories, poll finds," *The Times of Israel*, August 4, 2020. https://bit.ly/3CJdnNp.

[20] Mohammed al-Adzee, "Antisemitism In Sermons In U.S. Mosques," *Middle East Media Research Institute*, November 8, 2021. https://bit.ly/3Lvrkm3.

[21] Leon Watson, "'Honour' violence is acceptable, say one in five young British Asians," *The Daily Mail*, March 19, 2012. Updated April 17, 2012. https://bit.ly/3Sbv2Dd. See also Hollie McKay, "Honor killing in America: DOJ report says growing problem is hidden in stats," *Fox News*, May 3, 2016. https://fxn.ws/3eEepT4.

22 "'Islam is Peace' Says President," *The White House*, September 17, 2001. https://bit.ly/3ScHgLT.

23 Quoted in Ian Schwartz, "Obama: This 'Medieval Interpretation Of Islam' Is Rejected By '99.9%' Of Muslims, Not A 'Religious War,'" *RealClearPolitics*, February 1, 2015. https://bit.ly/3yQqeMA.

24 See Bruce Bawer, "The Fraud of Identity Studies," *FrontPage Magazine*, August 27, 2012. https://bit.ly/3g7r5lw.

25 Landes, "Judith Butler, the Adorno Prize, and the Moral State of the 'Global Left,'" *The Augean Stables*, August 31, 2012. https://bit.ly/3ERZUp6.

26 Marvin Folkertsma, "The Strange Case of the Secular Progressive-Islamist Alliance," *American Thinker*, November 25, 2015. https://bit.ly/3CJpcmN.

27 See "Islamist Terror and Antisemitism: The Mission against Modernity," *Stanford University*, March 10, 2008. Lecture by Matthias Küntzel. Audio, 47:12. https://stanford.io/3Crqnax.

28 Mohammed Dajani, "Dealing with Hate Sermons," *Fikra Forum*, September 5, 2017. https://bit.ly/3yuyjGH.

29 See Günther Jikeli, *European Muslim Antisemitism: Why Young Urban Males Say They Don't Like Jews* (Bloomington, IN: Indiana University Press, 2015).

30 Michelle Goldberg, "Anti-Zionism Isn't the Same as Anti-Semitism," *The New York Times*, December 7, 2018. https://nyti.ms/3MIaqRJ.

31 See Andrew Fleischer and Mary Markos, "Speakers Draw Protests at Stoughton Temple," *The Jewish Journal of the North Shore*, November 18, 2016. https://bit.ly/3ghVbTD.

32 See Phyllis Chesler, *The New Anti-Semitism: The Current Crisis and What We Must Do About It* (Jerusalem: Gefen Publishing House, 2015).

33 See Adam Shatz, ed., *Prophets Outcast: A Century of Dissident Jewish Writing about Zionism and Israel* (New York, NY: Nation Books, 2004).

34 Charles Jacobs, "What's up with Patrick?", *The Jewish Advocate*, June 4, 2010. https://bit.ly/3D7c641.

35 "Rabbis come to the defense of a colleague under fire," *The Jewish Advocate*, June 11, 2010. https://bit.ly/3MILp9d.

36 See Ilya Feoktistov, "Revealed: Jihadist Lessons at the Boston Marathon Bombers' Mosque," *Breitbart*, March 27, 2015. https://bit.ly/3VCHw9S. See also Feoktistov, *Terror in the Cradle of Liberty: How Boston Became a Center for Islamic Extremism* (New York, NY: Encounter Books, 2019).

37 Craig Bannister, "Kamala Harris Tells Student Who Accused Israel, U.S. of 'Ethnic Genocide' that 'Your Truth Cannot Be Suppressed,'" *CNS News*, September 30, 2021. https://bit.ly/3gn2s4I.

4

AMERICAN JEWS' POLITICAL KRISTALLNACHT

JOSHUA BLOCK

Of the eight billion people who live on this planet, just over fifteen million are Jews.[1] Of these, about six million reside in America (out of 320 million citizens) and there are now seven million in Israel.[2] The remainder are scattered about the globe. That means that just seven million Jews live in their natural habitat (if we were of the animal kingdom, the Jewish people would be classed an endangered species). Yet it seems the world will do more to preserve the spotted owl in its natural habitat than the last remaining Jews in theirs. Perhaps Israel, the nation state of the Jewish people, should liken itself to a bird sanctuary and hope that the world might make it a special crime to kill a Jew. But Jew-hatred is *not* a special crime it seems, even in America. On March 7, 2019, the U.S. Congress sent a clear signal that Jew-hatred would not be deemed special at all. With poetic license, I suggest we think of that specific moment as America's political Kristallnacht.

A growing anxiety now grips America's Jewish community as it contends daily with waves of ideological and physical assault. "It can't happen here"—the incantation once expressed with confidence while uttered by many with their fingers crossed—is now being reconsidered, at least in murmurs. Something new and truly dangerous is stalking the Jews, something they thought could not happen in this country.

Recent FBI hate-crime statistics validate an innate Jewish fear that, despite the decades of lives lived alongside their neighbors in prosperity and safety, Jews have become disproportionately singled out for hate-filled attacks. [3] One analysis of the FBI data shows that "a Jewish person is approximately twice as likely to suffer a hate crime than a black person or a Muslim, 10 times more likely than an Asian or a Latino and 20 times more likely than a non-Hispanic white."[4]

American Jews certainly had plenty of warning. But many, following most establishment Jewish leaders and organizations, did not want to see it. They specifically did not want to see that the drum beat against Israel that began in the media and was adopted energetically by the campus professoriate was, in fact—as the wiser voices explained—a "new anti-Semitism" that soon enough caught fire in the liberal churches, the student left, and has now become the received wisdom propagated in nearly all of America's cultural institutions. But, as always and for everyone, it was more comfortable, too, for the Jews to find a way to feel less threatened by real dangers. They saw the singling out of Israel just as Israel's detractors wanted them to perceive it—as nothing more than the "legitimate criticism of Israeli policy." And, so, the frog cooked slowly.

American Jews watched for decades as the media, the left, the human rights organizations, the Presbyterian Church, and others singled out Israel for condemnation while ignoring or downplaying actual horrors across the globe—especially horrors in the Arab and Muslim realms. Singling out Jewish behavior for special scrutiny is the very definition of anti-Semitism, but it is also what Jews themselves do, which added to the confusion of many. Jews sat and watched as many who imbibed the constant barrage of biased criticism came to question the Jewish people's right to self-determination. Jews saw the liberal churches passionately embrace the Palestinians while remaining silent about Christian persecution in Muslim societies,[5] including even Christians being made slaves.[6] The leaders of almost every legacy Jewish establishment organization failed to warn of where this animus against the Jewish state would inevitably end up.

We also saw intermittent flashes of the old anti-Semitism rise out of the more familiar classical hate pits. These, which had mostly been suppressed after the Shoah, were not very surprising, but we chose to focus on those "old" enemies and fretted at how the most well-known and widely recognized anti-Jewish racists would be returned to polite society, more predictably than the sunrise. (Brace yourself: Mel Gibson bringing you *Lethal Weapon 5* any month now.)

Out of the corner of their eyes, however, Jews watched Louis Farrakhan spew hatred for us, but then mostly averted their eyes when shown that photo of him standing with soon-to-be-president Barack Obama.[7] And then Jews were shocked when it took Adidas a month to do anything about its relationship with Kanye West—the man going "death con 3 On JEWISH PEOPLE,"[8] as he misspelled it on Twitter—while he urged others to follow his hatred,[9] just as he urged them to buy his sneakers.

Now all hell has broken loose. Violence on the streets of American cities and anti-Semitic assaults—not carried out by white supremacists but by other minorities, including racists and Jew-haters within the black community[10]—are cast upon the Jewish community at the same time as neo-Nazis hung banners over major highways blaring the black Jew-haters' message.[11] Jew-hate is super glue, able to bind those who usually hate each other together in order to hate us more.

For all the anti-Israelism that captured the media, the liberal churches, and the colleges—and for all the societal noise coming from the pop culture stars and social media influencers who either praise or fail to condemn those who would march to the sounds of "Jews will not replace us," or suggest that "Jews worship Satan"—it is the words and actions of our elected government officials that provide the most definitive indication as to whether Jews in America will be protected—or not.

The opinions of the mainstream media, the professors, the student groups, and the liberal churches are one thing. The kindling, perhaps. But for people to strike out at Jews physically, there needed to be a sign that the government would not rush to protect America's Jews. That signal came on March 7, 2019.

Up to this point, America had been sending a very different signal to this country's black community: that the black experience of racism and bigotry is indeed unique, that "black lives matter"—which means specifically that black lives need special protections when under assault or facing bigotry. But what about Jews?

The Democratic Party's embrace of the Black Lives Matter movement and its name was a pledge to use federal power to address the victimization of black people, but it should not have come at the expense of other minority groups. When some resisted the many negative implications and racist presuppositions packed into these formulations and retorted, "No! All lives matter," they were shouted down and defiled as racists. Jews, too, are told that their victimization—the greatest of any persecuted religious minority in history—is not special and does not deserve unique recognition.

It was in early 2019 that America's Jews were slandered by the new Democratic congresswomen Ilhan Omar (D-MN) and Rashida Tlaib (D-MI). The Jewish community asked the Democratic Party, the political home to most American Jews—to whom they gave their passion, money, and work—to publicly censure the defamers in their midst. The Democratic Party refused. Instead of calling out anti-Semitism as though it truly mattered because it was a live threat to a beloved constituency, the Democrats passed a resolution that made Jew-hatred seem a *lesser* danger. They passed a congressional resolution against "hate," in which every sort of hatred from the beginning of human history onward was listed. The response to the Jews who asked, at this one special time, for our government to say essentially that "Jewish lives matter" was "No! All lives matter." Instead of helping and standing by the Jews, H. Res. 183 abandoned the Jews. And everybody saw this.[12]

The signal was sent to the wolves: We have lifted our protection of the Jews. And that's when the beasts learned that they could strike. Here's the play-by-play:

With the swearing-in of radical left-wing politicians like Omar and Talib, pure anti-Semitic vitriol directed by sitting members of Congress against more senior Jewish colleagues,[13] and in support of foreign anti-Jewish terrorist groups,[14] was mainstreamed and reached a new height.

Omar attributed American support for Israel to Jewish "Benjamins"[15] and claimed Congress was being "hypnotized" into supporting "apartheid" Israel's "evil doings."[16] A supporter of the anti-Semitic BDS movement against Israel,[17] she also "chuckle[s]" that the U.S. even classifies Israel "as a democracy,"[18] and she received campaign funding from the CAIR, a Hamas front group.[19]

Tlaib, too, was linked to CAIR[20] and was a supporter of anti-Semitic Women's March leader Linda Sarsour in her struggle against Israel's "racist policies."[21] On the very day she was sworn into Congress, Tlaib tweeted out a picture of a world map with a Post-It note stuck next to Israel with the word "Palestine" written on it in red marker.[22] An open BDS supporter,[23] she posed with a supporter of Hezbollah in her congressional office[24] and tweeted that then-Senator Kamala Harris taking a picture with Benjamin Netanyahu was an example of her abandoning the "resistance to racism against ALL people."[25]

Clearly, these founding "Squad" members, Omar especially, were a major menace to American Jews. The government of which they were a part had a duty to denounce their bigotry. A woman who suggested that her colleagues were being "expected to have allegiance/pledge support to a foreign country" (namely Israel,[26] one of America's closest allies) had to be condemned—censured, not censored—for tainting her office with classic anti-Semitic rhetoric.

But under pressure from those who excused and defended Omar and her anti-Semitic bile, the Democratic Party shunted its responsibility to call out the hatred that Omar and Tlaib were normalizing—anti-Semitism—and did the opposite. On March 7, 2019, the Democratic House majority passed H. Res. 183. It reads in part:

> Condemning anti-Semitism as hateful expressions
> of intolerance that are contradictory to the values
> and aspirations that define the people of the United

States and condemning anti-Muslim discrimination and bigotry against minorities as hateful expressions of intolerance that are contrary to the values and aspirations of the United States.

[W]hite supremacists in the United States have exploited and continue to exploit bigotry and weaponize hate for political gain, targeting traditionally persecuted peoples, including African Americans, Latinos, Native Americans, Asian Americans and Pacific Islanders and other people of color, Jews, Muslims, Hindus, Sikhs, the LGBTQ community, immigrants, and others with verbal attacks, incitement, and violence...

...[O]n August 11 and 12, 2017, self-identified neo-Confederates, white nationalists, neo-Nazis, and Ku Klux Klansmen held white supremacist events in Charlottesville, Virginia, where they marched on a synagogue under the Nazi swastika, engaged in racist and anti-Semitic demonstrations and committed brutal and deadly violence against peaceful Americans...

[This resolution] encourages all public officials to confront the reality of anti-Semitism, Islamophobia, racism, and other forms of bigotry, as well as historical struggles against them, to ensure that the United States will live up to the transcendent principles of tolerance, religious freedom, and equal protection as embodied in the Declaration of Independence and the first and 14th amendments to the Constitution.[27]

The resolution paired its condemnation of anti-Semitism—of which Omar was guilty of espousing—with a condemnation of "Islamophobia"—of which Omar had falsely accused her critics[28]—and then condemned a list of almost every other form of prejudice under the sun. Omar turned a resolution that should have condemned her own anti-Jewish statements alone into a twisted proclamation, essentially absolving her of her own behavior and treating *her* and her fellow Muslims as the victims.

The message? That attacks on Jews were not especially noteworthy or terrible. Foreseeable consequences followed. One was immediate and spectacular. None other than the former Grand Wizard of the very Ku Klux Klan the resolution had condemned, infamous neo-Nazi David Duke, was among the first to understand this breakthrough moment: that a sitting member of Congress had slammed the Jews—and gotten away with it. He *praised* Omar: "By defiance to [the] Z.O.G. [Zionist-Occupied Government]," Duke announced the same day the resolution passed, "Ilhan Omar is NOW the most important Member of the US Congress!"[29]

Much worse was soon to come. Late 2019 saw a rash of anti-Jewish hate crimes in New York and New Jersey,[30] including outright murder.[31] In a pattern that refuses to abate, brutal physical assaults against Jews on the streets of New York City have since witnessed a massive uptick[32] and happen regularly.[33] Though some attacks are reported by the media—at least anecdotally[34]—many are not. And when anyone in the media occasionally chooses to take notice of this trend, they simply blame it on the "old" anti-Semites—the neo-Nazis and white supremacists.[35]

America was supposed to be different. First, structurally: As a salad mix of very different peoples, Jews could be just one more un-hated species of lettuce. Add to this the post-Holocaust shock and guilt that made it fashionable across America, at least in polite society, to keep the (intentionally insulting) Jew jokes at a hush. Yes, for many, it has been valuable politically or economically to do so. But still, for most of America's good people, it became a simple, natural, moral reaction to express outrage at and to chastise any who dared express anti-Semitism in public view, a thing not so true in the rest of the world.

Were our hopes that we had finally found a country where we'd be treated differently than in the past simply misplaced?

It is true that the *goldena medina* has always been tainted. There have been anti-Semites in Congress since its creation. Though, after the Shoah, the Second World War, and the civil rights advances of the 1960s and '70s, fewer have been willing to be seen as outright bigots, such as Ron Paul or Pete McCloskey, or as being associated with them and giving them plum committee assignments, such as Marjorie Taylor Green.

Yes, it was tragic that President Roosevelt didn't let the Jews on the *St. Louis* land in America and tragic that he failed to bomb the rail tracks to Auschwitz. Absorbing that reality pushed Jews to greater organizational zeal and a deeper participation in the civil and political life of the nation. It led to the emergence of a pro-Israel lobby, the American Israel Public Affairs Committee (AIPAC)—a rarity among foreign policy lobbies, as it lobbies for an American *ally*—and to a new willingness of Jewish citizens to speak out and be heard in the American way, unlike their craven leaders during the last war.

None of these structures, organizations, or political efforts provided Jews a guarantee of our safety. We came to believe that in times of fear and times of safety the Jewish community would be heard and would have a seat at the table. Even more, we came to believe that were the mobs to come again, we'd be defended by non-Jewish political leaders as legitimate, full members of American society and deserving participants in its public debate.

Some speak of the end of the Golden Age of American Jews. Perhaps that is because they have already heard the shattering glass of all those illusions being destroyed. Perhaps they sense that March of 2019 was America's Jewish political Kristallnacht.

Joshua Block is a Jewish activist with more than twenty-five years of experience in public relations and foreign policy advocacy, and was chosen by The Forward *as one of America's Top 50 Jewish leaders. A Clinton administration appointee, he was later a spokesman for the 1996 Clinton-Gore and 2000 Gore-Lieberman presidential campaigns. A senior AIPAC staff member for nearly a decade, Block served as CEO and president of the Israel Project from 2012 to 2019. Block now works at the Hudson Institute, where he focuses his scholarship on American national security, Middle East policy, and promoting a deeper U.S.–Israeli alliance.*

---

[1] Itamar Eichner, "On Rosh Hashanah, global Jewish population reaches 15.3 million," *Ynet News*, September 26, 2022. http://bit.ly/3hGf2wz.

[2] "Israel's Jewish population passes 7 million on eve of Rosh Hashanah," *The Times of Israel*, September 25, 2022. http://bit.ly/3FUcdSo.

[3] See Federal Bureau of Investigations, *Supplemental Hate Crime Statistics*, 2021 (Washington, D.C.: U.S. Department of Justice, March 2023), pp. 9, 12–14, 16, 17, 39–42. https://bit.ly/3KKiMZJ.

[4] George Flesh, "Anti-Semitism: The numbers don't lie," *JNS*, January 21, 2022. https://bit.ly/3DCafoF.

[5] See "Webinar | Fighting for Freedom in Iran," *Save the Persecuted Christians*, October 20, 2022. http://bit.ly/3huh6ra.

[6] Gary Lane, "Terrorists Spare Nigerian Christian Schoolgirl Leah Sharibu, Will Instead Make Her a 'Slave for Life,'" *CBN News*, October 15, 2018. https://bit.ly/3WN8cVp. See also "Slavery in Sudan," *Christian Solidarity International*. https://csi-usa.org/slavery/.

[7] See Aaron Klein, "More Than a Photo: Obama's Close Associations With Notorious Anti-Semite Louis Farrakhan," *Breitbart*, January 29, 2018. http://bit.ly/3Gd3tHf.

[8] Quoted in Lee Brown, "Kanye West claims 'Jewish underground media mafia' out to get him in Chris Cuomo interview," *The New York Post*, October 18, 2022. https://bit.ly/3zA5yc7.

[9] See Gadi Zaig, "Kanye says 'Jewish Zionists' control the media, Jews own the Black voice," *The Jerusalem Post*, October 17, 2022. https://bit.ly/3fgCSOF.

[10] See Kristina Narizhnaya and Gabrielle Fonrouge, "One suspect in anti-Jewish Brooklyn gel pellet attack held on bail, two other freed," *The New York Post*, November 10, 2022. http://bit.ly/3UVWHdd. See also Louis Keene, "As Black Hebrew Israelite group gathers outside arena, Kyrie Irving returns to NBA court," *The Forward*, November 20, 2022. http://bit.ly/3u98Tfj.

[11] See "Antisemites hang banner over LA freeway declaring Kanye 'right about the Jews,'" *The Times of Israel*, October 23, 2022. http://bit.ly/3hDIjbc.

[12] H.Res.183—116th Congress (2019–2020): "Condemning anti-Semitism as hateful expressions of intolerance that are contradictory to the values and aspirations that define the people of the United States and condemning anti-Muslim discrimination and bigotry against minorities as hateful expressions of intolerance that are contrary to the values and aspirations of the United States." March 7, 2019. http://bit.ly/3WYuyE4.

[13] See Michael Lee, "Rashida Tlaib comes to defense of Ilhan Omar after Minnesota lawmaker made comments comparing US and Israel to Taliban and Hamas," *The Washington Examiner*, June 10, 2021. http://bit.ly/3UAZ7xV.

[14] See Steven Emerson, "Rashida Tlaib: Terrorist-Affiliated Charities 'Inspire Me Every Single Day,'" *The Algemeiner*, October 26, 2022. https://bit.ly/3NLTHNV.

[15] Oren Litwin, "Ilhan Omar's 'Benjamins' Slur Was Deliberate," *Islamist Watch*, February 15, 2019. http://bit.ly/3ht3cpd.

[16] Jewish Telegraphic Agency, "Rep. Ilhan Omar defends 2012 tweet accusing Israel of 'hypnotizing the world,'" *The Times of Israel*, http://bit.ly/3Tsu7yU.

[17] "Newly elected Rep. Ilhan Omar backs Israel boycott movement after telling Jewish audience it isn't effective," *Jewish Telegraphic Agency*, November 14, 2018. http://bit.ly/3hxJFUB.

[18] Quoted in Lukas Mikelionis, "Rep. Ilhan Omar slammed for saying she 'chuckles' when Israel is called a democracy, compares it to Iran," *Fox News*, January 31, 2019. http://bit.ly/3GiDo9X.

[19] Morton A. Klein and Elizabeth A. Berney, "Rep. Ilhan Omar is funded by Israel-hating BDS promoters and PACs," *JNS*, February 15, 2019. http://bit.ly/3TzJSnR.

[20] "1000 Turn Out for CAIR-MI Banquet," *Council on American-Islamic Relations*, March 24, 2009. Archived December 13, 2018. http://bit.ly/3hGlLqb.

[21] Rashida Tlaib's Facebook page. Accessed December 21, 2017, at 5:20 P.M. http://bit.ly/3O3cDba. See also Linda Sarsour's Facebook page. Accessed January 3, 2019, at 10:37 A.M. http://bit.ly/3ErMgbU.

[22] Alyssa Fischer, "Israel Relabeled As 'Palestine' On Map In Rashida Tlaib's Office," *The Forward*, January 4, 2019. http://bit.ly/3UAZE2V.

[23] Ryan Saavedra, "Far-Left Democrats Ocasio-Cortez, Omar, Tlaib Are Normalizing Anti-Semitism In Democratic Party," *The Daily Wire*, February 4, 2019. http://bit.ly/3Eut65d.

[24] "Rashida Tlaib poses with Hezbollah-backing anti-Israel activist," *The Times of Israel*, January 15, 2019. http://bit.ly/3GbJ856.

[25] Rashida Tlaib. Twitter post. November 21, 2017. 8:50 A.M. http://bit.ly/3EtDtWG.

[26] Quoted in Chris Perez, "Ilhan Omar blasted over latest 'anti-Semitic' tweet about Israel," *The New York Post*, March 3, 2019. https://bit.ly/3UwaJSk.

[27] H.Res.183.

[28] See Washington Free Beacon. "Omar: I fear 'Jewish colleagues' think my criticism of Israel is anti-Semitic because I'm a Muslim." Filmed February 27, 2019. YouTube video, 9:54. Posted February 28, 2019. https://rb.gy/qfehqw.

[29] Quoted in Victor Morton, "David Duke praises Rep. Ilhan Omar," *The Washington Times*, March 7, 2019. http://bit.ly/3TzqIyl.

[30] Ryan Tarinelli, Michael R. Sisak, and Michael Balsamo, "5 stabbed at Hanukkah celebration in latest attack on Jews," *Associated Press*, December 30, 2019. https://rb.gy/kxwvh6.

[31] See John Bacon and Charles Stile, "'Act of domestic terrorism': Jersey City suspects had anti-Semitic, anti-police views, authorities say," *USA Today*, December 12, 2019. https://rb.gy/uhvafr.

[32] See David Israel, "NYPD: Hate Crimes Against Jews Up 409%," *The Jewish Press*, March 9, 2022. https://bit.ly/3dpIyEO. See also Amir Rosen, "It's

Open Season on Jews in New York City," *Tablet*, August 28, 2022. http://bit.ly/3Oifttf.

[33] See Janon Fisher, "Orthodox men attacked with fire extinguisher in possible hate crimes in Williamsburg, police say," *The Daily News*, August 22, 2022. http://bit.ly/3Et15La. See also Thomas Tracy, "VIDEO: Orthodox Jewish man struck with broken pieces of furniture in unprovoked anti-Semitic hate crime attack," *The Daily News*, July 9, 2021. http://bit.ly/3UP1Kfm.

[34] "New York Jewish Voters Divided On Governor's Race," *Matzav.com*, November 6, 2022. http://bit.ly/3UR2kt1.

[35] See "See how antisemitism is growing to become mainstream," CNN, August 19, 2022. http://bit.ly/3fZJe5k. See also Alex Safian, "CNN's Rising Hate: Antisemitism in America," *Committee for Accuracy in Middle East Reporting and Analysis*, August 23, 2022. http://bit.ly/3hzns8N.

5

HOW DID WE GET HERE?

REBECCA SUGAR

When I ran alumni programming for Birthright Israel participants in New York years ago, philanthropist Michael Steinhardt and I lamented that the best way to capture the attention of American Jews might be to hire gangs of thugs around the country to break some windows and yell anti-Semitic slurs. Anti-Semitism has a way of reaching out to even the most disengaged Jew. We didn't have to spend a dime, of course, because the anti-Semites already had their plans. The recent spate of anti-Semitic incidents across the country has had the effect we imagined.

Many Jews seem to be paying attention to Jewish life in America in a new way now. Rashida Tlaib, Apartheid Week on college campuses, social media influencers, Colleyville, and much more have come together in critical mass and shoved these "twice-a-year Jews" into the figurative Jewish communal room, many for the first time. They are stumbling around, wondering how we got here and what to do next. "I can't believe this is happening here, in the United States," they say in disbelief.

But, actually, it isn't at all hard to believe. After all, "this" has been happening here for a while. "This" has also happened in almost every diaspora Jewish community throughout history. If by "this" they mean the scapegoating of Jews during turbulent times and the subsequent increase in anti-Semitic activity, then "this" is neither new nor surprising. In fact, it is perfectly predictable.

What most American Jews are really shocked by, but couldn't see until it became inescapably obvious, is the fast-growing, unabashed anti-Semitism of the American political left where they themselves reside. The BDS movement, the Squad, attacks on Hassidic Jews in the streets, Black Lives Matters' charter, "pinkwashing," Deadly Exchange, the anti-Semitic leadership of the Women's March, biased mainstream media coverage of Israel, anti-Semitic professors at elite private high schools, Islamist apologists: It has all felt like a sudden landslide. But, in fact, it has been more like a slow, creeping mudslide that American Jews seem to have entirely missed—until it appeared as a daily feature on their social media feeds. Why do American Jews seem so caught off guard?

One explanation is historical ignorance. It's usually a bad blind spot. If you didn't study Soviet Jewry, perhaps it is difficult to understand that political collectivism is bad for the Jews. If you didn't learn about the implications of group "identity politics" in nineteenth- and twentieth-century Europe, you might not appreciate that the contemporary American manifestation of it is a threat to the Jewish community and Israel. If you don't know that the image of the money-hungry, usurious Jew is an anti-Semitic slur hundreds of years old, then when Ilhan Omar says, "it's all about the Benjamins," you might think the comment was merely an offensive one-off remark that you can overlook. These trends have been building for some time, but if you don't have historical sensitivity to them, you wouldn't guess that the politics you support are also hurting Jews. Then, when your favorite ice cream brand suddenly decides to boycott Israel, it comes as a shock.

Another explanation is a failure of leadership. American Jewish leaders certainly should know our history and concern themselves with helping us not to repeat it. They should be sensitive to signs that portend trouble and should sound the communal alarm bell well in advance of a crisis. Why didn't more of them do exactly that before we started racking up assaults on city streets, hostile Humanities Departments at major American universities, and members of Congress accusing the Jewish State of putting Palestinian kids in cages?

Some did, but too often they were sidelined and dismissed. Many heads of establishment Jewish organizations had long-standing relationships with members of Congress, directors of think tanks, and editors at *The New York Times*, which in the past had proven helpful when defending Jewish interests. They didn't want loud voices pointing out illiberal trends in liberal circles that might compromise the delicate balance of an important relationship. Political and social realities in America had changed, but these leaders and their organizations didn't. They confused their historical access with continuing influence and even as the latter waned, they held firmly to the former. So, they either ignored or explained away what the alarm-bell ringers were warning us about.

Others were committed to the political left and understood that their constituency, the majority of American Jews, were similarly committed. As Jewish organizational affiliation waned, its leadership reasoned that a Jewish world that mirrored liberal Jewish values might attract more members. But "liberal values" rapidly devolved into "left-ist ideology," and Jewish leaders who had committed to the left were now reinterpreting Judaism to keep up with it. They gave progressive buzzwords like "diversity and inclusion," "social action," and "ally-ship" a Jewish name: *tikkun olam.* They made "intersectionality" a Jewish communal priority and suggested that mutual benefit would result from Jewish investment in "the other." Many openly used their Jewish organizations to advocate partisan policy initiatives, claiming that advocacy was the natural outgrowth of authentic Jewish values. Jewish leaders brought Jewish organizational life into such close ideological alignment with the American political left, that a break between the two could not be tolerated.

The orthodoxy around this approach took hold quickly and few challenged it. It was hard to find a Jewish communal conference that didn't feature progressive outreach programs or social action initiatives on behalf of the environment. Jewish foundations couldn't fund them fast enough. At one of these conferences, I recall a courageous representative from a Christian, pro-Israel organization who stood up and cautioned the room that in its pursuit of partisan intersectional interests under the *tikkun olam* banner, the organized Jewish communal world might be marginalizing allies whose American political outlook may not always align but whose Judeo-Christian values did. The prioritization of the one over the other seemed not to be in the interest of the Jewish community in the long term, he pointed out. His message wasn't well received.

Even as the left continued to break away from classical liberalism and demonstrated an increasing tolerance for anti-Semitism in its ranks, Jewish leaders resisted changing course. They claimed the problem was relatively small and not representative. The way to beat it back was with more intersectional fervor and more support for partisan political issues in the name of the Jewish community. We needed more Jewish voices at immigration rallies, they claimed, to demonstrate the unbreakable alliance with the left that our leadership promised was still strong. Jewish leaders religiously pursued those who increasingly rejected them and downplayed that rejection to American Jews.

But the overwhelming reality of what has been happening on the left eventually overwhelmed our leadership's ability to manage the problem. Social media told a very different story than the one that mainstream Jewish leaders had been telling. The size and scope of it reached an unsuspecting American Jewish population who felt it hadn't been prepared. Jews seem to have awakened one morning to a world they didn't recognize. In it, anti-Semitism isn't new at all, and it is being perpetrated by the very people and ideas our leaders told us were our natural allies.

Jewish kids on campus who were taught "diversity and inclusion" as Torah in their temples back home weren't prepared when they were accused of "colonialist, white privilege" support for the Jewish State in philosophy class. No one explained that identity politics is not at all a Jewish concept, but, rather, a poisonous ideology that feeds anti-Semitism against Jews of *all* colors. That it got their "Rabbi of Color" profiled on NPR seemed so meaningful before, but it suddenly revealed itself to be part of the problem. It was stunning to realize that "inclusion" doesn't always include the Jews.

Maybe this is just how markets work: Buyer beware. There are synagogues and organizations to choose from if yours isn't serving you well. It would end there if these institutions didn't pretend to speak on behalf of all "American Jewry" or a large proportion of it. But many do.

Several years ago, I was in a meeting with the leadership of the Union for Reform Judaism (URJ). One of the senior executives in the room proudly declared that the Reform movement represents the great majority of Jews in America. But really, it doesn't. Most American Jews may in fact call themselves "Reform" (or "Reformed" as some of my friends mistakenly say). But most of my Reform Jewish friends can't name URJ president Rabbi Rick Jacobs or list three principles of Reform religious philosophy. When they say they are Reform Jews they usually mean "not Orthodox" or that they pay dues at a Reform Temple they hardly frequent. They show up on Pew Research study pie charts as "Reform Jews," but they don't feel "represented" by the central office or its pronouncements, if they even know what they are.

The Anti-Defamation League (ADL) is the media go-to when anti-Semitism bursts through the doors of an American institution. On whose behalf does it speak? Do politically conservative Jews see the organization as their representative when it issues statements on criminal justice reform or Supreme Court nominees? Do the majority of liberal Jews in America agree with the ADL's recent assertion that racism is an offense only perpetrated by white people? The ADL does have a following, but it is not "American Jewry." It is a particular slice of it, along with some donors from Google.

Whether or not American Jews realize it, Jewish institutions are not only responsive to the interests of non-Jewish audiences, but they are speaking on the entire Jewish community's behalf to the rest of the world: to the media, to politicians, and to foreign leaders. This has consequences. Legislation is passed, funding is allocated, and narratives are built based on what these institutions say are American

Jewish priorities. If left-wing anti-Semitism in America wasn't in the top three of those priorities over the past twenty years (and it wasn't), why would most American Jews have seen any of this coming?

By definition, we have to say that leadership has failed when it hasn't led. But it is also true that those who can't believe how we got "here" share some of the blame for their own confusion. American Jews are largely disconnected from their history and ignorant of their religion. Many don't participate in the very Jewish communal organizations whose leadership is questioned in this article. They don't read Jewish books or follow news about Israel. They don't speak Hebrew or know what Shavuot is. They have so abandoned their particularistic identities that their organizational leaders' penchant for universalism doesn't strike them as odd. They have so conflated their political outlooks with their Jewish identities that they can't see the connection between Jewish organizational partisanship and the worsening of the anti-Semitism problem. They may be attracting the leaders they deserve.

What would *Jewish* leadership specifically look like to most American Jews today? Put another way, if most American Jews were asked to conjure up the perfect Jewish leader, would they be able to make a top-ten list of character traits and priorities to fill out a job description that would be distinguishable from the requirements to lead, say, Habitat for Humanity? What other kind of Jewish leadership would such a fractured, unmoored Jewish community produce than the one we've had?

Michael Steinhardt once spoke to a group of roughly sixty Birthright alumni at an event I was hosting. He asked them a simple question: Who are your Jewish heroes? There was no reply, not from a single person in the room. Then, slowly, a smattering of celebrity names was offered up: Jerry Seinfeld, Steven Spielberg, You?!

Michael was shocked. He began prompting the group by describing a certain Russian refusenik who spent years in the Gulag and later became a member of the Israeli Knesset—and waited for someone to fill in the blank. Still nothing. "Ever heard of Natan Sharansky?" he asked, his eyebrows raised in disbelief. "I think I have heard that name," said one young man in the front row. A few others nodded.

The truth is, most young Jews don't have Jewish heroes. That matters because heroes model the kinds of traits and behaviors that we should be looking for in our leaders. You have to know that particularism defined Revisionist Zionist leader Ze'ev Jabotinsky's bold vision for a proud, unapologetic Jewish State if you want a proud, unapologetic defender of Israel to speak on your behalf today. You have to recognize that a great love of being Jewish (and love for every Jew) inspired the Lubavitcher Rebbe to build an international movement of Jewish revitalization. You have to remember that Abraham Joshua Heschel stood alongside Dr. Martin Luther King, Jr., not to beg his pardon for having marginally greater "privilege" in America but to promote their shared love of the Judeo-Christian values they were proud to say made America possible. You have to know that Hannah Szenes was a warrior and Moses was a humble man. Whoever they are, your Jewish heroes are likely to help you to identify Jewish leaders who can serve you well. If you don't have the former, it will be harder to locate the latter.

Most American Jews will only recognize Moses on my list, and that is a big part of the problem. We are going to continue to get the leaders we deserve, and the shock of our lives when we realize that they aren't leading us that well, so long as anti-Semitism remains the most reliable Jewish engagement tool in American Jewish life and intersectionality is our strategy for staving it off.

Judaism itself is at the core of Jewish survival and understanding that should be bullet point number one on every Jewish leader's job description. It is the thing worth defending when the anti-Semites come and the thing that endures when American political parties and their values change. Jewish leaders who attach themselves and their organizations too much to partisan political interests either miss or dismiss the reality they cannot or will not see, thereby putting all Jews in a dangerous position.

There is no political "forever home" for American Jews. Did we really need BLM to see that? Maybe we did.

Rebecca Sugar *is a philanthropic consultant and writer living in New York City. She has been published in* The Wall Street Journal, USA Today, The Christian Post, *JNS.org,* The Spectator, *and* The Jewish Journal.

6

THE TWO-STATE SOLUTION AND AMERICAN JEWISH SURVIVAL

CAROLINE B. GLICK

The twin forces threatening the survival of American Jews are assimilation and anti-Semitism. Reasonably, they feed off each other. It is the natural progression of human affairs that people fight less for things that are less important to them than they fight for things that are important to them. The weaker and more attenuated the Jewish identity of American Jews becomes, the less willing they are to fight for it.

The American Jewish community's embrace of the so-called two-state solution as its primary position on the Palestinian conflict with Israel has undermined communal efforts to provide a positive and sustainable non-religiously-based Jewish identity to American Jews of all ages. It has debilitated the community's capacity to fight anti-Semitic assaults on its political power and the civil and human rights of American Jews.

The two-state solution is shorthand for a policy model for resolving the Israeli–Palestinian conflict. It asserts that the only way to resolve the Israeli–Palestinian conflict is by transferring land that Israel controls—Judea and Samaria and large portions of sovereign Jerusalem—to the control of the Palestine Liberation Organization's (PLO) governing authority, the Palestinian Authority. According to the two-state model, that land, together with the Gaza Strip, which the Hamas terrorist group has ruled since 2007, is supposed to form a unitary Palestinian state. The formation of such a state is supposed to bring a peaceful resolution to the Israeli–Palestinian conflict and enable peace to break out throughout the Middle East.

The two-state solution is the issue that has most alienated American and Israeli Jews from one another. Since the Rabin-Peres government embarked on the so-called Oslo peace process (or Oslo Accord) with the PLO in 1993, support for the transfer of land to the PLO among Israelis has waxed and waned. Across most of those years, and certainly over the past generation since the PLO rejected the two-state solution outright at the Camp David peace conference in July 2000 and initiated a two-pronged terrorist and political warfare campaign against the Jewish state, public support in Israel for the two-state solution plummeted to single digits. In 2014, I wrote *The Israeli Solution: A One State Plan for Peace in the Middle East* to provide the argument for an Israeli and American abandonment of the failed paradigm in favor of one with a chance of succeeding.[1]

But while Israelis have largely rejected the two-state solution as a policymaking model, in the decades since 1993, American Jewish support for the two-state solution has remained solid and overwhelming. There are almost no major American Jewish organizations that either oppose or seriously question the reasonableness or desirability of the policy model.

Much has been written about how this disparity of positions has harmed relations between American Jews and Israel. But, to date, scant attention has been paid to how the American Jewish community's embrace of the long-failed policy model has caused devastating harm to the community itself.

The Underlying Assumption of the Two-State Solution

Supporters of the two-state solution policy model state axiomatically that it is "the only solution" to the Israeli–Palestinian conflict. In so asserting, they block debate about its nature and reduce the discourse to practicalities regarding how best to implement it. Over the years, decades, and generations, the answer at the end of all these discussions is always the same: Israel is the reason it hasn't succeeded. Israel must be pressured to do more.

This conclusion is unavoidable because the two-state model is based on one fundamental, but largely unremarked, assumption: Israel is to blame for the Israeli–Palestinian conflict. Since the two-state paradigm asserts as an axiom that the only way to resolve the conflict is for Israel to give up sufficient quantities of land that it presently controls to the PLO-controlled Palestinian Authority to satisfy the needs of the Palestinians, the absence of peace is necessarily due to Israel's failure to cough up the lands required for peace. This view is the reason why Israeli communities in Judea and Samaria, and neighborhoods in Jerusalem, are consistently demonized and their very existence viewed as, at best, the moral equivalent of terrorist attacks. The refrain that "settlement activity has to end" has been the routine refrain of most of the American Jewish and practically all international discourse on Israel and the Palestinians for thirty years—not because Jewish neighborhoods and communities are greater obstacles to peace than Palestinian rejection of Israel's right to exist, or because they are obstacles to peace per se. They "need to end" because they defy the foundational assumption of the two-state solution, namely that this is the only path to secure peace and establish justice.

As for "justice," it is notable that the two-state solution always discusses justice as something that the Palestinians alone require. The reason for this is also rooted in the assumption of Israeli guilt at the base of the two-state model. At the most fundamental level, Israel's very existence, which gives it land that it is supposed to surrender, is the reason there is no peace. Israel's existence in the absence of a Palestinian state is an "original sin." Israel needs to repent and expiate its sin through land transfers and the conferral of moral legitimacy on the Palestinians by accepting their narrative and appeasing their demands, wherever they lead.

As it happens, the basic, foundational premise of the two-state solution is entirely false, and it has been proven false repeatedly. The 1993 Oslo peace process was neither the first nor the last time that Israeli and international efforts have been made to resolve the Israeli–Palestinian conflict by dividing the land of Israel between the Jewish state and a Palestinian Arab state.

The first effort to reach this solution came in 1922 when the British partitioned the land they received as a mandate from the League of Nations two years earlier for the establishment of a Jewish state. Britain removed 65 percent of the territory of what was slated to become the Jewish state and established the Arab state of Transjordan—which later became the Hashemite Kingdom of Jordan. The Arabs to the west of the Jordan River, however, failed to make do with that 65 percent. Instead, they ratcheted up their terrorist and diplomatic efforts to block Jewish immigration to the remaining lands and extort the British into renouncing their commitment to establish a Jewish national home in the land of Israel, as they were required to do under the terms of their mandate. The Palestinian Arab war launched in those days against all Jewish presence and sovereignty in the land of Israel has been maintained to the present day.

In the aftermath of the failed Camp David peace summit in July 2000, and the Palestinians' subsequent turn to war, then-Israeli foreign minister Shlomo Ben-Ami ruminated on the implications of what had just happened in an interview with the *Haaretz* newspaper. Ben-Ami, a prominent dove and peace activist, served as Israel's chief negotiator with the PLO in the months that led up to the peace summit, and was a senior member of Israel's negotiating team at Camp David. In his interview, Ben-Ami explained that the problem with the two-state solution was that the Palestinians would not accept a Jewish state within any borders. As he put it:

> Camp David failed because [PLO chief Yasser] Arafat refused to put forward proposals of his own and didn't succeed in conveying to us the feeling that at some point, his demands would have an end.... We didn't expect to meet the Palestinians halfway, and not even two-thirds of the way. But we did expect to meet them at some point. The whole time we waited to see them make some sort of movement in the face of our far-reaching movement. But they didn't.[2]

Ben-Ami continued that the peace process with the PLO—predicated on the belief that peace is a function of Israeli land concessions to the Palestinians—was a hoax.

Speaking of Arafat's 1993 "concession" to recognize Israel's right to exist at the outset of the peace process, Ben-Ami explained, "Arafat's concession *vis-à-vis* Israel at Oslo was a formal concession. Morally and conceptually, he didn't recognize Israel's right to exist. He doesn't accept the idea of two states for two peoples... Neither he nor the Palestinian national movement accept us." Ben-Ami concluded by stating that:

> [W]e are in a confrontation with a national movement in which there are serious pathological elements. It is a very sad movement, a very tragic movement, which at its core doesn't have the ability to set itself positive goals... More than they want a state of their own, they want to spit out our state. In the deepest sense of the words, their ethos is a negative ethos.[3]

Despite Ben-Ami's recognition of its utter futility—for reasons that are beyond the scope of this discussion but have to do with social status, economic interests, and political power—neither Ben-Ami nor the Israeli left abandoned the two-state solution.

The American Jewish community also held fast to it, opting to ignore its fundamental (anti-Semitic) flaw. With almost no exceptions, the American Jewish leadership refused to acknowledge that the peace process collapsed and morphed into the Palestinian terror war against the Jewish state and its citizens because the two-state solution was a hoax predicated on a blood libel. It failed because it blamed the Jews for the Palestinian Arab rejection of Jewish self-determination, of Jewish nationhood, and of the Jewish people's right to justice, freedom, sovereignty, and security in their homeland.

The two-state solution failed because the Palestinians define themselves more by their pathological hatred of the Jews and the Jewish state than by their aspiration for a state of their own. The Palestinians didn't embrace the two-state solution. They used the two-state solution, and use it still today, to blame the Jews for their own pathological Jew-hatred.

In maintaining faith with a failed, anti-Jewish policy paradigm, the American Jewish community joined the Israeli left and the American and European policy elite in ignoring its bigotry. Following the Western foreign policy establishment's example, the Jewish community reduced its discourse on Israel and the Palestinians to the futile discussion of how to best implement the two-state solution, "the only solution" to the Palestinian conflict with Israel.

The first casualty of this position has been American Jewish Zionism, and through it, American Jewish identity.

American Jewish Zionism

What is the basis of a meaningful, sustainable Jewish identity for diaspora Jewry?

To the extent the question was ever asked, the answer for thousands of years was the Torah. From the time of the Exodus from Egypt 3,300 years ago, the Torah has been the basis for Jewish identity, family, faith, and nationhood. It attaches Jews to their religious tradition, to one another as the Nation of Israel, and to the Jewish homeland, the Land of Israel. While Torah-based Jewish identity is meaningful and sustainable, it is not immediately, or meaningfully, accessible to America's largely non-observant, secular Jewish community.

This brings us to Zionism.

More than any other story, Zionism is *the* Jewish story. Jews have been Zionists since the dawn of Judaism with Abraham 4,000 years ago. Zionism is the basis of the story of the Exodus from Egypt. It is through Zionism that Jews have been political actors within their own communities, in their homeland, and on the world stage. The Jewish people's continuous attachment to the Land of Israel, no less than the Torah and intertwined with the Torah, enabled the Jews to survive through 2,000 years of exile and homelessness. Jewish history and attachment to Israel attaches Jews in America to Jews in Israel and to Jews around the world who naturally share their Jewish attachment to Israel. So as a practical matter, Zionism attaches diaspora Jews to the center of the Jewish world—Israel—in a sustained and mutually beneficial way.

Zionism is also the most powerful non-religion-based source of a meaningful and sustainable Jewish identity. Whether defined as the Jewish national liberation movement, the attachment of Jews to the land of Israel and the State of Israel, or the Jewish migration to Israel from diaspora communities, Zionism was the basis of non-Orthodox Jewish identity in the U.S. for three generations. From the founding of the modern State of Israel in 1948 until 1993, these American Jews were informed, inspired, and motivated by this Jewish, Zionist education and disposition. It formed the basis of their identity and their communal attachments.

This began to change in 1993, as the American Jewish establishment at large embraced the two-state solution paradigm as the end-all-be-all of Israel policy. Growing numbers of communal institutions, organizations, activists, and thought leaders began significantly downgrading and watering down the meaning of Zionism. In Jewish day schools, Sunday programs, synagogues, Jewish publications, and local and national Jewish organizations, the meaning of Zionism was revised. It no longer meant supporting Israel and feeling connected to Israel. It no longer meant immigrating to Israel. Zionism was subsumed within the peace process. Its meaning was gutted and then revised. Being pro-Israel came to mean supporting the two-state solution model. That is, to be pro-Israel meant being supportive of the Palestinian national movement. The reasons for this shift are manifold. But among the most prominent are a desire to join the peace carnival, to fit in with the foreign policy movers and shakers, and, at least initially, to support the efforts of the Israeli government. Sober examination of the realities of the Middle East generally, or of the Palestinian national movement and the actions of the PLO on the ground in the Palestinian Authority specifically, rarely received attention.

So, if Zionism is the basis for your Jewish identity, and if being a Zionist has come to mean being part of an historic movement that creates a Jewish state and a Palestinian state that will live side by side, but the Jewish state is foiling the establishment of the Palestinian state, it becomes difficult, if not impossible, for you to remain part of that movement. It is better to join with opponents of Israel and attack Israel and its Jewish supporters for anti-Palestinianism—which, by the post–1993 definition of Zionism, is also anti-Zionism. Hence, J Street, for example, which bills itself as "pro-Israel and pro-peace," is effectively an anti-Israel organization. Since, under the two-state axiom, Israel is to blame for the absence of peace, being pro-Israel means being anti-Israel and being opposed to Jewish American supporters of Israel.

With Zionism thus subsumed in the fundamentally anti-Zionist, and hence anti-Jewish, narrative of the two-state solution, American Jews who have been schooled in this way of thinking have been left with few options. If they don't wish to become Orthodox Jews, and Zionism has become anti-Zionism, what meaningful basis for building a sustainable and positive Jewish identity do they have? In a real sense, the two-state solution not only facilitates assimilation; it compels Jews to assimilate.

Facing the Anti-Semites

As Jews were learning to support the PLO, the Palestinians' long-time supporters on America's political left followed the post-Camp David Palestinians in becoming more open in their rejection of Israel's right to exist. The BDS campaigns of today that make expressing support for Israel in any way impossible on university campuses, and increasingly impossible in corporate life in America, began with Arafat's rejection of the two-state solution and return to terror in 2000.

Confused by the two-state solution and weighed down by a morally ambiguous understanding of the conflict based on the false and anti-Israel assumptions embedded in the ostensibly neutral two-state solution, American Jews have been ill-equipped to handle the anti-Semitic mobs now gathered against them. Over the past two decades, we have seen untold instances of pro-Palestinian protesters calling for Israel's destruction (slandering it as a Nazi or apartheid state) and Jewish activists counter-protesting with peace signs and protestations of support for the two-state solution. These (dwindling) counter-protests have been ineffective because the protesters have ignored or been oblivious to the twin elephants in the middle of the room: (1) the intrinsic, unconditional justice and morality of Zionism and Israel, and (2) Jew-hatred. Young American Jews are no longer taught that Israel is moral and just in its own right, and so they cannot see that those who attack Israel for imaginary crimes are bigots.

These Jewish pro-Israel and pro-peace activists don't realize that the anti-Israel protesters arrayed against them seek Israel's destruction because it is the Jewish state, and their disenfranchisement because they are Jews. A growing number of American Jews cannot understand why anti-Zionism is anti-Semitism. And since they have become pro-Palestinian, conditional supporters of Israel, they cannot understand how to fight against pro-Palestinian anti-Semites.

The American Jewish leadership's embrace of the two-state solution has been a two-fold disaster for the community. It has denied non-religious Jews a meaningful, authentic, and sustainable Jewish identity. And even more disastrously, by acceding to and promoting the two-state solution's unstated slander that Israel is bad, they deny American Jews the truth they need to defend themselves and their communities from the most politically powerful and dangerous form of anti-Semitism now ravaging the American Jewish community—anti-Zionism.

Caroline B. Glick is an award-winning journalist and former senior columnist for The Jerusalem Post *and* Israel Hayom. *She is the author of* Shackled Warrior: Israel and the Global Jihad *(2008) and* The Israeli Solution: A One State Plan for Peace in the Middle East *(2014).* The Israeli Solution *has been endorsed by leading U.S. policymakers, including former Vice President Mike Pence and Senator Ted Cruz, and National Security Advisor John Bolton. She now hosts the podcast* The Caroline Glick Show *for JNS.*

---

[1]   See Caroline B. Glick, *The Israeli Solution: A One State Plan for Peace in the Middle East* (New York, NY: Crown Forum, 2014).

[2]   Ari Shavit, "End of a Journey," *Haaretz*, September 13, 2001. https://bit.ly/3D9A6nc.

[3]   *Ibid.*

7

WOKE IN CONTENT, JEWISH IN FORM: ON THE FAILINGS OF JEWISH EDUCATION IN AMERICA

NAYA LEKHT, PH.D.

"We know the Zionist perspective," a chorus of Jewish students at elite Jewish day schools across the nation continuously assure me. "We want to hear the other side. We want to know the Palestinian side." Indeed, the tagline of IfNotNow, one of the most virulent anti-Zionist Jewish youth groups, is, "You never told me."[1]

It was my latest visit to a prestigious Jewish day school in North America that prompted me to re-evaluate how it is that we got to a place where I question the efficacy of Jewish and Israel education in America. It was at one such lecture that I had given on anti-Zionism and antisemitism that students complained of my bias, presenting me with a plethora of grievances with Israel. In that moment, I decided to switch gears: "You have presented criticisms of Israel, and you claim that you come from Zionist homes and a Zionist school. So, you tell me: Why should Israel exist as a Jewish country?"

The Zionist challenge, as I have come to call it, was met with alarming rejoinders. One student proclaimed, "To be completely honest, as I am thinking out loud, I have to say, I would be willing to give up the land if human rights would be restored to the Palestinians." Her friend further explained: "Yes, because I can pray and practice my Judaism here [America] without ever having to be there [Israel]." Another student stated: "I can't trust Israeli courts when it comes to settling land disputes because they are majority Jewish and therefore, biased." And finally, a student settled it all: "I don't see a reason to call myself a Zionist. Zionism has fulfilled its purpose."

How did we get here? How do our brightest and most dedicated Jewish students surrender the land, the trust in their people, and their history?

It used to be that within Jewish families in North America, one sensible reason to send kids to Jewish day schools and to Jewish youth programs was to avoid anti-Israel bias in the classroom. This strategy, however, has proven to not only be ineffective, but more alarmingly, produced a generation of anti-Zionist Jews[2]—or, as Natan Sharansky and Gil Troy call them, the "un-Jews."[3] Likewise, having Israeli parents or joining Israeli youth movements, such as *tsofim*, provide little to no real shelter from the dangers of radical leftism, which has ushered in anti-Zionism, today's most potent form of Jew-hatred.

A stark example is a graduate of a K–12 Jewish day school, Simone Zimmerman, the founder of IfNotNow (a Jewish organization whose goal is to oppose "Israeli occupation"). Zimmerman is but one, although vivid, example of how Jewish education provides little refuge from an education steeped in Marxist thought.[4] But the phenomenon of Jewish young adults graduating Jewish day schools and joining anti-Israel groups such as J Street, Jewish Voice for Peace, IfNotNow, and even Students for Justice in Palestine, has been in the making for decades now. Indeed, Jewish day school graduates are at the helm of anti-Israel and anti-American movements on college campuses. They aren't just members, they are leaders. How did this happen?

To help answer this question, I turn to a Soviet policy enshrined during the Stalin years: "socialist in content, national in form." Having formed a nascent Soviet government in 1918, several ethnic minorities (that is, Jewish, Ukrainian, Uzbek, and Armenian) found themselves under Soviet rule. Party officials had a problem to solve: how to unite these diverse ethnic minorities under the *aegis* of a common ideology.

What the central committee devised was ingenious: Allow ethnic minorities to speak their native language, publish newspapers and books in their native language, and support the arts of the minorities. The only caveat: The content had to promote socialism. Indeed, in the 1920s and even in the 1930s, there was a burgeoning of Yiddish in the Soviet Union. This is why Jews scanning the globe in 1919 declared the Jewish future *not* in Palestine or America, but in the Soviet Union! How wrong they were is for another time (anti-Semitism returned in greater force in the Soviet Union with the murder of Yiddish poets, artists, and writers during Stalin's last years in power).[5]

In a rather twisted turn of historic events that would make Stalin chuckle, Jewish day schools in North America practice "woke in content, Jewish in form." Indeed, all major Jewish groups that oppose the "Israeli occupation" or promote the BDS movement have been started by Jews who either graduated from Jewish day schools or were involved in Jewish youth groups:

1. **Jewish Voice for Peace:** Founder Julie Ivny joined Hashomer Hatzair, a Jewish youth group focused on social justice and Judaism, when she was in the third grade: "The older teens in the youth group," a sympathetic article says, "encouraged their waist-high counterparts to think and talk about the world around them, to not ignore the inequality that persisted in Los Angeles' neighborhoods and schools."[6] According to the ADL, Jewish Voice for Peace is a "radical anti-Israel activist group that advocates for a complete economic, cultural and academic boycott of the state of Israel."[7]

2. **J Street:** Founder Jeremy Ben-Ami completed Hebrew school at Temple Rodeph Sholom in Manhattan, a Reform synagogue. Ben-Ami founded J Street as a reaction to the American Israel Public Affairs Committee (AIPAC), whose goal is to foster a strong relationship between the U.S. and Israel. According to J Street, the "ongoing Israeli occupation of Palestinian territory is a major obstacle to the achievement of Israeli-Palestinian peace, is a systemic injustice violating the rights of the Palestinian people, and poses a severe threat to Israel's long-term future as a democratic homeland for the Jewish people."[8]

3. **IfNotNow:** Founded by Simone Zimmerman, a graduate of two Jewish day schools in Los Angeles, the group calls itself a movement to end Israel's "occupation." In 2018, IfNotNow held a mourner's kaddish service for Palestinians killed by the Israeli army in a Gaza airstrike.[9]

This is not a coincidence. This is a pattern. And it comes from Jewish educational institutions that focus not on Judaism and anti-Semitism specifically, but on promoting "anti-racist" education, restoring "climate justice," and battling gender and racial "inequity." Moreover, at the root of it all is discomfort with Jewish particularism: a majority Jewish state with borders and, by extension, Jewish nationalism. Jewish mainstream institutions have abandoned Jewish particularism and gravitated toward universalism. Through universalism, we have re-written, so to speak, three major concepts in Judaism: *tzedek, tzedek tirdof; tikkun olam*; and *derech eretz*.

1. *Tzedek, tzedek tirdof*: "Justice, justice shall you pursue…"

    This phrase, taken from Deuteronomy 16:20, appears in most Jewish schools' mission statements, at times even emblematized on the front gates of the school. The original text reads: "Justice, justice shall you pursue, that you may thrive and occupy the land that Adonai your God is giving you." In its entire context, it is an imperative from God that the Jewish people occupy and settle in Eretz Yisrael by appointing magistrates and officials who will "not judge unfairly." Willfully forgetting the remainder of the passage, Jewish educators apply these words, "justice, justice shall you pursue," as an ethical permission slip to embrace social justice causes such as racial and gender inequity, inclusivity, and immigration reform, to name a few.

2. *Tikkun olam*: "Repair the world."

    While *tikkun olam* is a signature theme of Jewish tradition in North America, somewhere along the way Jewish educators came to believe that the goal for the Jewish people was to help to repair the world through solving world hunger, campaigning against occupations real or imagined, ending gender wage gaps, and fighting climate change; however, in its original formulation, *tikkun olam* is achieved through ethical and ritual *mitzvot*, such as keeping the laws of *kashrut* and observing the Sabbath. Similar to those who invoke *tzedek, tzedek tirdof* piecemeal, *tikkun olam*, which comes from the *Aleinu*, a seminal prayer in Jewish liturgy, appears in a passage that extends hope in "You, Adonai our God… to completely cut off all false gods; to repair the world, Your holy empire." We make a grave error, therefore, in thinking that *tikkun olam* means embracing a woman's right to choose, open immigration, or supporting equity of outcome policies.

3. *Derech eretz*: "Way of the land"

Although the literal translation is "way of the land," Jewish educators have applied *derech eretz* to embrace compassion, kindness, and "common decency." The problem, however, is that compassion and kindness to each person mean different things. I once asked my students to define kindness and received disparate responses. To one, kindness was giving something from oneself in order to benefit another person; to another, it was saying kind words in order to make someone else feel better.

Derech eretz appears in several iterations in rabbinic literature. Take, for example, the *midrash* from Exodus Rabbah (Shemot Rabbah 35:2). In this tractate, an example of *derech eretz* is "refrain[ing] from using wood from a fruit-bearing tree to build a house."[10] Here, *derech eretz* is not a commentary on kindness, but rather a frame to help people to make better economic and ecological choices. But as I once heard among a cohort of Jewish senior educators at a conference, practicing *derech eretz* was finding a way to incorporate LGBTQ awareness into the Jewish middle school curriculum.

To return to the dictum "socialist in content, national in form," Soviet officials relied on this policy in order to unite a society around a shared system of values. In its entirety, the slogan, taken from Stalin's 1934 essay "Marxism and the National-Colonial Question," reads: "The development of cultures national in form and socialist in content is necessary for the purpose of their ultimate fusion into one General Culture, socialist as to form and content, and expressed in one general language."[11] This "one General Culture" was emblematized by the "new Soviet man"—*novyj Sovetskii chelovek*—an archetype of the Leninist-Marxist ideals. Regardless of the *chelovek's* ethnic background, he was a highly conscious individual, hyper-aware of his role to oppose private property and the greed of capitalism and to support the worker against the petty bourgeoisie. The policy to conform was a success. Within five to ten years, ethnic minorities touted the Soviet policy line; and within fifteen to twenty years, as was planned, the "national form" had disappeared. By the 1960s, Jewish homes in the Soviet Union saw a 66 percent decline in spoken Yiddish.

But at least in the Soviet Union, it was done for a cause, granted a rotten one. What is the reason—the cause—for Jewish educators to practice "woke in content, Jewish in form"? Certainly, it is not due to external forces, as in the case of the Soviet government that mandated educational policy. In North America, we cannot point to a single leader, a legislative document, or unique event that demonstrates a widespread adoption of these principles. What we can do, instead, is look to the triad—*tzedek, tzedek tirdof, tikkun olam*, and *derech eretz*—and find a common denominator: the removal of God from each of the Jewish ideas. In each invocation of the triad, God is not present.

The consequence of an absent God is that man must step in to restore order. Therein lies the problem: The moral compass is thus defined by individuals and not the institutional codex from which the principles emanate. The lack of explicit theological grounding allows individuals to sanction ideologies and policies they see fit to promote.

My recent encounter with young Jews demonstrates that in each of their articulations—from discomfort with a Jewish majority court system to enshrining human rights, and, most significantly, finding no reason to be a Zionist since "Zionism has fulfilled its purpose"—somewhere along the way, Jewish educators, along with the institutions, have dropped the ball on Jewish identity. It was most painful to hear a young Jewish student surrender one of the holiest pillars of Jewish identity, the Land of Israel, in order to "restore" justice and human rights to the Palestinians. And what is most painful is that behind her reasoning is a well-oiled Jewish education system that has taught this young lady that, in order to be a Jew, she must repair the world, seek justice for the persecuted, and jettison her parochial Jewish nationalism. This young lady, therefore, surrenders the Land *because* she is a Jew, a Jew who has been taught social justice in content while national in form.

What then is the answer? How do we treat this alarming malaise? First and foremost, we address the root cause: discomfort with Jewish nationalism. Next, we unpack Jewish nationalism by reminding American Jews that we are, first and foremost, a people, *not* a religion. We are an indigenous people from the Land of Israel; the reason we have been dispersed around the globe is because we were exiled from our national homeland.

We need to stop capitulating to the *Zeitgeist*, that is the desire to fit Jewish identity into a woke framework. Yes, Zionism is a movement of justice; yes, Zionism sought to restore power to the persecuted Jewish people. But this is partial. We must inspire our Jewish youth in the idea that we are living in the most miraculous moment, a most supreme Zionist moment. Through Zionism, Jews have returned to history: We are not being written about, but rather are the scribes of history. What is Zionism? Zionism is a national Jewish movement—it is about returning the Jewish people to their homeland, with self-determination, with power, and with secure borders.

Naya Lekht received her Ph.D. from UCLA in Russian Literature, where she wrote her dissertation on how Soviet writers pushed communist-enforced boundaries of Holocaust representation in literature and film. A passionate educator and public speaker, Naya writes and teaches on the topic of antisemitism, and Soviet influences on contemporary anti-Zionism in particular. She is currently a research fellow at the Institute for the Global Study of Antisemitism and Policy (ISGAP) and education editor at White Rose Magazine.

---

[1] *YouNeverToldMe.org.* Archived June 12, 2019. https://bit.ly/3yPAVyU. The site has now been made "private." See also Daniel J. Solomon, "IfNotNow Launches #YouNeverToldMe Anti-Occupation Campaign," *The Forward*, September 11, 2017. https://bit.ly/3CNgFzr.

[2] Jewish Telegraphic Agency, "Jewish Harvard students form anti-Zionist organization," *The Times of Israel*, February 13, 2020. https://bit.ly/3MIASdZ.

[3] Natan Sharansky and Gil Troy, "The Un-Jews," *Tablet*, June 16, 2021. https://bit.ly/3eHCS9W.

[4] See "Simone Zimmerman," *Canary Mission*. https://bit.ly/3VDAuS5.

[5] See Lawrence W. Reed, "The Night of the Murdered Poets: Remembering One of Stalin's Forgotten Killing Sprees," *Foundation for Economic Freedom*, August 12, 2022. https://bit.ly/3ERNgXj. See also Aaron Reich, "On this

day: 13 Jews killed by Stalin in Night of the Murdered Poets," *The Jerusalem Post*, August 21, 2021. https://bit.ly/3TA7Akf.

6   Stacey Palevsky, "Oakland activist cornerstone of Jewish community," *JWeekly*, June 22, 2007. https://bit.ly/3CMokh5.

7   "Jewish Voice for Peace," *Anti-Defamation League*, July 19, 2013. https://bit.ly/3TAa0PU.

8   "Annexation, Occupation & Settlements," *J Street*. https://bit.ly/3CJ7WOz.

9   IfNotNow. Twitter post. May 17, 2018. 9:30 P.M. https://bit.ly/3eBMjYF.

10   Rabbi Peretz Rodman, "Derech Eretz," *My Jewish Learning*. https://bit.ly/3sbEOKM.

11   Quoted in Richard Taruskin, *Russian Music at Home and Abroad: New Essays* (Oakland, CA: University of California Press, 2016), p. 263.

8

WHERE JEWISH LEADERSHIP
WENT ASTRAY

RICHARD L. KRONENFELD, PH.D.

O n Sunday, July 11, 2021, an impressive array of more than one
hundred Jewish and interfaith organizations concerned about
the rising tide of anti-Semitism in America held a rally at the U.S.
Capitol.[1] Hoping to match the success of a rally for Soviet Jewry organized by famed Soviet dissident Natan Sharansky that drew more
than 250,000 American Jews, the organizers even provided free bus
transportation for people to come from Baltimore, Boston, across
New Jersey, New York City, and Philadelphia. Sadly, their good intentions weren't amply rewarded. Estimates of crowd size ranged from
300 by the ever-hostile media to 3,000 by the organizers, who con-
soled themselves that it was a hot summer day and millions of viewers
watched via Zoom.

Other Jewish activists saw it differently, however. Foreign policy analyst Mitchell Bard summarized as follows: "The country's

largest and most active organizations, which are spending millions of dollars to fight anti-Semitism, failed to convince their members it was worth their time to show the American public that Jewish lives matter."[2] Jonathan S. Tobin, editor-in-chief of the *Jewish News Syndicate (JNS)*, noted the difference in support of Israel from the politically and religiously liberal majority of the community versus those who are Orthodox, politically conservative, or pro-Zionist and questioned whether American Jews are really united against anti-Semitism.[3] CUNY professor Phyllis Chesler questioned whether rallies have any effect in general.[4] Respected commentator Jonathan Rosenblum observed:

> The fecklessness of American Jewish leadership was on full display at the recent rally. The organizers felt the need to emphasize that the rally was "against all hatred," not just anti-Semitism. That message both distorts and trivializes anti-Semitism.... The speakers at the anti-Semitism rally were carefully mooted to exclude any ardent advocates for Israel or anyone who might be charged with Islamophobia... No speakers were called upon to demonstrate the absurdity of claims of Israeli apartheid and genocide or to explain why they are anti-Semitic.

His conclusion: "The failure of the 'No Fear' rally represents the failure... of American Jewish leadership."[5]

How did we reach this point where political ideology outweighs what should be unified Jewish support for Israel? For answers, we can look back at our history. To begin, consider the interpretation of Isaiah 1:10–17, in which the prophet castigates Israel, saying that because of their sinful behavior, God finds the people's offerings worthless, rejects their prayers, and concludes, "Learn to do good, seek justice, vindicate the victim, render justice to the orphan, take up the grievance of the widow."

The simple meaning of these verses is to observe both the particularistic ritual commandments between the Jewish people and God and the universalistic commandments for ethical behavior toward people. A deeper meaning can be inferred: The two sets of commandments have equal standing. Thus, when the Enlightenment swept across Europe and many Jews came to regard the ritual commandments as archaic, the ethical commandments (which later came to be known as "social justice") became the core of their Jewish identity. They justified this substitution by improperly invoking a sixteenth-century Kabbalistic concept, *tikkun olam*,[6] literally "healing/repairing the world," thereby affording them a convenient way to escape the burden of being a Jew in Europe without converting to another religion. While Chabad, for example, regards *tikkun olam* as a basic religious obligation of everyone to bring the world closer to the state of perfection that God wants, the newly secularized Jews began to equate it with socialism. In twentieth-century America, with New Deal liberalism, they largely kept silent during the Holocaust to remain under the radar.

After the Holocaust, even Reform Jews (who had been reluctant to embrace Zionism) initially supported the new State of Israel. As the ideology of progressivism supplanted liberalism, however, and as Israel and its supporters were increasingly slandered with the bogus charge of "oppressing poor, darker-skinned, indigenous Palestinians," secularized Jews began distancing themselves from Israel. Under the rubric of *tikkun olam*, they instead embraced progressivism as a universalized view that allowed them to disassociate themselves from mainstream Judaism and Zionism, which they could then disparage as being too parochial as opposed to their wider vision of caring for all of humanity.

This process is discussed in much greater detail by Jonathan Neumann in his book *To Heal the World? How the Jewish Left Corrupts Judaism and Endangers Israel*. Neumann asserts that the Jewish left has effectively hijacked Judaism and misused *tikkun olam*, which he categorizes as having no place in Judaism, to conflate the religion with its social justice agenda, which is *political*, not religious. Charity and good works are not the same as *tikkun olam*, nor is *tikkun olam* a commandment. Neumann further asserts that, "Not only has tikkun olam enabled the misappropriation of Scripture, but its stridently universalistic aspirations undermine Jewish Peoplehood and in so doing give sanction to anti-Zionism and assimilation. This state of affairs is not sustainable."[7]

We can now analyze why, as well as how, established Jewish leadership went astray. As compassionate people with a history of persecution, as well as a Divine injunction to pursue justice, we are naturally drawn to the cause of civil rights and internationalism, both of which have been pre-empted by the left. Consequently, our leadership sides with minorities and ignores or excuses their anti-Semitism while concentrating on anti-Semitism from the far-right fringe. While its propensity for violence makes it a threat, it's small in numbers and has little popular support. Adding insult to injury, one man, Arab-American activist James Zogby, outsmarted the entire American Jewish establishment by portraying Palestinians as the victims of Israeli oppression, which enabled him to enlist first college students and then the media to support the Palestinian cause.[8]

Thus, the ADL (longtime lead Jewish defense organization) convened a summit conference, ostensibly to fight anti-Semitism, featuring radical leftist speakers but no supporters of Israel, which claimed that fighting anti-Semitism requires Jews to confront our own "racism." Daniel Greenfield hypothesizes that "the ADL is careful to cultivate an imaginary distinction between good leftist hatred of Israel and bad leftist hatred of Jews so as not to offend its political allies."[9] The ADL endorsed Black Lives Matter and critical race theory, despite the ideology identifying Jews as having "white privilege"—even Israeli Jews, the majority of whom are non-whites from North Africa and the Middle East. The ADL also adopted a definition of racism under which only whites can be racist, namely "[t]he marginalization and/or oppression of people of color based on a socially constructed racial hierarchy that privileges white people,"[10] which it had to withdraw after a wave of objections. Then, they hired left-wing activist Tema Smith, who has a long history of criticizing Israel, as its new director of Jewish outreach and partnerships.[11]

The same pattern of siding with the "progressives" predominates at the local level as well. For example, Patti Munter cited her local Rochester, New York, Jewish Federation as consistently inviting anti-Zionist, pro-BDS (Boycott, Divestment, and Sanctions) activists to speak while ignoring Zionists. She observed, "Rochester's community leadership has become so wedded to the new 'progressive' ideology that it forbids community discussions, inquiries, or challenges to it." Moreover, "[r]adical anti-Zionist activists and their allies are building a new religion inside of Judaism, and it has seeped inside the Jewish community's mainstream organizations.... An increasing number of us see that Jewish organizations have been enabling and even promoting groups ...which are now so visibly our foes."[12]

More disturbing yet is a developing trend for states, starting with California, to require ethnic studies courses in the public schools that are anti-Semitic and anti-Zionist, with support from the teachers' unions. Although Governor Gavin Newsom vetoed the first version of such a mandate that openly advocated for BDS against Israel before signing a second version that toned down the anti-Semitism, educational consultants with the Liberated Ethnic Studies Model Curriculum Consortium (LESMC) have made inroads with major California school districts, starting with Castro Valley, to adopt the original version. Even worse, as of this writing, the University of California is considering a mandate that would force every student in the state, even those attending Jewish day schools or other private schools, to take a course using the LESMC curriculum to qualify for admission to the University of California.[13]

Meanwhile, the Massachusetts Department of Elementary and Secondary Education now mandates a curriculum to be used in all public schools whose lesson plans about the Israeli–Palestinian conflict have been re-written to exclusively reflect the Palestinian point of view.[14] While there was opposition in California, CAMERA reported that Boston's ADL, Federation, and JCRC failed to properly vet these materials.[15] They have been informed, and yet we see no evidence that they will act. In a previous case in Newton, Massachusetts, they betrayed the community and defended the anti-Israel curriculum.[16] Jewish leadership seems conflicted between its progressive "woke" ideology and its fiduciary responsibility to the community. Instead of doing their job, Jewish leaders pretend that their political ideology is consistent with the best interests of the Jewish community.

The American Jewish community is threatened collectively as never before. In the fall of 2021, in an interview with *The Jewish Press*, Rabbi Yitzchok Adlerstein made an ominous statement: "The only prediction I make, despite my abhorrence of such predictions, is that the noose is tightening around American Jewry."[17]

Especially frightening is the situation at America's universities: The more elite the college, the more intense the anti-Semitism. It is chilling to think that these campus bullies will be the next generation of America's leaders throughout society. A majority of Jewish college students have felt the need to hide their identity,[18] and Jews are increasingly being excluded from student government and other campus activities.[19] Ironically, officials charged with enforcing "diversity, equity, and inclusion"[20] are among the worst promoters of anti-Jewish propaganda.[21]

As we have seen, the response of mainstream Jewish organizations has been inadequate. If that continues, they may spawn new, competing defense organizations (which is already happening), and a "revolt of the masses."

Domestic anti-Semitism is linked to international anti-Zionism, which has reached the point where Palestinians gleefully anticipate that their ludicrous charges that Israel is an apartheid state (which grossly insults black South Africans who experienced real apartheid) will succeed in delegitimizing Israel. Whereupon the dictators' club that is the U.N. and its Human Rights Council, supported by mendacious reports from Amnesty International and other so-called human rights groups, will call for global BDS and for arresting and trying Israelis for alleged war crimes. While their tactics succeeded in South Africa, as it is said in physics, a good idea works only once.

In this trying time, we need to remember being delivered from slavery in Egypt, from Haman's plans of genocide in Persia, and from the Seleucid Greeks' plans against Judaism. It is beyond the scope of this essay to discuss possible courses of action for us. Suffice it to say, in the words of the philosopher Yogi Berra, "It ain't over till it's over."

Richard L. Kronenfeld holds a Ph.D. in physics from Stanford University and has taught mathematics and physics as adjunct faculty at Arizona State University, and at six of the colleges in the Maricopa Community College District (Metro Phoenix area).

Editors' Note: In the face of backlash from some brave grassroots activists—most notably the AMCHA Initiative[22]—and even faculty, the University of California Academic Council—though it "lamented the hostility toward ethnic studies in academia from more traditional academic units"—reluctantly chose not to ratify the proposed ethnic studies admission requirement. Voting to "send the proposal back to BOARS [the Board of Admissions and Relations with Schools] for further consideration,"[23] as of this writing, the proposal appears lost in the bureaucracy for the present moment.

---

[1] "Rally against anti-Semitism draws 3,000 at US Capitol," *JNS*, July 12, 2021. https://bit.ly/3MMM9Kv.

[2] Mitchell G. Bard, "The 'not enough fear' rally," *JNS*, July 14, 2021. https://bit.ly/3TiKw9J.

[3] Jonathan S. Tobin, "Are Jews really united against anti-Semitism?", *JNS*, July 12, 2021. https://bit.ly/3To74WU.

[4] Phyllis Chesler, "Opinion: Is a rally the way to beat anti-Semitism?", *World Israel News*, July 14, 2021. https://bit.ly/3glNewO.

[5] Jonathan Rosenblum, "Two rallies: The contrast between the gatherings pretty much captures the trajectory of American Jewry," *Jewish World Review*, August 6, 2021. https://bit.ly/3TFs773.

[6] Edward Alexander, "Jonathan Neumann, *To Heal the World? How the Jewish Left Corrupts Judaism and Endangers Israel*," *Jewish Political Studies Review*, Vol. 29, Nos. 3–4, September 4, 2018. https://bit.ly/3eKBRhj.

[7] Jonathan Neumann, *To Heal the World: How the Jewish Left Corrupts Judaism and Endangers Israel* (New York, NY: All Points Books, 2018), p. xvii.

[8] Charles Jacobs, "How James Zogby Seduced Liberal America," *The Forward*, July 6, 2016. https://bit.ly/3gnpqIC.

9   Daniel Greenfield, "The ADL Convenes a Summit of Anti-Semites to Fight Anti-Semitism," *FrontPage Mag*, November 10, 2021. https://bit.ly/3Ddc5vA.

10 Quoted in Tobin, "The ADL's disturbing obsession with race," *JNS*, February 4, 2022. https://bit.ly/3DdJd6D.

11 Debbie Hall, "Tema Smith and the ADL: Controversy Explained," *Scholars for Peace in the Middle East*, February 25, 2022. https://bit.ly/3yRPQIX.

12 Patti Munter, "America's failing Jewish establishment: The case of the Rochester Federation," *JNS*, June 21, 2021. https://bit.ly/3MMOd5d.

13 Tammi Rossman-Benjamin, "New Proposal Would Force CA School Districts to Adopt 'Liberated' Curriculum if Students Want Admission to UC Schools," *The Jewish Journal*, February 23, 2022. https://bit.ly/3elL67H.

14 Karen D. Hurvitz, "From Texas to Massachusetts: Will Incitement Wake up Sleeping Jewish Leaders?", *JNS*, February 1, 2022. https://bit.ly/3fLrHgv.

15 Steven Stotsky, "Proposed Ethnic Studies Curriculum in Massachusetts Sparks Controversy," *Committee for Accuracy in Middle East Reporting and Analysis*, February 8, 2022. https://bit.ly/3epepWR.

16 Jacob Kamaras, "ADL downplays controversy over anti-Israel texts in curriculum of Newton, Mass.," *JNS*, April 15, 2013. https://bit.ly/3BtVzFB.

17 Eve Glover, "Rabbi Adlerstein On This And That In The Jewish World," *The Jewish Journal*, September 2, 2021. https://bit.ly/3ShYojp.

18 "Survey finds nearly two-thirds of Jewish students feel unsafe, half hide identity," *JNS*, September 20, 2021. https://bit.ly/3D8ARwR.

19 Kenneth L. Marcus, "Berkeley develops Jewish-free zones," *JNS*, September 29, 2022. https://bit.ly/3Ty69CP.

20 Tobin, "Why does 'diversity' have to lead to anti-Semitism?", *JNS*, December 29, 2021. https://bit.ly/3gno6FV.

21 Jay Greene, Ph.D. and James Paul, "Inclusion Delusion: The Antisemitism of Diversity, Equity, and Inclusion Staff at Universities," *The Heritage Foundation*, December 8, 2021. https://herit.ag/3MLhGMQ.

22 See Gabe Stutman, "Ethnic studies debate comes to UC system with proposed admission requirement," *JWeekly*, April 8, 2022. http://bit.ly/3UonQWV.

23 "University of California Academic Council: Minutes of Videoconference Meeting," March 30, 2022, p. 3. https://bit.ly/3Ulmxbk.

9

THE LEADERSHIP WE DESERVE?

BRUCE D. ABRAMSON, PH.D.

Liberty vs. Safety

Benjamin Franklin famously wrote: "Those who would give up essential Liberty, to purchase a little temporary Safety, deserve neither Liberty nor Safety."[1] That admonition goes straight to the heart of our problem. Our Jewish communal leaders reflect the priorities that we—America's Jews—have set for them. The leaders who have failed us may well be the leaders we deserve.

America's Jews have long wanted liberty to stand out as proudly Jewish while melting safely into the great American melting pot. Those conflicting desires have split our community. Many in America's Jewish "mainstream" have relegated their Judaism to a very minor part of their lives. That made the choice for mainstream leadership easy: Prioritize safety over liberty. Many smaller, mostly religious, communities prioritized the liberty to live Jewishly over personal safety. Their leaders reflect that priority.

How well have the strategies born of these priorities worked? To put the matter bluntly, mainstream American Jews today feel less safe, and more constrained in expressing their Judaism, than they have in decades. Religious Jewish communities are thriving, integrating themselves into large swathes of American life *as visible religious Jews,* and far more likely to be attacked by bigots than any other group in America.

Even a quick Internet search confirms that split over priorities. The Conference of Presidents,[2] the Religious Action Center of Reform Judaism (RAC),[3] Hadassah, and numerous JCRCs and regional Federations—such as those serving San Francisco,[4] Boston,[5] Washington,[6] Cincinnati,[7] and Minnesota and the Dakotas[8]—highlight their commitment to consensus and to a leftist view of social justice rather than to anything uniquely Jewish. Organizations focused on elements of the Orthodox community cast their visions in explicitly Jewish- and Torah-oriented terms. The home pages of Agudah, the National Council of Young Israel,[9] and the Coalition for Jewish Values[10] provide excellent examples.

The difference is stark. Our mainstream organizations express their greatest pride in unifying the Jewish community behind a particular interpretation of "justice." Our religiously observant organizations express their greatest pride in promoting uniquely Jewish expression. It's hard to miss their radically divergent priorities—and when it comes to strategy and effectiveness, priorities are the only things that matter.

Priorities vs. Preferences

It has become commonplace to confuse priorities with preferences. Public opinion polling has played an important role in spreading that confusion. Pollsters ask questions in isolation. Polls rarely, if ever, consider trade-offs. The real world, however, is a study in trade-offs. The preferences we may express about low priority items are of little but academic interest. They have almost no effect on behavior.

The American Center for Law and Justice's senior counsel Jeff Ballabon and I have previously shown how the AIPAC's misplaced priority on bipartisanship has neutered its ability to forward Israel's interests.[11] Worse, its elevation of bipartisanship over a race to the top has paved the way for a race to the bottom featuring increasingly anti-Israel Jewish groups like J Street, IfNotNow, and Jewish Voice for Peace.

We took a similar approach to making sense of the "Jewish vote" that has long perplexed observers.[12] Though most American Jews express sympathy and preference for a strong Israel and the right to practice their Judaism, only a minority prioritize such issues. Because priorities rather than preferences guide voting patterns and partisan affiliation, mainstream American Jews are politically indistinguishable from their non-Jewish neighbors of comparable education and income levels.

Most of our prominent Jewish organizations—like the mainstream voters they represent—have relegated identifiable Jewish issues to low-priority considerations. They're demonstrably more committed to cozying up to their selected allies and promoting their own concepts of justice than with preserving Jewish liberties.

A Personalized Case Study

From 2010 to 2012, I worked with the JCRC of the San Francisco Bay Area. I learned a great deal from my colleagues in this important regional organization. In relating these lessons—not all of which appear complimentary—it's important to emphasize the absolute commitment and dedication of everyone with whom I served. The Bay Area has an enormous Jewish population with the lowest affiliation rate among America's sizable Jewish communities. As a result, the relatively small cadre of Bay Area Jews who promote their Jewish connections and seek involvement in lay leadership are worthy of commendation whether or not I agree with the paths they may have chosen.

Most of them are also successful professionals. The group with whom I served represented a genuine cross-section of America's Jewish elite: urban, affluent, credentialed, and professional. Yet when it came to Jewish involvement, the strategic acumen that had helped them navigate other aspects of their lives evaporated. Their basic strategic approaches toward protecting and strengthening the region's Jewish community were textbook inversions of those that might have proven helpful.

As more than one of my colleagues patiently explained, their strategy for coalition-building began by identifying an organization or cause they liked (uniformly to the left of center). They connected these causes to something they claimed to be a Jewish value. Having determined that their preferred cause was true, just, and mandated under Jewish values, it was easy to conclude that opponents rallied behind values antithetical to Judaism. Every conflict on every issue thus became central to the local Jewish community. With the battle thus framed, the JCRC had little choice but to throw the community's unified Jewish voice behind the forces of virtue who, like us, were locked into an existential struggle against irrational, biased hatred.

That's where their strategy truly unraveled. My colleagues believed that once our chosen allies came to appreciate the work done on their behalf in the name of Jews and Judaism, and once they saw how our deep commitment to Jewish values compelled us to work for their cause, they would necessarily embrace our own concerns to become pro-Jewish activists.

When I inquired about how often that strategy had worked, I was pleased to learn that there had been some success stories. For the most part, however, the response was that just because this strategy failed to secure allies far more often than it succeeded, there was no reason to change approaches. After all, doing the right thing even in the face of adversity is a Jewish value.

I proposed a different strategy: First, carve out a small number of issues critical to the safety and survival of our Jewish communities. Second, jettison all preferences on all other issues. Third, shop around for allies. By all means, start with the side you believe has the better and more just argument. Approach that side with an offer. Describe the assets we can bring to bear. Enumerate the benefits of working in coalition with the Jewish community. Tell that side clearly what we expect in return. Be specific about the foreseeable conflicts in which we expect the members of that side to raise their voices, mobilize their people, or otherwise deploy their assets on our behalf.

In other words, I proposed offering all potential allies a deal. If they take it, we can feel good about supporting a just cause aligned with Jewish values while knowing that we had secured an important ally in our own future struggles. If they balk, take the offer to the other side. If the other side accepts it, we'll know that we've done our work on behalf of our community—even if it feels less rewarding. If both sides balk, we'll know that we have no place in their fight. There need not be a "unified Jewish position" on every issue, conflict, or struggle. If there's no potential advantage that the Jewish community can squeeze from an unrelated conflict, why not let the range of Jewish opinion mirror the full range of American opinion?

I also advocated embracing the adage "once burned, twice foolish." We can afford to stick our necks out trusting those we believe to be most just—once. If those to whom we have provided support fail to support us when we need them, they will have squandered our good will. We won't reach out to them or offer further support until they prove that they've become trustworthy. Any organization that has ever mobilized against a Jewish interest bears the burden of proving that it has changed before we ever again trust it.

The typical responses to my strategic proposal included incredulity and disgust: It was worse than a total abandonment of Jewish values. It exemplified the sort of mercenary deal-making at the heart of so many antisemitic stereotypes. It was precisely the sort of thinking that had given Jews a bad name for millennia.

This strategic debate highlighted our divergent priorities. I believe that a leading regional Jewish organization should turn the Jewish community into a powerful political force with a clear message: Support Jewish interests and we will move mountains on your behalf. Challenge Jewish interests and we will mobilize forces against you, your interests, and your cause. Arrayed against me were colleagues elevating a different goal: Demonstrate the Jewish commitment to justice even when that means promoting those who seek to harm us.

Theirs is a feel-good strategy doomed to fail on all grounds. Mine prioritizes Jewish survival over the feelings of individual Jews. Given the choice, of course, we'd all be happiest feeling virtuous while thriving. The challenge comes when those two goals point in different directions. The feel-good direction has come to define the American Jewish mainstream's quest for enlightened assimilationist safety. My survivalist instincts are far more common among those elevating the liberty of Jewish distinctiveness.

A Very Public Case Study

I raise my experience with the Bay Area JCRC not to condemn an organization that seems attuned to the desires of its members and that provides a coherent voice for a disconnected, unaffiliated, otherwise disjointed, and Judaically illiterate community. I raise it because I believe that it's emblematic of mainstream American Jewish leadership.

That's a problem. Nearly everything I've seen coming from our most prominent organizations exudes misplaced priorities, twisted notions of Judaism, and blinkered strategy. Not only have Jewish leaders failed to secure the Jewish distinctiveness that their organizations have given a low priority, they have failed to ingratiate us to the groups whose approval the American Jewish mainstream most craves: those at the core of the "intersectional" struggle for social justice.

No group exemplifies this better than the Anti-Defamation League (ADL), an organization that has always leaned left but has recently dropped all pretense of being anything other than a Democratic Party operation. Consider, for example, its Glossary of Extremist Terms, a centerpiece of the ADL's online offerings in its fight against extremism. As of April 2023, the glossary listed 970 entries; 223 qualify as "Groups/Movements." Of those 223, the ADL classifies 176 as "Right Wing," five as "Left Wing," and eighteen as "Islamist," with the outlying twenty-four fitting extraneous categories like "Anti-government."[13]

Four of the five left-wing organizations are eco-terrorists or animal rights activists; Jews are very far from their crosshairs. The fifth addresses, but largely excuses, Antifa:

> A decentralized, leaderless movement composed of loose collections of groups, networks and individuals who are vigorously opposed to fascism, and focused on countering right-wing extremists both online and on the ground. While some antifa adherents have engaged in violence or vandalism at rallies and events, this is not the norm, despite disinformation campaigns that suggest otherwise.[14]

Of the eighteen Islamist entries, fifteen are based overseas. The two American entries, the Holy Land Foundation[15] and the Virginia Jihad Foundation,[16] are both defunct; the former funneled charitable contributions to jihadis overseas while the latter consisted of nine men. Louis Farrakhan's radical, extremist Nation of Islam (NOI), perhaps the single most influential and virulently antisemitic group in America today, appears nowhere in the glossary. The eighteenth Islamist entry defines Islamist extremism, as "a marginal and rigid interpretation of Islam."[17] How such a "marginal" view managed to take over entire countries and form a cross-border caliphate apparently warrants neither comment nor thought.

The glossary makes no mention of important domestic groups that are, at the very least, sympathetic to Islamism. The CAIR and the Islamic Society of North America (ISNA) apparently do not warrant mention, even to say that some sources have accused these groups, their affiliates, or their spokesmen of antisemitic statements and actions.[18] Is the ADL's implicit message that these are fine groups promoting civil rights while their accusers are entirely illegitimate? The inference certainly seems plausible.

The 169 "right-wing" extremist groups, on the other hand, represent a deep dive into obscurity. A few, like the Ku Klux Klan, were very dangerous in their heyday—but, as even the ADL notes: "In the 2020s, there aren't many Klan groups and the ones that do exist are quite small and often short-lived."[19] Newer organizations like the Proud Boys are unquestionably too rough and coarse for the genteel tastes of most American Jews. They do a poor job of vetting their members—and even their leaders. As the ADL notes, they're frequently accused of the full litany of ills: "Their ideology is primarily misogynistic, Islamophobic, transphobic and anti-immigrant." Are those accusations grounded in legitimate concerns? Should Jews worry about them? The worst the ADL could find is that "some members espouse white supremacist and antisemitic ideologies and/or engage with white supremacist groups."[20]

Black Lives Matter (BLM)—some of whose members espouse black supremacist and antisemitic ideologies and engage with black supremacist groups, and whose platform and history are so blatantly antisemitic that even as staunch a Democrat as Alan Dershowitz has called it out repeatedly[21]—does not warrant an entry. White Lives Matter does, even though it's not actually an organization, but rather a "phrase that originated in early 2015 as a racist response to the Black Lives Matter movement."[22] What does the exclusion of one and inclusion of the other suggest about the ADL's priorities?

Turning Point USA (TPUSA), according to the ADL, works to "identify educate, train, and organize students to promote the principles of freedom, free markets, and limited government." Yet the ADL is concerned because it "was connected to many controversial incidents including problematic comments by TPUSA spokespeople or activists."[23] Unlike CAIR, ISNA, or any other organization not to the right of center? Apparently so. The ADL has no evident problem with the Women's March, whose leadership was so undeniably antisemitic that even former Democratic National Committee (DNC) Chair Debbie Wasserman Schultz felt compelled to distance herself from it until the organization recruited new leaders[24]—who proved to be just as antisemitic.[25]

What antisemitic evil has this vast array of right-wing extremists wrought? According to the ADL, it's central to the growth of online extremism—a phenomenon the ADL attributes almost solely to surging white supremacism. In 2020, it writes, "three groups—Patriot Front, New Jersey European Heritage Association and Nationalist Social Club—were responsible for 92 percent of the [anti-Semitic] activity."[26] In 2021, the Folkish Resistance Movement replaced the Nationalist Social Club as part of the troika.[27] Who are these groups? According to Wikipedia (at least in July 2022), the Patriot Front has a membership of about 300 (citing a source reporting that it's stuck in the 220–230 range).[28] None of the other groups even warrants Wikipedia pages. The ADL refers to them as "small."

Any reasonable observer chasing down this glossary's entries would conclude that the greatest problem facing America's Jewish community today is a few hundred hateful, annoying, and largely immature Internet trolls. Does that match *any* Jewish person's lived experience?

In America today, a handful of dangerous, psychotic, violent loners imbibe the work of these "right-wing extremist" groups, self-radicalize, and wreak carnage on those unlucky enough to fall within their purview. Some Islamists take the same route. Other Islamists—notably the leadership of CAIR and ISNA—align with various "unlisted" extremist groups spouting leftist ideologies to make campus life inhospitable for Jews; rally against the Jewish state; curtail opportunities for Jewish education and ritual observance; harass, beat, and vandalize visibly Jewish targets; promote the myth of "privileged white Jews" as oppressors; and turn ice cream parlors into epicenters of antisemitic boycott campaigns.[29]

The ADL's messaging is so imbalanced that mere incompetence cannot possibly explain it. The misrepresentation must be intentional. Is there any plausible explanation other than that in an increasingly polarized America, the ADL has subverted its mission of combating antisemitism to its goal of ingratiating itself into today's left?

How's that strategy working? An entire faction of the Democratic congressional caucus is proudly anti-Israel. The "Squad" rarely even tries to hide its overt antisemitism. The Congressional Black Caucus—the allies over which left-leaning Jews most salivate—fetes blatant antisemites like Louis Farrakhan.[30] Al Sharpton, a man who fomented actual pogroms,[31] remains a power broker. Prior to joining the White House, Press Secretary Karine Jean-Pierre explained: "You cannot call yourself a progressive while continuing to associate yourself with an organization like AIPAC that has often been the antithesis of what it means to be progressive."[32] Squad member Rashida Tlaib took it further, explaining the inherent conflict between progressivism and Zionism.[33]

Deserving Better

America's mainstream Jewish leadership has only "failed" if we judge it using objectives that it has rejected. In their own words, the primary values animating our most prominent mainstream organizations are consensus, unity, alliance with pre-selected groups, and the promotion of particular concepts of social and environmental justice. Judged as they've asked to be judged, these organizations may have succeeded. The spate of antisemitism flying off campus and across America, the emergence of a powerful and overtly anti-Israel bloc in Congress, and the antipathy to religious practice may be small and acceptable sacrifices necessary for the emergence of a more just American society. Perhaps, given the visceral leftist distaste for God, Jews, Judaism, religion, national identity, and distinctiveness, mainstream American Jewish leadership has done the best work possible within the constraints it set for itself.

A majority of America's Jews consistently articulate and demonstrate those same priorities. Perhaps the reason that mainstream American Jewish leadership has proven so ineffective at preserving either Jewish safety or Jewish liberty is that most American Jews prioritize neither goal.

A Jewish community that assigns communal safety a low priority and Jewish distinctiveness an even lower one lacks self-respect. Perhaps, as a community that disrespects so much of our own distinctive traditions, we have the leadership we deserve.

The message is clear to both individual American Jews and the broad American Jewish community: If we want better, we must be better.

Bruce D. Abramson, Ph.D., J.D., is the author of five books, most recently The New Civil War: Exposing Elites, Fighting Utopian Leftism, and Restoring America *(RealClear Publishing, 2021). He is the founder of the strategic consultancy Informationism, Inc., and a member of the board of directors of the American Center for Education and Knowledge.*

---

[1] Benjamin Franklin, "Pennsylvania Assembly: Reply to the Governor, 11 November 1755," *National Archives*. https://bit.ly/3WI35W7.

[2] "About the Conference," *Conference of Presidents of Major American Jewish Organizations*. https://bit.ly/3sav4Av.

[3] "About the Religious Action Center of Reform Judaism," *Religious Action Center for Reform Judaism*. https://bit.ly/3suZnSZ.

[4] "Who We Are Jewish Community Relations Council," *Jewish Community Relations Council of of San Francisco, the Peninsula, Marin, Sonoma, Alameda, and Contra Costa Counties.* https://jcrc.org/who-we-are/.

[5] "Our Mission," *Jewish Community Relations Council of Boston.* https://www.jcrcboston.org/our-mission/.

[6] "History," *Jewish Community Relations Council of Greater Washington.* https://www.jcouncil.org/history.

[7] "Who We Are," *Jewish Federation of Cincinnati.* https://jewishcincinnati.org/about/who-we-are.

[8] "Who We Are: A Brief History," *Jewish Community Relations Council of Minnesota and the Dakotas.* https://bit.ly/3TqgwsQ.

[9] "Welcome to the National Council of Young Israel." *National Council of Young Israel,* January 24, 2023, https://www.youngisrael.org/.

[10] "About Us," *Coalition for Jewish Values.* https://coalitionforjewishvalues.org/about-us/.

[11] See Bruce D. Abramson and Jeff Ballabon, "The End of AIPAC's Israel Monopoly," *Tablet,* July 11, 2016. https://bit.ly/3VGOM4x.

[12] See Abramson and Ballabon, "How to Think Politically About the Jews," *Mosaic,* July 21, 2020. https://bit.ly/3DeZmZt.

[13] See "Glossary of Extremism," *Anti-Defamation League.* https://extremism-terms.adl.org.

[14] "Antifa," *Anti-Defamation League.* https://extremismterms.adl.org/glossary/antifa.

[15] See "Holy Land Foundation," *Anti-Defamation League.* https://extremism-terms.adl.org/glossary/holy-land-foundation.

[16] See "Virginia Jihad Foundation," *Anti-Defamation League.* https://extrem-ismterms.adl.org/glossary/virgina-jihad-network.

[17] "Islamist extremism," *Anti-Defamation League.* https://extremismterms.adl.org/glossary/islamist-extremism.

18 See Steven Emerson, "CAIR's Antisemitism Fails to Draw Media Scrutiny," *The Investigative Project on Terrorism*, December 8, 2021. https://bit. ly/3yWEa83. See also Erin Dwyer and Eric Rozenman, *The Islamic Society of North America: Active, Influential and Rooted in the Muslim Brotherhood* (Boston, MA: *Committee for Accuracy in Middle East Reporting and Analysis*, September 2012). https://bit.ly/3SiJ3iu.

19 "Ku Klux Klan (KKK)," *Anti-Defamation League*. https://extremismterms. adl.org/glossary/ku-klux-klan-kkk.

20 "Proud Boys," *Anti-Defamation League*. https://extremismterms.adl.org/ glossary/proud-boys.

21 See Alan M. Dershowitz, "Black Lives Matter must rescind anti-Israel declaration," *The Boston Globe*, August 12, 2016. https://bit.ly/3Skqlaj. See also Yossi Lempkowicz, "Alan Dershowitz: 'Black Lives Matter Platform Guilty of Serious Sin & Crime of Antisemitism,'" *European Jewish Press*, July 14, 2020. https://bit.ly/3seItl6.

22 "White Lives Matter," *Anti-Defamation League*. https://extremismterms.adl. org/glossary/white-lives-matter.

23 "Turning Point USA (TPUSA)," *Anti-Defamation League*. https:// extremismterms.adl.org/glossary/turning-point-usa-tpusa.

24 Representative Debbie Wasserman-Schultz, "Debbie Wasserman Schultz: Why I refuse to walk with the Washington Women's March," *USA Today*, January 18, 2019. https://bit.ly/3yXP3GA.

25 "The Women's March still has an anti-Semitism problem," *The New York Post*, September 21, 2019. https://bit.ly/3eOyNAU.

26 "ADL: White Supremacist Propaganda Hits All-Time High in 2020," *Anti-Defamation League*, March 16, 2021. https://bit.ly/3TqOkWM.

27 "U.S. White Supremacist Propaganda Remained at Historic Levels in 2021, With 27 Percent Rise in Antisemitic Messaging," *Anti-Defamation League*, May 3, 2022. https://bit.ly/3TyrewI.

28 See Sergio Olmos, "'We are desperate for new people': inside a hate group's leaked online chats," *The Guardian*, January 28, 2022. https://bit. ly/3VNYty3.

29 See "Where We Stand on Ben & Jerry's," *BDS Movement*, August 17, 2021. https://bit.ly/3ySF99d.

30 Dennis Lund, "Why Does the Congressional Black Caucus Get a Pass on Farrakhan?", *American Thinker*, March 27, 2018. https://bit.ly/3yWXXEh.

31 See Jeff Dunetz, "How Al Sharpton Inflamed The Crown Heights Riot and How The Media Lied," *The Jewish Press*, August 15, 2018. https://bit. ly/3o554pn. See also Dunetz, "20 Years After the Firebombing of Freddy's

Fashion Mart, Sharpton's Still Inciting Hate," *Media Research Center*, December 11, 2015. https://bit.ly/3u8yxjg.

[32] Karine Jean-Pierre, "Why 2020 Democrats Skipped AIPAC: Pro-Israel Group Is Often the Antithesis of Progressive Values," *Newsweek*, March 26, 2019. https://bit.ly/3TjDSAh.

[33] See Benjamin Kerstein, "Rashida Tlaib and the coming purge of progressivism," *JNS*, September 25, 2022. https://bit.ly/3EWVihw.

10

WHERE ARE TODAY'S MACCABEES?

THANE ROSENBAUM

Where are the Maccabees when we need them? And do they work overseas?

Those are serious questions, because aside from the amusing paradox of the American Jewish Mafia, those clever ruffians who saw no contradiction between Bar Mitzvahs and Murder Incorporated—Dutch Schultz, Meyer Lansky, Bugsy Siegel, Mickey Cohen, and the more recent Russian variety from Brighton Beach, Brooklyn—Jewish muscle in America, and assertive leadership, in general, shies away from calling attention to itself. Defending the tribe is a tough sell, even among those who identify as proudly Jewish.

Indeed, the fight instinct within American Jewry has been perpetually repressed. So, too, in Europe. Conflict is usually resolved with conciliatory gestures if not outright capitulation. Explain it away. Call it an aberration. Dismiss its severity. Pretend it didn't happen.

Worse still, American Jewish leaders, such as they are, often extend greater efforts crusading on behalf of other communities rather than their own. Being liked by the "gentiles" remains a singular preoccupation. After all, one can't be expected to win elections by getting out the Jewish vote alone. Other constituencies and alliances must be built. Favoritism should always be held in reserve.

Jews born in the Middle East, however, are a rougher lot and made of sturdier stock. The reprisal reflex is always at the ready. When the smoke clears from the Iron Dome, the Israeli fist soon follows. It was once true with the Maccabees, and it's even more true now with the Israel Defense Forces (IDF).

The diaspora traveled earnestly and compliantly with Torah and Talmud. But the cult of heroic hardness—the Sabra's creed—was left behind in the deserts and mountaintops of biblical Judea.

No wonder that in today's America, Jewish leadership is imperceptible—even though its absence is widely felt. Fisticuffs are not essential, although the Jewish Defense League enlivened New York City in the gritty 1970s with the sight of Jewish boys carrying baseball bats who had no interest in hitting balls. But what is needed, now more than ever, is a full-throated defense of the Jewish people—right here in the U.S.

Surely there is one American David with a slingshot somewhere.

Certainly, there's no shortage of Jewish elected officials—in both Houses of Congress, governors' mansions, and city halls. Many identify as Jews, observe holidays, and attend synagogues. But when it comes to speaking out as a Jew, for Jews, on matters of Jewish concern—especially when it comes to the defense of Israel—their Jewish voice loses its accent (all except Bernie Sanders, who retained the accent but abandoned everything else), and their ethnic origins take on Protestant refinements. The refrain seems to be: Being Jewish should *not* guide one's politics.

Jewish leadership these days seems to reside mostly in charitable works—raising money, outfitting local synagogues with stained glass windows, establishing a wing at a hospital, endowing a chair at a university, or renovating a campus Hillel center. The Jewish community long ago graduated from *tzedakah* boxes and planting trees in Israel to more formidable gift-giving.

But such worthy acts are, nonetheless, charitable in nature. They have little to do with the exercise of moral or political leadership, which is an entirely different level of involvement. Not quiet, behind-the-scenes negotiations, but unabashed rallying on behalf of Jews and the Jewish state.

This kind of leadership is rare these days, whether from elected officials, private citizens, rabbis, or legacy organizations. Jews simply won't make much noise as Jews. The grogger that is so grating on Purim is reserved, one night, for Haman, but never for Hamas. Jewish outrage is tempered; Jewish leadership has all the visibility of Elijah the Prophet.

In November and December 2019, Hasidic Jews were being assaulted, mostly by African Americans, in Brooklyn and Jersey City; one was killed in Monsey, New York.[1] Law enforcement, shockingly, at first wasn't entirely sure whether these acts qualified as anti-Semitic hate crimes—not even those that were committed on Hanukkah. Hardly any Jewish elected public officials rallied their colleagues to put an end to the violence, conducted press conferences on the steps of City Halls, shouted from the rooftops (or even whispered), or made it their own personal crusade to defend the defenseless members of the Hasidic community.

Similarly, in May 2021, after thousands of rockets were fired from Gaza into Israel and the Israelis were forced, once again, to do something about it, Jews were beaten and assaulted on the streets of Los Angeles, New York, and Miami, mostly by Muslims.[2] Aside from quietly signing letters or standing beside other equally taciturn, cowering Jews, who among the Jewish leaders stepped out from the anonymous crowd, condemned the attacks, and demanded the protection of Jews from marauding Muslims? Who had the clout or charisma to galvanize Jews and non-Jews alike?

More recently, Representative Alexandria Ocasio-Cortez (D-NY) accused Israel of placing Palestinian children in cages in the West Bank.[3] Jew-haters apparently know there are no costs to repackaging age-old anti-Semitic libels, even when the falsity of the accusation is easily proved.

Abraham Foxman, the longtime national director of the Anti-Defamation League, used to be front and center in situations like these. But his old job has been redefined, and retitled, as that of a CEO. Other Jewish legacy organizations have adopted the same models that have more in common with faceless corporations than town criers who have something to truly cry about. Jewish advocacy has gone corporate, answerable to a board of directors, fearful of fickle consumers, and obsessed with product placement. Calling attention to African Americans or Muslims assaulting Jews will lead to accusations of racism or "Islamophobia." And that would be bad for their brand.

Ironically, due to their knack for social and economic advancement, Jewish Americans have never wielded more cultural clout. But they are far too timid, and obsessed with corporate titles, to leverage that power into anything that resembles unapologetic political leadership.

All throughout the presidency of Franklin Delano Roosevelt—which coincided with the beginning and end of the Holocaust—Rabbi Stephen S. Wise was the most significant Jewish political figure in the U.S. He was president of both the American Jewish Congress and the World Jewish Congress. What's more, Rabbi Wise had the ear of President Roosevelt. He was a frequent guest of the White House. (Even his daughter and her husband once dined there.) His access to the seat of American power was extraordinary and, for a Jew in the twentieth century, unprecedented, even by today's standards.

Yet, none of his visits to the Oval Office resulted in the U.S. bombing the railroad tracks leading to Auschwitz. Indeed, when the first reports of Nazi atrocities committed against European Jewry surfaced, Wise dismissed them as propaganda. It didn't take long for Wise to glean that Roosevelt had no interest in rescuing Europe's Jews. When Wise was finally convinced that a Holocaust was truly underway, he politely raised his concerns with the president, but to no avail.[4]

The Maccabees were never polite in dispatching the Greeks.

Yet, Wise adamantly opposed other Jews protesting America's inaction. He knew that calling out the president's failure would upset Roosevelt. For more than twelve years as an informal advisor to President Roosevelt, Wise served as a quiet Jewish diplomat who didn't wish to press and thereby alienate the president. A similar complaint could be made against then-Secretary of the Treasury Henry Morgenthau, Jr., whose friendship with Roosevelt dated longer and who, after all, served in the president's Cabinet. Other Jews in Roosevelt's inner circle—Supreme Court Justice Felix Frankfurter, Sam Rosenman, and Ben Cohen—were all equally to blame.

You might call them Court Jews.[5] Throughout the diaspora, many Jews served in rarefied advisory roles that enabled them to skip the line and improve their social standing. Even in biblical times, Joseph in Egypt and Mordecai in Persia functioned in this capacity. But the American variety, historically, demonstrates what a colossal failure these advancements have proven to be for Jews. Henry Kissinger may be America's best example of a Jewish public official who attained great political power but who gave his fellow Jews, especially Soviet Jewry—and, to a lesser extent, the Jewish state—little thought.

Perhaps staying in the good graces of the king requires repressing one's Jewish commitments. It's nice getting invited to the ball. Just think of the new dances. Why let tribal loyalties get in the way of a good time?

Of course, there are Jews who happily turn down invitations to Court. Peter Bergson is virtually unknown today but was widely admired when silence dominated all discussions concerning the fate of European Jewry under the Nazis. He was unique as a genuine Jewish leader—a model that simply has not been duplicated, surely not in America in the nearly eighty years since he created what became known as the Bergson Group.

Bergson had a very different response to the unfolding Holocaust. The Bergson Group staged mass rallies, purchased full-page ads in major newspapers, and even recruited Hollywood and Broadway celebrities to participate in a pageant, *We Will Never Die*. Written by Kurt Weill and Ben Hecht, it was showcased twice in Madison Square Garden before taking to the road for performances in other major cities throughout 1943. The storyline and music focused entirely on saving Europe's Jews.

When the show was presented in Washington, D.C., in attendance were many congressmen, along with First Lady Eleanor Roosevelt.

Apparently, the First Lady enjoyed the performance so much she devoted one of her syndicated columns to this crusading production.

Her husband was none too pleased. He wanted the show to bomb.

The efforts of the Bergson Group did not stop there. The group's members pulled off an even more dramatic stunt, one the president could hardly miss because it happened outside his Oval Office. At the gates to the White House, 400 Orthodox rabbis petitioned the president to rescue Europe's Jews. As Orthodox Jews, many of them dressed in the manner of their European counterparts—long beards and coats, sidelocks and *tefillin*.[6] No one was concealing his identity. No one feared that he would attract the attention of anti-Semites, nor were the rabbis troubled that their actions might get them disinvited from lavishly un-kosher Beltway parties.

Not surprisingly, the activities of the Bergson Group enraged Rabbi Wise and other Jewish "leaders." He feared a backlash against Jews by other Americans, or repercussions from the president himself. But perhaps what angered Wise most was the damage being done to his reputation: The most powerful Jew in the country, a rock star of a rabbi, was outplayed by Bergson's street theatrics, and upstaged by a bunch of Hollywood stars.

More recently was the case of Nobelist and Holocaust survivor Elie Wiesel, a personal friend of mine,[7] who was slight of build and soft-spoken, but yet responded to anti-Semitism, anti-Zionism, and the desecration of Holocaust memory like a fearless Goliath.

Three times, he personally offended a president of the United States—twice in person! At a ceremony where he received the Congressional Gold Medal, Wiesel chastised President Ronald Reagan for planning to visit a cemetery in Bitburg, Germany, where some Nazi officials were buried. He embarrassed President Bill Clinton at the opening of the U.S. Holocaust Memorial Museum in Washington, D.C., when he pleaded that America should stop the genocide in Bosnia. He was in attendance in the Capitol when Republican leaders invited Israeli Prime Minister Benjamin Netanyahu to warn Congress about the impending Iran deal, which was President Barack Obama's signature foreign policy achievement.

This is what moral courage looks like. Leadership without exercising moral courage, without undertaking risks and performing selfless acts, is not leadership. Influence peddling, resume padding, and calling cards are not leadership.

Like Rabbi Wise, most Jewish leaders today have similar trepidations about antagonizing important constituencies, appearing to be "too Jewish," accused of "dual loyalty," or wrongly engaged in "special pleading" for Jews who already occupy the upper wrung of "white privilege."[8]

If you believed that American Jews had long abandoned the *sha stil* ethos of "not in front of the gentiles," think again.

Yet, Jewish leaders will knock each other over to get to the head of the line for any Black Lives Matter protest. They'll jockey for a seat on "diversity, equity, and inclusion" committees, even though these committees, in their deliberations, exclude and discount Jewish concerns—because, at their core, they hate Jews. Is it any wonder that Rabbi Wise was also a co-founder of the NAACP?

The term Jewish leadership might actually be an oxymoron. Once ascending to a position of elected or appointed office, moral courage and tribal loyalties disappear, spinelessness sets in, and the impulse to appear neutral in all things predominates. Denouncing Israel becomes a form of Jewish virtue-signaling, the shameless flashing of moral narcissism.[9] For others, Israel is such a divisive issue, best to simply dodge the topic altogether and recite the meaningless words "two-state solution."

There are two meaningless words in Hebrew, *tikkun olam*, that could stand to be discarded. Overused and misapplied, "repairing the world" is a nice impulse, but it doesn't mean that God has directed the Chosen People to express their Judaism solely by doing good deeds for others.

There is one Jewish leader dominating the news cycle at this very moment, but he lives and governs in Ukraine. Volodymyr Zelensky is winning well-earned plaudits for leading and rallying his people against the invading Russians. Fighting on his front lines, however, is an extremist right-wing paramilitary force, the Azov Battalion, wearing uniforms bearing insignia similar to that of the Nazis.[10] Perhaps one day we'll learn whether Zelensky will stand as aggressively, and valiantly, in defense of Jews.

Thane Rosenbaum is a novelist, essayist, law professor, and Distinguished University Professor at Touro College, where he directs the Forum on Life, Culture & Society. He is the legal analyst for CBS News Radio. His most recent book is Saving Free Speech... from Itself *(2020).*

---

[1]   Thane Rosenbaum, "The December doldrums in full force," *JNS,* December 31, 2019. https://bit.ly/3D65MtO.

[2]   Rosenbaum, "Welcome to Europe, American Jews," *The Jewish Journal,* May 24, 2021. https://bit.ly/3EPIlWX.

[3]   Carl Campanile, "Queens Jewish leader slams AOC for suggesting Israel 'cages' Palestinian kids," *The New York Post,* February 20, 2022. https://bit.ly/3Sb8FOb.

4   See JBS. "The Jews Should Keep Quiet: Franklin D. Roosevelt, Rabbi Stephen S. Wise, and the Holocaust." Filmed 2019. YouTube video, 1:28:47. Posted September 24, 2019. https://bit.ly/3S74Idv.

5   Rosenbaum, "The Golden Age of the Court Jew," *The Jewish Journal*, November 30, 2020. https://bit.ly/3MEAtcJ.

6   See "Bergson Group," *The David S. Wyman Institute for Holocaust Studies*. https://bit.ly/3g7mrE7.

7   Rosenbaum, "A Protégé Remembers Wiesel, And His Unfinished Business," *New York Jewish Week*, July 3, 2016. https://bit.ly/3VGuNTq.

8   See Rosenbaum, "Jewish Westerns and Peddler Power," *The Jewish Journal*, February 14, 2022. https://bit.ly/3TBIcdT.

9   Rosenbaum, "Israel, it's not you—it's them," *The Times of Israel*, August 4, 2016. https://bit.ly/3MFZAMa.

10 Rosenbaum, "Oligarchs and Bedfellows," *The Jewish Journal*, March 14, 2022. https://bit.ly/3VFkHT2.

PART II
PROOF POINTS

11

OUR GREATEST WEAPON IS EXPOSING THE TRUTH. SO WHY DO JEWISH LEADERS FAIL TO DO SO?

MORTON A. KLEIN

As the president of the Zionist Organization of America (ZOA), I'm gratified that the Jewish Leadership Project consistently points to the ZOA as a courageous exception to the general failures of mainstream Jewish organizations.

Summary

Anti-Israel and anti-Jewish hatred is based on lies. Accordingly, the Jewish people's greatest weapon in the battle to combat anti-Israel and anti-Jewish hatred is to expose the truth.

Conversely, when Jewish leaders and organizations fail to tell the truth about our enemies' intentions and actions, and fail to combat them, the Jewish community is left defenseless.

Unfortunately, there are countless instances of certain mainstream Jewish leaders and organizations failing to speak the truth, and following useless diversion strategies. Even worse, such Jewish leaders and organizations have praised and promoted harmful acts and actors which should have been condemned, confronted, and fought.

There are several reasons for those mainstream Jewish leaders' failings, including fear; ignorance of history and current facts; and the psychological difficulty of facing the reality of intractable radical Islamist hatred and radical left-wing hatred of Jews. The refusal to face reality leads to the mistaken belief that radical Islamist and leftist hatred will end "if only the Israelis will make more concessions." But, in fact, more concessions lead to more terror. Those Jewish leaders' failures to expose the truth ends up doing grievous harm to the Jewish state and entire Jewish people.

The Best Strategy is to Expose and Combat Antisemitic Lies

The best strategy for combatting antisemitism, and its modern manifestation of Israel hatred, is to expose, counter, and tell the truth about anti-Israel propaganda and lies. This is ZOA's strategy. If other mainstream Jewish organizations had adopted the same strategy, the Jewish people would be in a far better situation today. Sadly, many mainstream groups have instead adopted useless, counterproductive appeasement and diversion strategies, and have ignored or downplayed dangers to our people.

From time immemorial, Jew-hatred has been based on lies. The antidote and the Jewish people's greatest "weapon" is to simply expose the lies and directly spread the truth. Indeed, Judaism teaches that delegitimizers fail when we directly counter those who spread falsehoods. The great prophet Isaiah foretold: "Any weapon whetted against you shall not succeed, and any tongue that contends with you in judgment, you shall condemn" (54:17).

But, unfortunately, too many Jewish leaders failed to counter the Islamist-Palestinian-Arab propaganda wars against Israel and the Jewish people.

People side with Israel and the Jewish people, and oppose anti-Israel boycotts, divestment, and sanctions ("BDS") when they learn the truth that the Palestinian Authority ("PA") pays Arab terrorists lifetime pension rewards of $400 million a year to murder Jews.[1]

People side with Israel and the Jewish people when they learn that the PA glorifies Jew-killers and incites antisemitism in the media and government-controlled mosques and schools, including by accusing Jews of blood libels and naming schools, streets, and sports teams after Jew-killers.[2]

We also need to impress upon the public that the PA imposes the death penalty for selling land to a Jew;[3] that they planned and incited intifadas in which Arabs murdered or maimed 10,000 Jews; that Palestinian Arabs failed to create a state during the 19 years after six Arab nations invaded Israel and seized lands lawfully designated for the Jewish state; and that the Palestinian Arabs refused repeated, over-generous peace offers to create a state on Israel's lawful land because they didn't want to sign an agreement to stop attacking the remainder of Israel. Imagine how different our situation would be if the American people knew these easily documentable facts.

People stand with the Jewish people when they learn that the Hamas charter calls for the murder of every Jew throughout the world,[4] and that Hamas' leaders give so-called "protestors" maps of the routes to Jewish kindergartens,[5] and instructions to breach the border in order to "eat the livers" of innocent Jews.[6]

People side with us, when they are informed of the 3,500-year-long history of the Jewish people in Israel, including in Jerusalem and Judea-Samaria; and that there never was a "Palestinian" Arab state; and that a series of binding international agreements guaranteed these lands to the Jewish people (San Remo, the Mandate—which codified the Balfour Declaration, the League of Nations Charter, the Anglo-American Treaty, and the U.N. Charter).

In light of Farrakhan/Black Nationalist antisemitism and deadly attacks against innocent Jews in Jersey City, Monsey, Brooklyn, and elsewhere, it is also essential to tell the truth that Black Lives Matter and its parent organization, the Movement for Black Lives, are antisemitic. It's important to point out that Farrakhan-supporting BLM leaders incited the vicious 2020 pogrom against Jews in Los Angeles;[7] held antisemitic "days of rage" in U.S. cities;[8] and are involved with the Popular Front for the Liberation of Palestine (PFLP) and its front groups.[9]

But, unfortunately, many people do not know any of the foregoing facts. Too many mainstream Jewish leaders have failed to say and emphasize the simple truths that would win the ongoing war for hearts and minds. Too many Jewish organizations have failed to use their skill and resources to counteract anti-Israel propaganda lies with these truths. When I speak at synagogues and other fora throughout the United States, many audience members are shocked, and tell me that they've never heard any of the facts. Every Jewish organization should be making these truths known.

Examples of the Harm Caused By Mainstream Organizations Ignoring the Truth

The Failure to Expose and Push Back Against President Biden's Hostile Policies Towards Israel

During President Biden's trip to Israel in July 2022, Biden announced numerous policies hostile to Israel. The ZOA objected.[10] But other mainstream groups such as AIPAC, the Anti-Defamation League (ADL) and the Conference of Presidents of Major American Jewish Organizations (the "CoP") praised Biden's trip or irrelevant aspects of it, while ignoring the raft of dangerous policies Biden pursued.

Strong pushback from the Jewish community could have convinced the administration to change at least some of its dangerous policies. Thus, AIPAC, the ADL and the CoP *should* have joined the ZOA in exposing and opposing these hostile policies, which included the following:

1. Biden called for creating a "contiguous" Palestinian state "on the 1967 lines" with illusory "land swaps mutually agreed to by the Israelis and Palestinians." Abba Eban famously called the 1967 lines the "Auschwitz lines" because they would leave Israel indefensible. President Lyndon Johnson also stated that the 1967 lines would cause more war. These lines would divide Jerusalem in half, subject all of Israel to rocket attacks, and endanger Israel's very existence.

2. Biden increased the amount of U.S. tax dollars that his administration sends to Palestinian Arabs, including the Hamas-allied United Nations Relief and Works Agency (UNRWA), to more than $1.5 billion.

3. Biden kept pressuring Israel to allow the U.S. to re-open an illegal consulate for Palestinian Arabs in western Jerusalem. This would promote dividing Jerusalem and undermine Jerusalem as Israel's capital.

4. Biden falsely compared Palestinian Arabs' situation to oppression of the Irish.

5. Biden promoted and pressured Israel to provide "increased access" for Palestinian Arabs to enter Israel from Gaza and Judea-Samaria—shortly after such access resulted in Palestinian Arabs murdering 19 Jews and others.

6. Biden called ordinary Israeli checkpoints, which are necessary for security, "indignities" against Palestinians and otherwise portrayed the terrorists as victims.

7. Biden continued ignoring sanctions on Iran and insisted on continuing negotiations with Iran for a disastrous nuclear deal.

8. Biden encouraged Palestinians to emulate anti-Israel *Al Jazeera* propagandist Shireen Abu Akleh, and falsely claimed that she was telling the "truth."

9. Biden undermined Israeli security and sovereignty by calling for the Palestinian Authority to share control of the Israeli-Jordanian crossings.

10. Biden met with and held a smiling joint press conference with Palestinian Authority/PLO terrorist dictator Mahmoud Abbas, legitimizing and mainstreaming him, despite Abbas' incitement of terrorism and "pay to slay" payments to terrorists to murder Jews and Americans.

11. Biden removed the Israeli flag from his limo when he traveled to eastern Jerusalem, insulting Israel and undermining Israeli sovereignty over Israel's unified capital.

12. Biden falsely claimed that Palestinian Arabs have "deep and ancient roots in this land" in order to try to justify creating a Palestinian Arab terror state on Israel's land.
13. Biden refused to allow Israeli officials to accompany his visit to an Arab eastern Jerusalem hospital.
14. Biden refused to visit Hadassah Hospital in eastern Jerusalem.
15. Biden pressured Israel to legalize massive illegal Arab building in Area C—the area of Judea-Samaria lawfully under full Israeli administrative control, and Israel's left-wing interim government acceded to Biden's demands in key areas.[11]

Certain Mainstream Jewish Groups' Failure to Oppose Biden's Hostile-to-Israel and Antisemitic Appointees and Nominees

Another serious issue is that from the outset of his administration, President Biden nominated and appointed to key positions numerous individuals who had records of extraordinary hostility towards Jews and Israel. For example: Biden's U.S. Special Envoy to the Palestinians, Hady Amr, stated that he was "inspired by the Palestinian intifada"[12] (the anti-Israel terror wars); White House Press Secretary Karine Jean-Pierre helped orchestrate several Democratic presidential candidates' boycott of a major pro-Israel conference;[13] Biden's Senior Director for Intelligence at the National Security Council, Maher Bitar, organized anti-Israel conferences where he taught attendees how to best demonize Israel;[14] and Biden's Deputy Director of the White House Office of Legislative Affairs, Reema Dodin, legitimized and even encouraged suicide bombings against Jews.[15]

The ZOA opposed these appointments; informed and warned the Jewish community about this; and established a "Biden Appointments Watch" webpage with articles about hostile nominees' and appointees' records.[16] But, unfortunately, other mainstream groups failed to oppose the Biden administration's raft of horribly antisemitic, anti-Israel appointees and nominees.

Every Jewish group should have joined the ZOA in screaming about and opposing the numerous such horrific appointments. If every mainstream group did so, Biden could not have gotten away with appointing antisemites and Israel-haters. Notably, the nominees needed Senate confirmation: widespread Jewish opposition to hostile nominees could have blocked confirmation and forced President Biden to nominate less problematic officials.

Certain Mainstream Jewish Groups' Failure to Oppose Biden's Pressure to Surrender Israel's Maritime Border and Gas Fields to Hezbollah-Controlled Lebanon

In October 2022, under severe pressure from the Biden administration, Israel's interim Prime Minister Yair Lapid surrendered all of Israel's territorial waters, exclusive economic maritime zone, and gas fields that were demanded by Hezbollah-controlled Lebanon. The deal will enrich Hezbollah with billions of dollars and deprive Israel of her natural resources and defensive maritime line. Israel gained nothing for capitulating to Hezbollah's demands: no recognition and no peace. Lapid knew that the deal was so bad that it could not obtain the legally-required votes. So Lapid pushed the deal through without submitting it to mandated Knesset approval and national referendum.

The ZOA condemned this disastrous deal. Likewise, commentators such as Caroline Glick, and the Protectors of Israel Movement in Israel (*HaBithonistim*), comprised of 12,000 former high-level security and military officials, condemned the deal for endangering Israel's security, harming Israel economically, and enriching Hezbollah.

Sadly, other American mainstream groups praised this unlawful maritime territorial surrender and the Biden administration's role in forcing the surrender down Israel's throat. AIPAC tweeted that it "welcomes" the Lebanon deal and praised the Biden administration for it.[17] The American Jewish Committee (AJC) likewise "welcomed" the agreement and called it an "impressive achievement" negotiated by the U.S.[18] The ADL also "welcomed" the deal and tweeted that it was "grateful" to the Biden administration for making it happen.[19] The Conference of Presidents of Major American Jewish Organizations (the CoP) also praised the deal, and falsely claimed that Lebanon recognized Israel's shared border.[20] These reactions will only encourage more U.S. pressure on Israel to surrender her sovereign territory to terrorists.

Certain Mainstream Jewish Groups' Support for and Failure to Condemn the Antisemitic, Anti-Israel Black Lives Matter Organization

Many mainstream Jewish groups' response to the Black Lives Matter organization (BLM) and BLM's intertwined parent organization, the Movement for Black Lives (M4BL), was another case in which those Jewish groups offered praise and support when strong condemnation was needed.

The M4BL platform (which has never been abrogated) and BLM/M4BL social media posts continue to promote antisemitic BDS, promote the major BDS group in the U.S., and libelously accuse Israel of perpetrating genocide, ethnic cleansing, and apartheid against Palestinian Arabs.

BLM's Los Angeles leader incited a horrific pogrom in Los Angeles, in which BLM burned, defaced and looted Jewish synagogues, schools, and businesses. BLM participated in an anti-Israel "day of rage" in multiple U.S. cities. BLM/M4BL collaborated with and held joint demonstrations with anti-Israel groups such as Adalah and "Dream Defenders," which is intertwined with the Marxist designated terror organization PFLP. (Those groups co-authored the M4BL/BLM platform.) BLM also promoted the agendas of, and held joint events with, PFLP front groups Al-Haq and DCI-Palestine.

The ZOA condemned all these BLM activities, and established a web page (the "BLM Organization Files") to document the truth about BLM's antisemitic and anti-Israel activities, including pictures of the schools, synagogues, and Jewish businesses burnt, defaced, and destroyed during BLM's antisemitic pogrom.[21]

Some mainstream Jewish groups initially condemned the extremely antisemitic M4BL/BLM platform when it was first promulgated in 2016—but, quickly afterwards, ignored or downplayed the platform's continuing presence and import. They even claimed falsely that the platform was abrogated and then made excuses for it. For instance, the San Francisco JCRC claimed that "not all parties that signed onto the platform were fully informed about the inclusion of anti-Israel language."[22]

Moreover, such mainstream Jewish groups ignored BLM's antisemitic pogrom and numerous other antisemitic posts and activities, and then supported and promoted BLM instead of condemning it. The ADL, the Reform and Conservative movements, HIAS, and other left-leaning and far-left Jewish groups even signed a full-page newspaper ad supporting BLM, which they co-signed together with extremist Israel-bashing groups—including Jewish Voice for Peace (JVP), New Israel Fund (NIF), and IfNotNow.[23] The ADL also disseminated educational materials *promoting* BLM.[24]

Even worse, several left-leaning groups attacked the ZOA and me personally for telling the truth about the BLM organization. Attacking those who try to help fellow Jews and save Jewish lives depletes the resources which our tiny people desperately need to defend ourselves.

The Failure to Expose and Demand Action against the Squad

Then there's the failure to call out and combat the "Squad" of vicious Jew-haters and Israel-bashers in Congress, including Ilhan Omar, Alexandria Ocasio-Cortez ("AOC"), Rashida Tlaib, Ayanna Pressley, Cori Bush, Betty McCollum, and others.

The ZOA stood virtually alone in calling for Squad members to be removed from their committee assignments.

Incredibly, ADL CEO Jonathan Greenblatt *praised* Ilhan Omar, essentially giving her a free pass to defame Jews. In response to an unconvincing "apology" she was forced to make—which was accompanied by yet more antisemitic Israel-bashing—he said: "...[H]ats off to Rep Omar for her honest apology & commitment to a more just world."[25]

We need to expose and directly combat the antisemitism, blood libels, and dangerous anti-Israel legislation constantly promoted by the squad in the U.S. Congress, because those libels are encouraging increased antisemitic attacks in the U.S. Yet too many establishment leaders fear to displease their "progressive" allies.

I've provided even more examples of these problems later in this essay.

Fear, Ignorance, and Difficulties Facing Painful
Realities Underlie Certain Mainstream Groups'
Failures to Stand Up for the Jewish People

The $64,000 question that I'm often asked is: Why do certain mainstream Jewish groups embrace instead of condemn anti-Jewish and anti-Israel organizations and policies, when this is hugely harmful? Why do certain Jewish groups take positions that are against Jewish interests? There are several reasons.

Fear: The first and primary reason is fear. Professor Ruth Wisse's book *If I Am Not For Myself...: The Liberal Betrayal of the Jews*, published in 1992, explained that frightening, overpowering antisemitism results in several different reactions within the Jewish community. Proud Jews stand up, and fight for their people. Other Jews try to remove themselves from the fray, but help our people when they can without personal risk. And the third group joins with those who oppress the Jewish people. They cast themselves as the "good Jews," who should not be attacked because they oppose so-called "Zionists" or supposed evil Israeli settlers.

It is easy to attack fellow pro-Israel Jews. Standing up against enemies of the Jewish people is much more difficult. At the root of those who attack fellow Jews or fail to stand up to our enemies is overwhelming fear.

Ignorance: The second cause is ignorance. Anti-Israel propaganda lies—including the big lies that Israel is an occupier of her own land and an apartheid state, and that Jewish communities on Jewish land are illegal or an obstacle to peace—are so prevalent that many Jews believe them.

Jewish leaders who do not know Jewish and Israeli history are unable to dispel these anti-Israel lies.

Delusions: Another cause is the psychological difficulty of understanding the painful, intractable nature of certain Jew-hatreds, and the difficulty of coming to grips with our own powerlessness to change this. Psychiatrist Ken Levin's book *The Oslo Syndrome: Delusions of a People Under Siege* explains that some Jews don't want to believe the hard fact that Hamas and the Palestinian Arab regime want us to be dead and want to demolish all of Israel, and that there's nothing we can do to change their desires. So instead of facing reality, some Jews convince themselves if we just give the Palestinian Arabs a state, just give them more money, just lift the weapons blockade and the checkpoints, we'll have peace. But, of course, we will just create more danger for ourselves and our brothers and sisters in Israel.

Promoted Appeasement Strategies: The fourth reason is that mainstream groups were encouraged to adopt the counter-productive appeasement strategy discussed below.

The Failed ADL/Reut Strategy (of Agreeing with Israel's Enemies and Appeasement) Adopted by Certain Mainstream Jewish Organizations

A "secret" 30-page report issued in January 2017 by two leftwing Jewish groups, the ADL and Reut Institute (Reut), revealed and promoted the failed "strategy" used by the ADL and others both before and after the report's issuance. The report was distributed to select Jewish groups, *not* including the ZOA. The ZOA was only able to read the ADL/Reut report when the vicious anti-Israel website *Electronic Intifada* published a leaked copy.[26]

The report was entitled *The Assault on Israel's Legitimacy* and purported to provide a "coherent global Jewish response" to the "delegitimization" of Israel.[27]

But, in stark contrast to the ADL/Reut report's claimed purpose of combatting delegitimization, the report was a slick piece of Israel-bashing propaganda. It blamed Israel, Jewish communities in Judea/Samaria (which the report calls "settlements"[28]), and Israel's Rabbinate, Knesset, and administration for the propaganda assaults against the Jewish State, and pushed a left-wing political appeasement agenda, under the guise of combatting delegitimization of Israel. The report aligned with the views of hostile-to-Israel groups including J Street and Ameinu, who were listed among the "experts" consulted for the report.[29]

For instance, the ADL/Reut report justified and portrayed delegitimization assaults against Israel as reactions to "genuine injustices that require change";[30] as reactions to "the mistreatment of the indigenous population—the Arab citizens of Israel";[31] as "reactions to Israel's military campaigns [in Gaza] in 2009, 2012 and 2014";[32] as reactions to the "erosion" of the perception that Israel is a "peace-loving, pluralistic and democratic state (PPD)";[33] and Israel's perceived "lack of commitment" to a "two-state solution" (a euphemism for creating a Palestinian terrorist state on land lawfully designated for the Jewish state).[34] The ADL/Reut report also justified boycotting Jews living past the artificial 1949 armistice lines in order to remedy "a loss of trust by liberal Zionists regarding the commitment of the current Israeli government to peace."[35]

In other words, the ADL/Reut report said in essence that Israel deserves to be delegitimized. Not surprisingly, *Electronic Intifada* gleefully recited the ADL/Reut report's "blame Israel" narrative as "acknowledgements" of Israel's culpability.

The ADL/Reut report made no effort to correct the glaring falsehoods used to justify delegitimization. For instance, the ADL/Reut report did not explain or advise spreading the truths that the Jewish people are the indigenous people of Israel; that Jews were the largest religious group in Jerusalem since at least the first census in 1840; that the Jewish people have the international legal right to Israel, Jerusalem, and Judea/Samaria; that Israel's Arab citizens receive equal rights; and that the Palestinian Arabs rejected repeated, generous peace offers.

Instead of promoting countering lies with truth, the ADL/Reut report called for emphasizing Israeli "innovation" and "creativity"; forming alliances with left-wing groups, and adopting and promoting those anti-Israel groups' causes; and meaningless jargon such as "focusing their efforts on areas where their attributes create a unique value proposition in the field" and "altering the unfavorable Zeitgeist in which Israel's legitimacy is determined."[36]

None of the ADL/Reut report's strategies work. Alliances to promote the causes of groups that hate Israel end up strengthening Israel-hatred. Indecipherable jargon about "creating a unique value proposition" is useless.

The big lies that Israel is an "occupier" that "stole Arab land" and "kills Arab children" cannot be answered by saying: "But we're so innovative! There are 13 Israeli Nobel prize winners."

Anyone who believes the lie that Israel kills Arab children doesn't care about Israeli Nobel prize winners and inventions. The answer is the truth, that the PA and Hamas target Jewish children, and Israel goes out of her way to avoid harming civilians when defending herself.

In addition, instead of combatting delegitimization, the ADL/Reut report *legitimized* extreme hostility to Israel by advocating narrowing the definition of "delegitimization" to include only those entities which insist that Israel has no right to exist and must be eliminated. Under this narrow definition, persistent Israel-bashers, blood-libelers, and defamers are not actually "delegitimizing" Israel.

The same sleight-of-hand is often used to claim that vicious antisemites are not antisemitic: The left narrows the definition of "antisemitism" to only include the use of specified "tropes" by their political enemies. Indeed, a 2022 CNN antisemitism special quoted a far-left fringe Jewish leader, Jill Jacobs, who similarly restricted the definition of antisemitism. Jacobs claimed that anti-Zionism is only antisemitism when an antisemitic "trope" (such as Jews wanting money) is involved.[37] In fact, anti-Zionism denies the Jewish people's right to self-determination in the Jewish homeland, and is thus both discriminatory and antisemitic. Anti-Zionism is a major manifestation of antisemitism today. On college campuses and elsewhere, antisemites use the terms "Zionist" and "Jew" interchangeably.

The ADL/Reut report also made the absurd claim that "liberal and progressive groups are probably most effective in engaging with soft critics of Israel, who are often also of similar outlooks."[38] In fact, the progressive Jewish groups who persistently criticize and condemn Israel are *not* "most effective" as advocates for Israel. When critics of Israel are presented as pro-Israel, this *increases* delegitimization.

The ADL/Reut report approach is reminiscent of the cartoon entitled "debate between a Palestinian Arab and a liberal Jew." The bubble above the Palestinian Arab debater shows him saying: "*Everything is Israel's fault*" and the bubble above the liberal Jewish debater likewise shows him saying: "*Everything is Israel's fault.*"

The best and most persuasive advocates for the Jewish state are those who tell the truth about Israel's rights and the Arab war against Israel, as the ZOA does. Truth is not a political position. The ZOA often speaks to liberal groups, with excellent results. Lies undermine Israel and our people; the antidote is the truth.

More Examples of the Harm Caused By Mainstream
Organizations Ignoring the Truth:

It is heartbreaking and dangerous when other mainstream Jewish organizations ignore or downplay the truth about Islamic, Black Nationalist, and left-wing antisemitism, refuse to help, or outright hinder and condemn our efforts to protect the Jewish people. I discussed several recent instances of this earlier in this essay, but there are even more examples.

I encountered this problem even before I became president of the ZOA in 1993, when the ADL dismissively refused my request to help remove anti-Israel falsehoods from textbooks used in my daughter's school and throughout the country. I then initiated my own successful campaign to correct the textbooks.

Since then, at the ZOA, we've had dozens of run-ins with the ADL and certain mainstream groups, that were harming efforts to combat antisemitism. Incredibly, the ADL lobbied *against* anti-BDS laws, falsely claiming that they violated free speech. ZOA testified about and wrote articles pointing out the legality and necessity for such anti-discrimination laws. For years, the ADL refused to condemn so-called "targeted" boycotts against Jews living in Judea-Samaria and Jerusalem.[39]After years of pressure from the ZOA, the ADL finally quietly began supporting such laws.[40] (Sometimes, change is possible.)

In 2014, the Metropolitan Opera performed an antisemitic opera that demeaned American Jews as materialistic and petty, and falsely claimed that Jews were interlopers who brutally drove out Arabs from Israel in 1948.[41] (In fact, the Arab High Command ordered the Arabs to leave to clear a path for them to invade and murder all of Israel's Jews. The Jews urged the Arabs to stay.)

The opera glorified the Palestinian Arab terrorists who hijacked the *Achille Lauro* cruise ship and murdered an elderly, disabled, wheelchair-bound American Jew and threw him overboard.[42]

The ZOA helped organize massive demonstrations in front of the Met Opera house, attended by thousands of people, 50 organizations, and major speakers. The ZOA also contacted and persuaded the film company AMC to cancel its planned worldwide broadcasts of the opera.[43] We probably would have also succeeded in also canceling the Met's 2014 performances—but then the ADL stepped in and wrongly declared that the opera wasn't antisemitic,[44] thereby giving the Met Opera "cover" to perform this Jew-demeaning travesty.

The 2015 Iran deal was another instance where mainstream groups fell short. The ZOA helped organize huge demonstrations against the deal—including the New York demonstration with 20,000 attendees, but most mainstream groups were absent.

Hope for the Future:

Despite all this, I am hopeful. I am seeing some changes for the better. More and more mainstream groups have signed on to letters to public officials the ZOA has initiated, demanding specific actions to counteract Iranian regime threats, BDS activities, and other issues. We've even occasionally obtained virtually across-the-board support from other mainstream groups, such as for our effort to return to the Iraqi Jewish community Jewish artifacts stolen by Saddam Hussein. Our policy critiques are being heard, and are promoting change. Smaller pro-Israel groups have joined with us and are raising their voices. The Jewish Leadership Project is doing critical work calling attention to this important issue.

Let's continue to work for Jewish leaders and organizations that are unafraid to tell the truth about and combat the real sources of danger to our people.

Morton A. Klein is national president of the Zionist Organization of America (ZOA), the oldest pro-Israel group in the U.S., founded in 1897. Mr. Klein is widely regarded as one of the leading Jewish activists in the United States. His more than four hundred articles and letters have been published in newspapers, magazines, and scientific journals around the world, including the New York Times, Washington Post, Wall Street Journal, L.A. Times, Washington Times, New Yorker, Commentary, Breitbart, Jerusalem Post, *and many others.*
Elizabeth A. Berney, Esq., the ZOA's Director of Research and Special Projects, assisted with this essay.

---

[1] See, *e.g.*, Brigadier-General (Res.) Yossi Kuperwasser, *Incentivizing Terrorism: Palestinian Authority Allocations to Terrorists and their Families*, (Jerusalem: Jerusalem Center for Public Affairs, 2016). https://bit. ly/45iscTY; Edwin Black, "PA Salaries: Kill More Israelis, Get More Cash," *Israel National News*, February 8, 2015. https://bit.ly/3qqNJLl; "Palestinian Authority Financing of Terrorism," *Jewish Virtual Library*. https://bit. ly/442eiUI.

[2] See *Palestinian Media Watch*. https://palwatch.org.

[3] See Khaled Abu Toameh, "PA: Death penalty for those who sell land to Jews," *The Jerusalem Post*, April 1, 2009. http://bit.ly/39BMqhp. See also Jacob Magid, "Palestinian Authority boasts it 'thwarted' major land sales to Jews in Jerusalem," *The Times of Israel*, December 23, 2018. http://bit. ly/3GAGNAX .

[4] See "Hamas Covenant 1988: The Covenant of the Islamic Resistance Movement," *Yale University*. http://bit.ly/35zKoLE.

[5] See Ronen Manelis, "The Truth About Hamas and Israel," *The Wall Street Journal*, May 20, 2018. http://bit.ly/3Oom3y4.

6   Quoted in Abu Toameh, "Hamas head Sinwar says Gaza protests will continue until border is erased," *The Times of Israel*, May 30, 2018. http://bit.ly/3hVz6eh.

7   See Daniel Greenfield, "A Farrakhan Supporter Led the LA Black Lives Matter Rally That Became a Pogrom," *FrontPage Magazine*, June 19, 2020. http://bit.ly/3gd4zs3.

8   See Dan Diker, "The Alignment of BDS and Black Lives Matter: Implications for Israel and Diaspora Jewry," *Jerusalem Center for Public Affairs*, July 16, 2020. http://bit.ly/3vLzqig.

9   See *Ibid.*

10   See, *e.g.*, "Biden's Policies Voiced at Israeli and Palestinian Mtgs. Demanding Israel Return to '67 "Auschwitz" Lines, End Checkpoints, Open Jerusalem Arab Consulate—and More—Show Biden's No Friend to Israel," *Zionist Organization of America*, July 18, 2022. http://bit.ly/3UMC0AG; "Readout of President Biden's Meeting with President Abbas of the Palestinian Authority," *The White House*, July 15, 2022. http://bit.ly/3UTlBKY; "Remarks by President Biden and President Abbas of the Palestinian National Authority in Joint Press Statement, Bethlehem, West Bank," *The White House*, July 15, 2022. http://bit.ly/3Oe1qEX.

11   See *Ibid.*

12   Quoted in "Biden Admin. Disrespects Israeli Sovereignty and International Law By Separating 'Palestinian Affairs Unit' Reporting and Elevating 'Intifada-Inspired' Hady Amr to Special Envoy to Palestinians," *Zionist Organization of America*, May 31, 2022. http://bit.ly/3Gs79VS.

13   Morton A. Klein, "Top contender for Biden's press secretary is an Israelophobe," *JNS*, November 19, 2020. http://bit.ly/3hTgYSn.

14   Greenfield, "Biden Puts Maher Bitar, Anti-Israel BDS Activist in Charge of NSC Intel," *FrontPage Magazine*, January 29, 2021. http://bit.ly/3hZ8BEP.

15   "ZOA: Biden's Troubling Appointments: Apologizer-to-Sarsour Tony Blinken; Anti-Israel Platform-Promoter Avril Haines; Suicide Bombing-Supporter Reema Dodin; and Alejandro Mayorkas," *Zionist Organization of America*, November 30, 2020. http://bit.ly/3UNKbwG.

16   See "Biden Appointments Watch: Joe Biden's Hostile-to-Israel Appointments," *Zionist Organization of America*. https://zoa.org/biden-appointments-watch/.

17   AIPAC. Twitter post. October 11, 2022. 1:28 P.M. http://bit.ly/3ViVOvw.

18   AJCGlobal. Twitter post. October 27, 2022. 6:30 P.M. http://bit.ly/3TUK01h.

19   ADL. Twitter post. October 27, 2022. 1:09 P.M. http://bit.ly/3EuY5gl.

20 Conf Of Presidents. Twitter post. October 13, 2022. 1:40 A.M. http://bit. ly/3tPmkRb.

21 See also "The BLM Organization Files," *Zionist Organization of America.* https://zoa.org/the-blm-organization-files/.

22 "An Update on The Movement for Black Lives and Israel," *Jewish Community Relations Council of San Francisco, the Peninsula, Marin, Sonoma, Almeda, and Contra Costa Counties,* August 24, 2016. http://bit.ly/3tD01Ov.

23 "ZOA Criticizes ADL, Reform/Conservative Movements, JCRCs, HIAS, Etc. Signing Ad Supporting Israel-Hating & Jew-Hating Black Lives Matter Organization, Co-Signed With Israel-Haters," *Zionist Organization of America,* September 13, 2020. http://bit.ly/3ge3rUS.

24 "BlackLivesMatter Platform Falsely Accuses Israel of Genocide, etc.—Yet ADL Still Promotes BLM," *Zionist Organization of America,* August 9, 2016. http://bit.ly/3TMgk6g. See also "Fox News Joins ZOA in Exposing ADL's Dangerous, Extremist 'Educational' Programs & Joins JNS Editor Tobin in Urging Firing ADL CEO Jonathan Greenblatt," *Zionist Organization of America,* September 12, 2022. http://bit.ly/3gcSGSM.

25 Quoted in "Breitbart: ZOA Slams ADL for Accepting Ilhan Omar's Non-Apology for Antisemitic Rhetoric," *Zionist Organization of America,* February 6, 2019. http://bit.ly/3EhBrb1.

26 See Ali Abunimah, "Leaked Report Highlights Israel Lobby's Failures," *The Electronic Intifada,* April 28, 2017. http://bit.ly/3GvAmiJ.

27 Anti-Defamation League and the Reut Institute, *The Assault on Israel's Legitimacy: The Frustrating 20X Question: Why Is It Still Growing? Condition, Direction and Response* (New York, NY: Anti-Defamation League, January 2017), pp. 1, 2. http://bit.ly/3XbzSnG.

28 *Ibid.,* p. 5.

29 *Ibid.,* p. 31.

30 *Ibid.,* p. 19.

31 *Ibid.*

32 *Ibid.,* p. 18.

33 *Ibid.,* p. 19.

34 *Ibid.,* p. 5.

35 *Ibid.,* p. 22.

36 *Ibid.,* p. 4.

37 See Klein, "What CNN Left Out of Its Special on Anti-Semitism," *JNS,* August 29, 2022. http://bit.ly/3gf9R6q.

38 *The Assault on Israel's Legitimacy: The Frustrating 20X Question: Why Is It Still Growing? Condition, Direction and Response,* pp. 26–27.

[39] Klein and Elizabeth A. Berney, "Why Does the ADL Continue to Hinder Anti-BDS Efforts?", *The Algemeiner*, June 28, 2016. http://bit.ly/3gnTunU.

[40] Amir Tibon, "Anti-Defamation League Supports Controversial anti-BDS Bill: Act 'Won't Limit Free Speech,'" *Haaretz*, August 10, 2017. http://bit.ly/3Xomblc.

[41] See "ZOA Urges Cancellation of Metropolitan Opera's Planned Anti-Semitic Anti-Israel Performances and Worldwide Broadcast of 'Death of Klinghoffer," *Zionist Organization of America*, June 13, 2014. http://bit.ly/3EuOBRV.

[42] See Alan M. Dershowitz, "The Right to Protest the Metropolitan Opera Decision to Put on 'The Death of Klinghoffer,'" *Gatestone Institute*, September 24, 2014. http://bit.ly/3tMKTOD.

[43] See "Met Opera Cancels Broadcast of Anti-Semitic 'Klinghoffer' Promoting Anti-Israel Lies/Humanizing Terrorists, ZOA Had Spoken To Movie Officials, Donor Connections," *Zionist Organization of America*, June 18, 2014. http://bit.ly/3OFdT4R.

[44] See "ZOA is Shocked, Mystified That ADL/Foxman Wrongly States 'Klinghoffer' Opera is Not Anti-Semitic," *Zionist Organization of America*, June 19, 2014. http://bit.ly/3Vc6vzh.

12

THE PERSISTENT FAILURE OF AMERICAN JEWISH LEADERSHIP: A CASE STUDY

ALAN M. DERSHOWITZ

P rotecting the interests of American Jews and Israel is the central task of America's Jewish leadership. Its performance has ranged, over the course of America's history, from moderate success to abject failure. Tragically, it has tended more toward failure during the most critical of times.

The reason is that Jewish leaders are generally selected by the wrong criteria. Jews who become Jewish leaders are often successful, wealthy, influential members of the community and have often tended to put their own interests (and those of their social and economic peers) ahead of the interests of the general community and the nation state of the Jewish people.

There are many instances throughout history where Jewish leaders have sought to preserve their own status instead of advocating positions that might disturb a status quo that benefits them, their families, and their friends. We know how Jewish leaders, many of them from Central and Western Europe, failed to do enough to open America's gates to much poorer Eastern European Jews. We know of the shameful and massive failure of Jewish leadership during the Holocaust, represented most dramatically by Rabbi Stephen Wise, Justice Felix Frankfurter, and many of their associates in refusing to confront their patron and political hero, Franklin Delano Roosevelt, with the realities of the Nazi extermination. We know of the lukewarm attitude of many Jewish leaders toward Zionism and the establishment of the state of Israel. More recently, we are coming to understand the failure of most leaders of our mainstream, establishment Jewish organizations to take on the universities—which they and their off-spring attended and wish to attend—and to combat anti-Zionism and anti-Semitism on campuses.

When one compares the Jewish leadership in America with early Zionist leadership in Europe, the Jewish pre-state, and then Israel, the distinction becomes most apparent. American leaders in general have refused to rock the boat on which they were first-class passengers. Zionist leaders, on the other hand, were generally not of the same elite status. They had far less to lose by rocking their sinking ship. Inevitably, therefore, they were far more aggressive and successful in their leadership roles while American Jewish leaders maintained success in their personal roles precisely by not truly representing their constituents' needs.

I have long observed this disturbing phenomenon of leadership failure and have written about it in several of my books, most especially *Chutzpah* (1991) and *The Vanishing American Jew* (1997). Then, I experienced it personally, when I was falsely accused of sexual misconduct by a woman I never met. Although several leaders told me they knew the accusation was false, they "didn't want trouble." So, they "cancelled" me and silenced my voice in defense of Israel and in support of Zionist students on campuses throughout the country.

Another reason for the cancellation was my defense of the Constitution on behalf of President Donald Trump, during which CNN deliberately mischaracterized my arguments and my answers to questions during the 2020 senatorial impeachment trial.

These personal experiences, which I tell more out of sorrow than anger, demonstrate the failure of Jewish leaders because they prioritized guarding their reputations among their elite social circles over truth and the good of the Jewish community.

Here is a brief account.

Before I defended President Trump and Jeffrey Epstein, and before I was falsely accused by Virginia Roberts-Giuffre (who ultimately admitted that she "may have made a mistake" in identifying me as someone with whom she claimed to have had sex), I was the second-most sought-after speaker by Jewish organizations: synagogues, schools, book fairs, fundraisers, pro-Israel rallies, and the like. The most sought-after was my dear friend and colleague of blessed memory, Elie Wiesel.

For several years, I was the "defense lawyer" for Biblical characters who were put "on trial" at Temple Emanu-El in New York City, the most important Reform synagogue in the world. The trials—of Abraham, Moses, David, Noah, and others—were the most popular and well-attended events at the Temple. Upwards of 1,500 people would attend, listen to the trial, and vote "guilty" or "not guilty." I was always the "defense attorney," and different "prosecutors" were selected to present the case against the "defendant." These prosecutors included Senator Joseph Lieberman (D-CT), TV commentator Chris Cuomo, former New York governor Eliot Spitzer, and others. King David was found guilty. All the others were found innocent.

In the fall of 2019, the trial of Joseph's brothers for selling Joseph to the Egyptians was scheduled and announced. A prosecutor was selected, and I was preparing my case. The event was cancelled.

The following year was COVID-19, and there were no in-person events at the Temple. When public events resumed in the fall of 2021, I called the rabbi and asked him to schedule another trial. He said there would be no more. I asked why. He told me that the president and the board had decided against any more trials involving me. A few days later, he informed me that the president and the board had decided that I could not speak at the Temple on any subject whatsoever. He assured me that no one—certainly not he—believed that the sex charges were true, but they were in the media. He implied that the Temple did not want to be identified with or tainted by any accusation, even if false.

I reminded the rabbi that this is exactly how McCarthyism worked in the 1950s. The institutions that banned people accused of being communists did not necessarily believe the accusations or think that they justified the ban, but they did not want to be tainted even by false accusations. So, they went along with the ban—just to be safe. So did many prominent French Jews when Captain Alfred Dreyfus was falsely accused of espionage and treason in 1894. They didn't want trouble.

The result of the cancellation is that more than 1,500 people were denied the opportunity to see trials they loved and from which they learned. They were also denied the opportunity to hear—and having their children hear—my arguments in defense of Israel and against anti-Semitism at a time of increasing anti-Zionism and anti-Jewish attitudes in universities and among the hard left. I offered to speak on how to combat these dangers, but the Temple preferred to hear from Peter Beinart, who advocates the end of Israel as the nation state of the Jewish people and who supports boycotts against Israelis. At the same time that I was cancelled, Beinart received a substantial speaker's fee from the Temple to make his case against Israel.

Temple Emanu-El has silenced my voice while amplifying the voice of one of Israel's most toxic detractors. What does this say about the Temple's priorities and values? These Jewish leaders evidently believed that Jewish congregants' hard-earned donations were better spent on blatant anti-Israel propaganda than on good-faith, pro-Israel advocacy.

Moreover, the fact that I have been cancelled by a prominent Jewish institution gives cover to non-Jewish institutions—such as universities—to cancel me as well, without being accused of anti-Zionism or anti-Semitism. Temple Emanu-El has thus contributed to the silencing of my pro-Israel voice where it is most needed today. Shame on the Temple.

Silence is not the option in the face of unjustified McCarthyite censorship by a synagogue that claims to be a house of study, open-mindedness, and Jewish values of dialogue and dissent.

Nor is Temple Emanu-El the only prominent Jewish institution to cancel me. For more than a quarter of a century, I have been among the most sought-after and popular speakers at the 92nd Street Y— the primary venue for Jewish talks in America. I had spoken there at least once a year and introduced nearly all my new books there since I published *Chutzpah* three decades earlier. I always filled the auditorium and got thousands of viewers on the Y's feeds to synagogues and Jewish community centers around the world.

In 2019, I published *Defending Israel: The Story of My Most Challenging Client*. It was a natural fit for the 92nd Street Y. But when my agent approached the Y, it refused to allow me to speak. It, too, offered every phony excuse—crowded schedule, not enough interest. Finally, the Y admitted it: I had been banned because of the false accusation. It, too, said it didn't believe the accusation, but "we don't want trouble." Exactly what the practitioners of McCarthyism said when they complied with "blacklists," "red channels," and other bans on accused communists and "fellow travelers."

This cancellation by the Y had been even more effective in silencing me than the cancellation by Temple Emanu-El, because talks at the Y are circulated more widely. So, its ban has prevented tens of thousands of people who would have wanted to hear my defense of Israel from doing so.

Other Jewish institutions have also followed Temple Emanu-El and the Y in banning me. This includes a prominent Manhattan Jewish high school—Ramaz—which asked me to speak to the juniors and seniors to help to prepare them for the anti-Zionism and anti-Semitism they can expect when they get to college. I agreed to speak. Then the headmaster called and told me that some people on the board did not want me to speak.

In all these cases, the McCarthyite censorship was blamed on nameless and faceless "board members" and "contributors." The rabbis, directors, and principles always say they want me to speak, and they don't believe the accusations. But they don't control "the board," and "the board" doesn't want to hear from me. Tragically, that is how decisions—immoral, un-Jewish, and indefensible—are made by many Jewish institutions, which act without accountability and against the interests not only of their members but of the Jewish community in general.

Jewish leaders' first priority must be to defend the community. This dark time of rising anti-Semitism and anti-Zionism must be a time of unity and fortitude, not petty partisanship or skittish kowtowing to the kangaroo court of public opinion.

As long as Jewish leaders are selected by a self-anointed elite which is more concerned with its privilege and status than its fiduciary responsibilities to the community, we will continue to be poorly represented. We cannot afford their incompetent and self-serving "leadership."

How can American Jewry survive its failed leaders' warped, inappropriate priorities? We must act now to do all in our power to make Jewish leadership respond effectively to the needs of the Jewish community and Israel.

Alan M. Dershowitz, the Felix Frankfurter Professor of Law Emeritus at Harvard Law School, is perhaps America's most famous advocate for the state of Israel. He is the author of fifty-three books, including Chutzpah *(1991),* The Case for Israel *(2003),* The Case for Peace: How the Arab-Israeli Conflict Can Be Resolved *(2005),* The Case Against Israel's Enemies: Exposing Jimmy Carter and Others Who Stand in the Way of Peace *(2008),* Defending Israel: The Story of My Relationship with My Most Challenging Client *(2019),* Cancel Culture: The Latest Attack on Free Speech and Due Process *(2020), and* The Case Against the New Censorship: Protecting Free Speech from Big Tech, Progressives, and Universities *(2021). His most recent book is* Get Trump: The Threat to Civil Liberties, Due Process, and Our Constitutional Rule of Law *(2023).*

13

THE REFORM MOVEMENT LEFT ME

RABBI CARY KOZBERG

Thanks to the man on a blue notebook, I became a rabbi instead of a doctor.

That blue notebook was called a *machberet*, and it was given out to students in afternoon Hebrew Schools during the 1950s. On the front was the likeness of Maimonides, the renowned twelfth-century rabbi. Until I was a freshman in college, my total knowledge of Maimonides was the little I remembered from Hebrew School: He was a famous rabbi, philosopher, and physician who lived in medieval Spain.

Until I was a freshman in college, I had planned to become a doctor. My high school and college freshman course work included the required math and science courses. But because a high GPA was a requirement for acceptance into medical school, I searched for electives that would help me maintain at least a 3.5 GPA. I heard about a course titled "The History of the Jews in Spain," which was reputed to be "an easy A," requiring only class attendance and a term paper.

Planning to become a physician, I decided to write my term paper on "Maimonides as Physician." As I began my research, I discovered an abbreviated translation of his most famous philosophical work, *A Guide for the Perplexed*.

It was 1970, and the political and social upheaval occurring in this country at that time was causing a lot of people to be "perplexed." That perplexity was echoed in a popular song of the time: *"There's somethin' happenin' here / But what it is ain't exactly clear."* My biggest concerns at the time were getting good grades, getting through my fraternity's pledge program, and getting dates for Saturday night. When it came to "perplexing" questions, I was like the son at the Passover seder who doesn't even know how to ask.

The writings of the man on the blue *machberet* changed all that. I began to ask questions I had never even considered—questions that people had been wrestling with for millennia, but were a jolting "wake up call" to this eighteen-year-old kid: Why are we here? Why is there evil? If there is evil, how can G-d allow it? What exactly is G-d's role in this world, and what is ours? Realizing that what I was reading was offering answers to these questions made them all the more compelling.

I was raised in a home that was a kind of religious "mixed marriage." My dad's parents were Orthodox immigrants from Russia; my mother's family was completely assimilated and she had no Jewish education. The compromise was joining a Conservative synagogue where my dad could pray in Hebrew with his head covered, and there was enough English to keep my mother's attention. Our Jewish observance was limited to Shabbat candles, a fairly strict Passover observance, and observing two days of Rosh Hashanah and, of course, Yom Kippur. I looked forward to my Bar Mitzvah but chose not to continue my formal Jewish education after Confirmation. All my friends were Jewish, but the Jewish youth organization we belonged to did not really stress Judaism per se. In short, Judaism to me was more of a somewhat cherished hobby, and not the life commitment that it would eventually become.

With the encouragement of my rabbi, I spent the summer of 1970 at a program for college students at the Jewish Theological Seminary (JTS). Returning from that summer, I came home more religiously observant and eager to begin pre-rabbinic studies. I changed my major from biology to Hebrew Studies, with the hope of entering JTS's rabbinical program after college graduation.

But a funny thing happened on the way to becoming a Conservative rabbi: I became a Reform rabbi.

Back then, JTS expected prospective students to have a minimum of Talmud knowledge before being accepted into its rabbinic program. Those lacking this knowledge had to take an extra year or two of preparatory work. I was prepared to make the commitment, but then a recruiter from the Reform movement's Hebrew Union College's (HUC's) Jewish Institute of Religion came to my campus. Out of curiosity, I met with him. When I told him of my background and journey, he assured me I was the kind of student HUC was looking for. When I asked if my newly acquired level of religious observance might not make me such a "good fit" in a movement that had jettisoned so much of traditional Jewish practice and belief, he assured me that the Reform movement was "re-forming" itself in some significant ways. He pointed out that:

- The "classical Reform" familiar to many non-Reform Jews (such as services reminiscent of church worship, *yarmulkes/*

head coverings and *tallesim*/prayer shawls discouraged, dietary laws rejected) was becoming less the norm. *Yarmulkes* were showing up in Reform synagogues, and guitars were being introduced to supplement—or even replace—the Protestant-sounding organ.

- The Reform movement's historical ambivalence toward a Jewish state had significantly changed after Israel's victory in 1967. Reform rabbis were now preaching full-throated support of Israel, and many were introducing more Hebrew into worship services.

- Many HUC students were also becoming more religiously observant—covering their heads during prayer, keeping kosher, even putting on *t'fillin*/phylacteries. Some, he assured me, were even more observant than I was. (Several fellow students eventually joined the Conservative movement; one went through HUC's five-year rabbinical program while living as an Orthodox Jew. He eventually became a Chabad rabbi.)

Finally, he added: "In order to strengthen their Hebrew skills, our students are now required to spend the first year in Israel. We don't have a 'prior knowledge' requirement to be accepted into our program, but we'll give you the skills to learn as much Talmud and other traditional texts as you want."

This was an offer I couldn't refuse.

To be sure, everything he told me during that conversation was true. During my time at HUC, my level of religious observance never made me feel out of place. Back then, the Reform movement was committed to true religious diversity and to creating a "big tent" that included different approaches to Judaism, from "radical" to "classical" to "traditional." This diversity became evident when the new Reform prayerbook *Gates of Prayer*—with its ten different Erev Shabbat services—replaced the *Union Prayerbook.*

During my time at HUC, I gravitated to those teachers whose understanding of Reform Judaism was more committed to holding on to traditional Jewish beliefs and practices. They themselves had been raised as Orthodox Jews (some with Orthodox *s'micha*/ordination), but their exposure to twentieth-century modernity had led them away from their Orthodox roots. Nevertheless, unlike advocates of "classical Reform," their embrace of modernity had not erased their commitment to traditional core beliefs and practices. Acknowledging that "personal autonomy" was the watchword of enlightened Western culture, they sought to create a synthesis of personal autonomy and commitment to the requirements of the Sinai Covenant, as delineated in the teachings of the Torah and the Sages. From them I learned that:

- An authentic Reform Jew was an *in*formed Jew.
- While personal autonomy is a positive value, Jewish religious choices are authentically "Jewish" *only* if they are demonstrably connected to the Covenant our people made with G-d at Sinai.
- "G-d, Torah, and the people of Israel" were still at the heart of Reform Judaism and nothing in Jewish tradition should be *a priori* foreign to a Reform Jew.
- Struggling to maintain a dynamic balance between covenantal commitment and personal freedom is the challenge a serious Reform Jew faces daily.

Throughout my rabbinic career, I believed that these are what defined me as a Reform Jew. Since my ordination in 1977, I've served as a rabbi in both Reform and Conservative congregations, a campus Hillel director, and a healthcare chaplain. Although most of my work has not been in Reform congregations, I continued to belong to the Central Conference of American Rabbis (the professional organization of the Reform rabbinate). I always considered myself a Reform rabbi and a Reform Jew.

That is, until a few years ago.

A few years ago, it became apparent that Reform Judaism—through the efforts of its rabbinic and lay leaders—was moving away from these core Jewish beliefs. Although the words "G-d, Torah, and the people of Israel" were still invoked, they were now equivocal terms, with meanings very different from the traditional ones. It was reminiscent of 1885 when Reform Judaism set down its principles in the Pittsburgh Platform. That statement affirmed a decidedly progressive approach to religious belief and observance, one that called for adapting to "the views and habits of modern civilization."

Once upon a time, that approach encouraged creating a "big tent" in which debate and discussion would help modern Jews to better understand what G-d wants from us.

But as today's Reform leaders have increasingly embraced the values and worldview of *contemporary* progressivism, the big tent that once accommodated diverse beliefs and approaches has metamorphosed into a confining cement bunker of theological and political progressive orthodoxy. That orthodoxy has one objective: the promotion of "social justice."

The notion of "social justice" is not an organic Jewish concept but rather has its beginnings in Catholic theology. Nevertheless, progressive Jews have "Judaized" it by identifying it (albeit inaccurately) with the rabbinic notion of *tikkun olam*. Literally meaning "repair of the world" and identified with inaugurating the Kingdom of the Almighty (*malkhut Shaddai*) here on earth, *tikkun olam* was understood by the Talmudic sages to be efforts to make the world more humane, more *menschlikh*. Today, *tikkun olam* is promoted (1) as a mitzvah given at Sinai that virtually trumps all other mitzvot—including the ones Reform Jews usually ignore; and (2) often without any reference to the Kingdom of the Almighty. Moreover, *tikkun olam*/social justice is the larger rubric under which other "adjective-added" justices are promoted (such as environmental justice, transgender justice, restorative justice). This is at odds with Jewish teachings because nowhere in Jewish religious texts are adjectives ever used when "justice" is discussed.

From my perspective, it is Reform's singular devotion to this tenet that has caused it to be a movement in which noun and adjective are reversed. Reform Judaism used to be a synonym for "progressive Judaism;" now it is a religion of "Jewish Progressivism." And that greatly concerns me.

It greatly concerns me that the age-old, honored rabbinic methodology of discussion and debate to learn and deduce holy behavior is no longer encouraged. Indeed, Reform rabbis who dissent and challenge progressive ("woke") wisdom discussed in online chats have been admonished, personally attacked, sometimes suspended, and even expelled from the conversations.

It greatly concerns me that a Reform rabbi would tell an adult Bat Mitzvah student that, despite Hebrew's use of masculine pronouns when referring to G-d, she had to remove them from her speech because the synagogue only permitted "gender-neutral" language be used when referring to the Deity.

It greatly concerns me that rather than teaching her students that "nothing in Jewish tradition should be *a priori* foreign to a Reform

Jew," the teacher of that same class told her students that when it comes to certain commandments and observances, "we Reform Jews don't do that."

It greatly concerns me that during an online Shavuot discussion about the meaning of the covenantal obligations originating at Sinai, an HUC faculty member would declare categorically "but we Reform Jews *have been given* autonomy."

It greatly concerns me that there are Reform rabbis who discourage *brit milah*, declaring that circumcision is "barbaric."

It greatly concerns me that Reform's commitment to social justice promotes universalism and "inclusivity" over Jewish particularism and the mandate that we Jews remain "a separate people" and focus on caring for our own before caring for others.

It greatly concerns me that the invited speaker at an HUC rabbinic graduation ceremony would call for an end to endogamy (marrying within one's own group), with the response of "academic freedom" in response to criticisms of the speaker's remarks.

It greatly concerns me that the singular focus on "inclusivity" now allows non-Jews to take leadership positions in synagogues and has resulted in some Reform synagogues removing all references to "chosen-ness" from worship services, lest guests and non-Jewish family members be offended.

It greatly concerns me that, rooted in progressive political ideology:

- Reform clergy—rabbis and cantors—are increasingly becoming "anti-Zionist," publicly labeling Israel an "apartheid state," and continuing to engage in actions that help and support Israel's implacable enemies.

- Rabbis are preaching from their pulpits the doctrine of critical race theory, which includes the nefarious lie that Jews, by virtue of sometimes "passing as white," are automatically racist.
- The Reform movement's political lobbying organization, Religious Action Center, invited the well-known and unapologetic anti-Semite Al Sharpton as a keynote speaker.
- A Reform rabbi, choosing to virtue-signal "welcoming the stranger" and throwing caution to the wind, invited a terrorist into his synagogue and almost got himself and his congregants killed.
- A member of URJ's board expressed on social media his wish for the painful death of a sitting president and was not removed from his board position, but merely "reprimanded."

These are specific examples of how Reform Judaism is embracing the values and teachings of political progressivism while moving away from Jewish values and teachings derived from Jewish texts. They are examples of a massive failure of Jewish moral leadership from spiritual leaders, too many of whom are rarely "spiritual" or "leaders." Their teachings and actions have weakened our people and our people's commitment to our unique covenant with G-d at a time when we need more, not less, spiritual strength and confidence in that legacy bequeathed to us by our ancestors.

But what most concerns me is not just *how* they have moved us away, but how *far* they will move Reform away before it is no longer recognizably a Jewish movement.

It's happened before.

When Jews lived in the Greco-Roman diaspora around the Mediterranean Sea, there were different Judaisms practiced, many significantly influenced by the cultural Hellenism of the time. Those Judaisms ultimately disappeared on their own or became so inundated by members and influences of the outside culture as to break with the Jewish community and its traditions, evolving into faith systems that sought to eclipse the mother faith.

Fast forward 2,000 years and it is easy to see the circumstances in which history could repeat itself. Should that happen, G-d forbid, wherever the man on the blue notebook is, he will be very, very blue indeed.

As will so many of us.

Rabbi Cary Kozberg has served as a congregational rabbi, Hillel director, and healthcare chaplain. He currently serves as rabbi of Temple Sholom in Springfield, Ohio.

14

JEWISH LEADERS MUST COUNTER
ISLAMIST SUPREMACISM

M. ZUHDI JASSER

The first question any American Jew may contemplate asking me, an American Muslim activist, is how does this guy have the chutzpah to tell our diverse Jewish communities what we should or should not do *vis-à-vis* American Muslim communities, Islamism, and especially anti-Semitism? Anyone who has followed our public work in this area of expertise knows that we at the American Islamic Forum for Democracy (AIFD) and the Muslim Reform Movement are certainly not delusional and are fully aware and engaged in the hard work necessary to begin change toward long-overdue reforms within the Muslim consciousness. We know that this road is arduous and may take a generation. But we also would have never guessed that some of our most significant obstacles to fighting Islamists like those of the Muslim Brotherhood would come from within the Jewish community.

We know that most, if not all, of this work can only be done by Muslims needing essentially nothing short of revolution after revolution against the Islamist establishments, theocrats, patriarchs, autocrats, and kleptocrats across the planet; however, no one should for a second believe that we can right this ship alone. Our non-Muslim, and especially our Jewish community, partners play an invaluable role in our success and failures, obviously and especially, when it comes down to countering anti-Semitism. We understand that this condition of endemic bigotry against the Jewish community emanates from centuries-old Islamist interpretations of Islam as well as pan-Arab racial supremacism, to name a few root-cause afflictions of the majorities of almost a quarter of the world's population who happen to be Muslim.

The reality, however, is that if the Jewish community's greatest allies within Muslim and Arab populations are, in fact, the "modern," "liberal" reformers who stand up within our own faith and ethnic communities against the anti-Semitic, Islamist, and Arabist demagogues, then they must be supported and augmented, not marginalized. If any of us reformers are going to ever make any headway at all, then the leadership of leading Jewish political and religious organizations must make strategic alliances—with eyes wide open, please. The importance of those alliances cannot be overstated as it provides important legitimacy to American Muslim groups domestically and abroad, and, also contrarily, what can be a very dangerous sense of complacency when it comes to Islamist dissimulation and their *façades* of reform.

I am here to tell you that, all too often, leading Jewish organizations grossly underestimate the profound impact they have in marginalizing their real allies by lifting up the lowest hanging fruit of our faith community's current Islamist leadership across mosques and activist Islamist organizations in America. The reason the Muslim

Brotherhood and Deobandi legacy groups like the Islamic Society of North America (ISNA), the Muslim American Society (MAS), the Islamic Circle of North America (ICNA), the Council on American-Islamic Relations (CAIR), and the Muslim Public Affairs Council (MPAC), to name a few, have such a greater audience and bandwidth is because they have had a two-plus-generation head start in the West organizing, and also being funded by, the worst government actors and terror-sympathizers in the Middle East—bolstered essentially across the greater "neo-caliphate" of today, with the fifty-six nations of the Organization of Islamic Cooperation (OIC) behind them.

My goal here is simple. It is to shed the antiseptic of sunlight upon the relationships that many Jewish organizations make with American Islamists. It is one thing to proclaim that anti-Semitism is pervasive and Jewish leadership must make allies wherever it can. It is, however, quite another thing to fall for the dissimulation of Islamists and refuse to acknowledge their core ideologies as they tell groups like the Anti-Defamation League (ADL) and the American Jewish Committee what they want to hear. It is not even a zero-sum game. In fact, the elevation of Islamists by any leading non-Muslims in the West is just another nail in the coffin of reformers. Don't be deceived.

It is important to truly understand the deep layers upon which the horrifically pervasive anti-Semitism of Muslim and Arab majority populations is based. As wise sages have said, the only way to prevent history from repeating itself is to truly understand it and learn from it. As a faithful Muslim, it is my obligation to be transparent about our own history and make sure that Muslims and non-Muslims alike learn from it and prevent the theocratic and ethnic supremacists from staying in power and ever gaining it again.

First, it is key to understand the history and ideology of Islamism, or *political Islam*. The link between Islamism (also known as Islamist supremacism) and anti-Semitism is fairly simple. It is self-evident that supremacists from within a particular faith community will create and exploit hatred toward another faith community in order to collectively rally their own followers against a common enemy. Much as Jew-hatred was a fundamental part of Christianity before the Protestant Revolution and the Enlightenment separated church and state, predominant interpretations of Islam (a much newer religion) promoted anti-Semitic imagery, profiling, and demonization of Jews as a tool for its devoted members' own ascension into power among Muslim-majority communities and nations, or in Arabic, the *Ummah*. My entire work and our mission at AIFD are founded on the precept that the primary cancer from which all hate within the Muslim community emanates is the idea of the "Islamic state." From that theocratic shariah "state" come obligations to jihad, anti-blasphemy laws, and the current oppressive shariah legal system that puts Muslims above all others.

Understanding this inextricable connection between the demonization of Jews and the advancement of Islamist movements whether violent or not, lawful or not (distinctions without a difference), is essential in order to break the link and finally give reformers the space to even begin the hard work of reforming various Muslim interpretations of the faith of Islam, as we have seen happen within Christianity. And yet, it breaks my heart to see so many in the Jewish community itself actively hampering and preventing such a positive change from occurring. We can all do better than this.

If the public goal is to simply fill dining halls with thousands of Muslim supporters and do "photo ops" with what appears to be large

Muslim populations, then go ahead—the Islamist dissimulators of moderation are the only way to go and the only Muslim "partners" who can give you that today. They have summarily dismissed anti-Islamist dissenters from the ranks of the Muslim communities they control. But Muslims who may simply, for example, recognize the horrific realities of the Holocaust and condemn Holocaust denial while certainly exemplifying a very good step forward, are far from reformational. That was the apparent low bar required by the AJC with its Islamist partners at ISNA.[1] Sadly, many Islamists cannot even do that, but when they do, all they are doing is dismissing a radical conspiracy theory.

It does nothing to treat the primary cancer of political Islam, the religious legitimacy of the Islamic state, and its theological underpinnings across all schools of current-day Islamic jurisprudence in both the Sunni and Shia traditions. I would submit that such a low bar is insulting to those of us with the honesty to address the more deep-seated fundamentals of Islamism and its anti-Semitic jihad.

Unlike the other Abrahamic religions, Judaism has always had a strong liberal streak running through it, encouraging questions and varied interpretations. The Talmud makes this fact crystal clear. And this liberalism has carried through into politics with the majority of Westernized Jews voting Democrat. That liberal history—influenced by query, reform, and the politics of immigration—has had an impact on the partisanship of various Jewish organizations in America. As such, the tendency toward "politically correct" approaches to sensitive issues of race and identity, even when Muslim leadership conflates Islamist ideologies with race and identity in such contrived notions as "Islamophobia," is mind-numbing. The avoidance by leftist Jewish communities of the pervasiveness of such deep-seated ideological threats as Muslim anti-Semitism has been at their own peril.

Instead of tackling the phenomena head-on—acknowledging how widespread it is and how increasingly problematic it has become given the recent influx of millions of Arab and Muslim refugees into Western Europe—many leaders in the Jewish community, in line with the media, academia, and the majority of Western governments, have preferred the nebulous and generic concept of "violent extremism" in developing targeted solutions against this domestic and global threat. But programs that only counter violence address the means of those who threaten the Jewish community while wholly ignoring the ideology or the ends that their movements seek. The common ideological thread running through the security threat that comes from Islamist extremism is the inherent supremacism of Islamism or political Islam. As I've testified to Congress many times, this country's programs should be titled "countering violent Islamism."[2] Full stop. Legitimate partners of Jewish communities should be anti-Islamist at best and non-Islamist at worst.

Anti-Semitism should not be viewed as just another "radical" symptom that arises from the supremacist mentality of Islamism. It is far more than that. It is its foundation. Translations and interpretations of our *Holy Qur'an* and *Hadith* (sayings of the Prophet Mohammed) distributed by virtually all Islamist governments are rife with anti-Semitic narratives, including translations and interpretations of some of the most commonly recited verses. Educational materials teach blatant Jew-hatred, with children throughout the Muslim world raised to believe that Jews are the enemies of the believers and the descendants of apes and pigs. For example, the most repeated verse in the Qur'an among faithful Muslims in their daily prayers is the short opening to

Surat al-Fatihah (chapter 1). It states, "Guide us in the straight path. The path of those upon whom you have bestowed favor, not of those who have evoked your anger or of those who have gone astray." The only Saudi version approved by its Wahhabist regime footnotes the phrase in that Sura—"or of those who have gone astray"—with "*not like the Jews and Christians." Modern reformist Muslims interpret those in the "straight path" in an egalitarian way among all believers in God of all faiths; however, Wahhabists, Islamists, and other Muslim supremacists read this as exclusive to Muslims. This small example, repeated many times a day, is but one of thousands of examples of explanatory interpretations that radicalize Muslims away from more moderate interpretations and toward the supremacist Islamist ones. Genuine Muslim-Jewish discourse should demand transparency over apologetics about the grim realities of these interpretations and so many more.

The importance of the underlying role of anti-Semitism and its rot in our communities here cannot be overstated. A Pew Research poll confirmed that "anti-Jewish sentiment" is endemic in the Muslim world. If Islamists are a plurality, upwards of 30 percent to 40 percent of the population, as was proven in the Arab Awakening, then pan-Arabist supremacists are another 30 percent to 40 percent, giving many of these nations astronomical rates of anti-Semitism—up to 80 percent to 90 percent-plus when their theological and racial hatred is combined. "In Lebanon," the study reported, "all Muslims and 99% of Christians say they have a very unfavorable view of Jews. Similarly, 99% of Jordanians have a very unfavorable view of Jews. Large majorities of Moroccans, Indonesians, Pakistanis and six-in-ten Turks also view Jews unfavorably."[3]

As many of these nations slide back and forth from one fascism to the other, from secular fascism to Islamist or theo-political fascism, one has to plainly see how the anti-Semitism long fueled for generations by Arab dictators like Hosni Mubarak, Zine El Abidine Ben Ali, Saddam Hussein, Bashar al-Assad, Muammar Qaddafi, and King Abdullah bin Abdulaziz was a harbinger of the type of violent and hate-filled societies they were sowing. These predominantly secular fascists and kleptocratic monarchs effectively used national media to propagate anti-Semitism in an "us versus them" mentality. They also effectively demonized Zionism in order to lift up pan-Arabism as a Machiavellian tool to keep the masses from questioning their authority. Their media propaganda machines made this happen.

For example—and there are thousands—under Egyptian President Mubarak (and later), Egypt annually aired a TV adaption of the virulently anti-Semitic, czarist Russian forgery *The Protocols of the Elder of Zion*.[4] State media regularly denied the Holocaust while at the same time irrationally labeling Zionism as a new Nazism. Conversely, on April 18, 2001, the government-sponsored newspaper *Al-Akhbar* published a paragraph extolling praise on Hitler for the Holocaust and complaining that it did not go far enough: "Thanks to Hitler, of blessed memory, who on behalf of the Palestinians, revenged in advance, against the most vile criminals on the face of the earth. Although we do have a complaint against him for his revenge on them was not enough."[5]

That propaganda and threat continues today in state-run media throughout the Middle East including the *Al Jazeera* media group. During the Obama administration, Qatari state media purchased potential access to more than 40 million American homes through its acquisition of Al Gore's Current TV for $500 million.[6] Only a few years later, that venture, *Al Jazeera America*, failed miserably, and is now defunct and unable to get high-level journalists or viewer traction;[7] however, its goal of influencing the American government, media, and academia continues unabated. Its strident Islamist correspondents, such as Mehdi Hasan, are now anchoring leftist news media like MSNBC.[8] When *Al Jazeera Arabic* journalists posted a horrifically anti-Semitic, Holocaust-denying "news report" in 2019,[9] *Al Jazeera Arabic* unleashed its lawyers across the planet to threaten anyone who hosted the video,[10] claiming it had "fixed" the problem by suspending the rogue journalists.[11] Our American Islamic Forum for Democracy was one of the sources that broke the story and still has its translation online.[12]

The hate created by the Arab secular fascists also tellingly fueled a mass exodus of the Jewish people that began in 1948 at Israel's founding, when there were over 800,000 Jews living in Arab lands. Today, it is believed that there are fewer than 20,000 remaining. That exodus has carried over to the Christian community, where it is believed that more than two million Christians have fled the Middle Eastern Arab world in the past twenty years. This vacuum of religious diversity only feeds the Islamist supremacist mentality.

The exploitation of Israel among Islamists is also virtually a litmus test for anti-Semitism. Apparent is the use of conspiracy theories by Islamist demagogues to portray a false narrative and fiction against Israel, and thus, by association, all Jews. These conspiracy theories then spread like wildfire and are exploited by fellow global Islamist movements of all stripes in order to broaden the conspiracy against all Muslims and provide more excuses for the failures of Muslim-majority nations. When the OIC, the neo-caliphate umbrella group of fifty-six Muslim-majority nations, met in Malaysia in 2003, Prime

Minister Mahathir Mohamad told the crowd, "The Europeans killed 6 million Jews out of 12 million. But today, the Jews rule this world by proxy. They get others to fight and die for them."[13] Reports were that the crowd responded with a "resounding ovation."[14] This is consistent with opinion polls in nations like Malaysia.[15] Nothing short of revolutions will change this entrenched bigotry. Muslims who are anti-caliphism, anti-Islamist, and anti-jihadi should be the only partners who rise to a level of reform, modernity, and respect acceptable for their Jewish brothers and sisters to embrace.

Yet, sadly, apart from the Israeli government, virtually nothing is said to Muslim audiences by the Jewish diaspora about the central need to combat the institutional ideas of anti-Semitism. In fact, far-left progressive Jewish groups, such as Jewish Voice for Peace, IfNotNow, and Bend the Arc, have expressed sympathy and made common cause with anti-Semitic Muslim groups, such as CAIR, or murderously hateful regimes, such as Iran's. These groups go so far as to collaborate with and regularly feature anti-Semitic speakers at their webinars, conferences, or national conventions. Except for notable exceptions due to how rarely they happen, larger groups like the ADL have sat on the sidelines as American Islamist groups born out of the Muslim Brotherhood have radicalized American Muslims and poisoned the discourse against reformist groups like the Muslim Reform Movement. Choosing party over substance when it comes to combating Islamist anti-Semitism, the likes of Keith Ellison (D-MN), Ilhan Omar (D-MN), and Rashida Tlaib (D-MI) receive little to no critique, while, instead, their bandwidth is filled with other priorities like attacking the American right.

Nothing epitomizes the damaging nature of their silence more than the response of Democratic Party leadership to Representative

Omar's and Representative Jan Schakowsky's (D-IL) deceptive Combating International Islamophobia Act, which was a patently obvious Islamist influence operation to put into place a legislative proposal seeking to establish an "Office to Monitor and Combat Islamophobia" within the State Department.[16] A more appropriate name for this proposed legislation would have been "The American Caliph Act."[17] They simply wanted to empower a government official with the ability to label criticism of Islam hate speech—an anti-blasphemy czar in our own government. The silence in the face of this legislation by established groups like the ADL and the American Jewish Committee says everything one needs to know about how far off the mark so many American Jewish organizations are from identifying what is in the best interests of America, modern American Muslims, and, dare I say, their own Jewish communities.

And it was not just about this one act. Since day one, the Biden administration began peppering its rolls with Islamists and their sympathizers in all its corners. These included Palestinian Islamist sympathizer Reema Dodin at the White House,[18] CAIR fundraiser Khizr Khan at the U.S. Commission on International Religious Freedom (USCIRF),[19] and the long-controversial Rashad Hussain as ambassador-at-large for International Religious Freedom at the State Department.[20] All of these appointments are flagrantly pro-Islamist, and, thus, by definition, facilitating anti-Semitism.

What these groups dominated by universalist and collectivist Jews fail to understand is that to patronize Muslim societies and communities with a different set of human standards than those embodied in the Universal Declaration of Human Rights is a moral relativism that insults every Muslim and citizen inclined otherwise in those nations. It also expects less of Muslims living in the West who remain silent about the obvious intimations of anti-Semitism that beset so much of the Arabic and Muslim-dominated media.

Tough love is the highest form of respect. Demanding a minimum standard of non-violence is by no means enough.

Moral relativism is exactly what the theocrats of the Muslim Brotherhood want in order to widen rather than close the divide between the ideas of liberty and Islamism.

That the Jewish community does not confront the scourge of Muslim anti-Semitism also makes it more challenging for those few Muslim imams, scholars, or activists with the courage to publicly take on the anti-Semitism of Islamist leaders. When these brave reformers arise, instead of being embraced by their Jewish brothers and sisters, they are either silenced or not given sufficient attention or support. The examples of Islamist-inspired anti-Semitism leading to terror against Jews are sadly too numerous to list.

Common among Islamist thought of all stripes is the utilization of hatred of Jews to marginalize their antagonists from within and thus avoid substantive debate about their own theological authenticity within Islam. Islamism depends on conspiracy in order to explain the weakness of the Muslim condition and the need for Muslim collectivism and Islamic statehood and, ultimately, neo-caliphism.

Anti-Semitism has long been a tool utilized by Islamists in order to invoke common sympathy from secular nationalists, who also fostered a hatred for Jews, in order to avoid national introspection. In fact, anti-Semitism is the one ideological litmus test shared by both secular autocrats and Islamists across Muslim-majority nations. At the U.N., the radical far Left and the Islamists work hand in hand to turn the world community of nations against Israel and all Western values.

When Venezuela, China, and Russia work together with Iran, Syria, and Qatar, this is the global version of the Red-Green Axis.[21]

And, at home, the Red-Green Axis is epitomized by the likes of radical progressive Representative Alexandria Ocasio-Cortez (D-NY) working together with Islamist Ilhan Omar. They normalize anti-Semitism and its anti-Zionism. Through 2020 and 2021, too many American Jewish organizations stayed silent as the Black Lives Matter (BLM) movement used the politics of identity and race in order to stifle free speech and destroy the foundations of America, essentially lifting a page right out of Islamist movements across the Arab world.[22] Rewriting history is their goal. Whether it is the Taliban destroying statues of the Buddha in Afghanistan or BLM rioters destroying statues of our Founding Fathers in the U.S., the goals are similar. The affiliation of BLM leaders with deeply anti-Semitic movements like the Nation of Islam and the Black Panthers is hardly a coincidence. How can we Muslims, ready to combat them within our communities, do so when they are blindly tolerated or even endorsed by essentially everyone on the American left, including leading Jewish organizations?

And, despite all of this, too many American Jews have failed to develop the understanding and conviction to directly confront the anti-Semitism of global Islamist movements and unravel the very fabric and platform through which Islamist leaders spread their ideas. Because where anti-Semitism thrives, so, too, does the eventual threat against other faith minorities and the very foundations of democracy. Only with bold new partnerships that lift up honest allies and confront the dissimulators will our chances of victory against Islamists be realized.

Here are a few obvious things that Jewish leaders who care about the threats to their community (and to America) from Islamist anti-Semitism should do:

1. Stop participating in the cover-up of instances of Islamist anti-Semitic activity.

2. Educate the Jewish community about the history, nature, and extent of Islamist Jew-hatred and the specific threats posed by Islamists who seek to radicalize America's Muslim community. Don't fall for the absurdity that it is somehow anti-Muslim bigotry (so-called Islamophobia) to expose the anti-Semitism and separatism of Islamist leaders. In fact, accepting Islamists as *de facto* leaders of what are far more ideologically diverse communities is far more anti-Muslim.

3. Monitor and expose anti-Semitic speeches and sermons of radical imams across the country, much of which is already available online at www.memri.org.

4. Ask your local Muslim dialogue partners about what they teach their communities and congregations about who the Jews are. Ask them to show you the materials they use to educate their youth about America, democracy, women, gays, Jews, and Christians.

5. Ask your local Muslim dialogue partners what they feel about the Declaration of the Muslim Reform Movement,[23] and if they would sign on to it. If not, their explanation should be very revealing. Therein are core principles on rejection of the Islamist shariah state and the foundations of the modernity of the West. Do they reject the Cairo Declaration

of Human Rights and support the Universal Declaration of Human Rights?

6. Ask if they would allow Jews to address their communities about Jews, Judaism, and Israel.

*M. **Zuhdi Jasser** is the founder and president of the American Islamic Forum for Democracy, based in Phoenix, Arizona, and the co-founder of the Muslim Reform Movement. He is a former U.S. Navy Lieutenant Commander and former vice chair of the U.S. Commission on International Religious Freedom. He is author of* A Battle for the Soul of Islam: An American Muslim Patriot's Fight to Save His Faith *(2012) and a senior fellow at the Center for Security Policy. He is also a physician in private practice.*

---

[1] See Lauren Markoe, "Jewish-Muslim alliance formed against anti-Semitism, Islamophobia," *Religion News Service*, November 14, 2016. https://bit.ly/3SeqBHS.

[2] See M. Zuhdi Jasser, "Willful Blindness: Consequences of Agency Efforts To Deemphasize Radical Islam in Combating Terrorism," testimony before the Subcommittee on Oversight, Agency Action, Federal Rights, and Federal Courts of the United States Senate Committee on the Judiciary, June 28, 2016. https://bit.ly/3ggPdCp.

[3] "Islamic Extremism: Common Concern for Muslim and Western Publics," *Pew Research Center*, July 14, 2005. https://pewrsr.ch/3CKKKQ8. See also Amir Mizroch, "Poll: 90% of ME views Jews unfavorably," *The Jerusalem Post*, February 9, 2010. https://bit.ly/3MMknhd.

[4] "Decade-Old Antisemitic TV Series 'Horseman without a Horse' Is Resurrected by Post-Revolution Egyptian TV," *Middle East Media Research Institute*, May 17, 2012. https://bit.ly/3SgOhLx.

[5] Ahmad Ragab, "Half a Word," *Al-Akhbar*, April 18, 2001. See "'Thanks to Hitler,'" *Middle East Media Research Institute*, April 24, 2001. https://bit.ly/3SgpYNK.

6   Jeff Bercovici, "Current TV Sold To Al Jazeera; $500 Million Deal For Al Gore and Co.," *Forbes*, January 2, 2013. https://bit.ly/3Shx44P.

7   Gilead Ini, "Al Jazeera America Failed, But Qatar Stilled Has AJ+," *Committee for Accuracy in Middle East Reporting and Analysis*, July 19, 2016. https://bit.ly/3sfHffn.

8   Sam Westrop, "NBC Hires Islamist-Linked Journalist with a History of Hate," *Middle East Forum*, October 5, 2020. https://bit.ly/3CQ8MJc.

9   Luke Rosiak, "Al Jazeera Says Its Holocaust Denial Video Was A Mistake, But Has A Long History Of Anti-Semitism," *The Daily Caller*, May 23, 2019. https://bit.ly/3eNPtbJ.

10 See Seth J. Frantzman, "Why is Twitter helping Al-Jazeera hide evidence of Holocaust denial video?", *The Jerusalem Post*, May 21, 2019. https://bit.ly/3Dy08AR. See also Rosiak, "Al Jazeera Gets Twitter To Silence Critics Of Its Video Implying Jews Benefited From Holocaust," *The Daily Caller*, May 20, 2019. https://bit.ly/3U0WEfH.

11 "Al Jazeera suspends two journalists over Holocaust report," *Al Jazeera*, May 20, 2019. https://bit.ly/3TyLWge.

12 Zuhdi Jasser's Facebook page. Accessed May 20, 2019, at 1:14 P.M. https://bit.ly/3TDBDXZ.

13 Quoted in "Mahathir attack on Jews condemned," CNN, October 16, 2003. https://cnn.it/3CMuWfE. See also AP Archive. "WRAP Wraps day's developments and speeches at IOC summit." Filmed October 16, 2003. YouTube video, 4:13. Posted July 21, 2015. https://bit.ly/3TAvrQJ. The relevant portion begins at 2:29.

14 Rabbi Abraham Cooper, "In Malaysia, When in Doubt, Blame the Jews," *The Huffington Post*, July 22, 2011. Updated September 21, 2011. https://bit.ly/3yTOZHR.

15 See "Malaysia," *Anti-Defamation League*. https://bit.ly/3DbCI3U. The ADL's 2014 worldwide poll found that 61% of Malaysians hold unfavorable opinions of Jews.

16 H.R.5665—117th Congress (2021–2022): "Combating International Islamophobia Act." December 15, 2021. https://bit.ly/3sagSaJ.

17 Jasser, "The American Caliph Act," *Center for Security Policy*, November 30, 2021. https://bit.ly/3TDnbiG.

18 See Evie Fordham, "Senior Biden staffer called Palestinian suicide bombings 'the last resort of a desperate people,'" *Fox News*, November 24, 2020. https://fxn.ws/3eR8ji1.

19 See Ibrahim Hooper, "CAIR Applauds Appointment of Rashad Hussain, Khizr Khan to Religious Freedom Posts," *Council on American-Islamic Relations*, July 30, 2021. https://bit.ly/3eI5Arl.

20 See "Radical Islamist Groups Welcome Appointment of Rashad Hussain as Special Envoy to the OIC," *Militant Islam Monitor*, March 3, 2010. https://bit.ly/3Sf025o. See also "Rashad Hussain," *Global Muslim Brotherhood Daily Watch*. https://bit.ly/3VHU0gf.

21 See Jasser, "How To Understand the Red-Green Axis," *Newsweek*, June 25, 2021. https://bit.ly/3EWmwFk.

22 Jasser, "The World's Red-Green Axis Has Come to Our Streets," *Newsweek*, July 24, 2020. https://bit.ly/3D6SLPB.

23 See "Our Declaration," *Muslim Reform Movement*. https://bit.ly/3DcdT89.

15

PLAYING DEFENSE IS NOT WORKING ON CAMPUSES

WILLIAM A. JACOBSON AND JOHANNA E. MARKIND

The ancient Chinese strategist Sun Tzu said, "Security against defeat implies defensive tactics; ability to defeat the enemy means taking the offensive."[1] In other words, you don't win a war by playing defense.

Major Jewish and pro-Israel organizations have reacted to specific campus incidents of anti-Semitism (usually masquerading as anti-Israelism), such as student government boycott resolutions, but have consistently failed to counter the growing narrative that Israel and Jews are racist colonialists. That false narrative has now been joined by a related one, that Israel and Jews are white, anti-people-of-color oppressors, a narrative often promulgated by anti-Israel activists deeply embedded within the "social justice" and Black Lives Matters movements.

Both narratives have become primary weapons against Israel. Rather than disarming the narratives, establishment groups too often simply deny the former and pledge support for the latter "anti-racism" movement out of a sense of progressive solidarity—solidarity that is not reciprocated. Below we explore the trajectory of these narratives, and how groups like the Anti-Defamation League (ADL), which promotes progressive solidarity, have made the problem worse instead of better.

The Problem: Durban Set the Formula for Delegitimizing Israel

After the 2001 Durban anti-racism conference was hijacked into an anti-Semitic and anti-Israel hate-fest,[2] campus anti-Israelism soared and became ever more clearly anti-Semitic. The Durban conference, as summed up by journalist Naomi Grant, "gave birth to the Boycott, Divest and Sanctions [BDS] movement and marked the beginning of baseless comparisons of Israel to apartheid South Africa."[3] The century-old anti-Jewish boycott was repackaged in social justice language to appeal to Western leftists.[4]

Since then, BDS ideology has increasingly pervaded American universities, where anti-Israel activists have pursued a no-holds-barred campaign to delegitimize Israel as a pariah state.[5] Faculty, students, and administrators have treated unfounded smears against Israel as fact, while actively shutting down expression of actual facts and pro-Israel opinions. They also stirred up hostility against Israel supporters and Jews in general, hostility that occasionally erupted into violence:

- On May 7, 2002, as a "Peace in the Middle East" rally at San Francisco State University was winding down, Jewish attendees were assaulted by anti-Israel counter-demonstrators who surrounded them screaming threats.[6]

- On September 9, 2002, violent pro-Palestinian protesters at Montreal's Concordia University stormed a university building and forced the cancellation of a speech by (at that time) former Israeli prime minister Benjamin Netanyahu.[7] The university student union—which reportedly organized the protest—urged the government not to prosecute the rioters and authorized the use of student fees to cover rioters' legal fees.[8]

The Problem Worsens: The Red-Green Alliance

Jewish organizations responded to Durban by working to correct factual inaccuracies about Israel and to expose problems on campus. Unfortunately, the problem got worse instead of better.

Following Israel's 2008–2009 Operation Cast Lead response to rocket attacks from Gaza,[9] anti-Israel campus activists further ratcheted up their activities to stifle pro-Israel voices and advance their agenda. The various branches of the University of California (UC) were particular hot spots:

- On February 8, 2010, the Muslim Student Union (MSU) disrupted a speech by Israel's then-ambassador to the United States, Michael Oren, at UC Irvine.[10] Ten students were criminally charged and convicted of disturbing a public event,[11] and UC Irvine suspended the MSU chapter for a year.[12]
- On March 5, 2010, the leader of UC Berkeley's Students for Justice in Palestine chapter rammed a shopping cart into a pro-Israel Jewish student who was holding a placard reading "Israel Wants Peace."[13]

- During the 2010 spring semester, divestment resolutions were put forward at both UC Berkeley[14] and UC San Diego,[15] and only narrowly defeated.[16]
- College professors at UC Santa Cruz and elsewhere increasingly inserted gratuitous and false anti-Israel commentary into classes and conferences.[17]

After the spate of anti-Israel attacks on American campuses that accompanied and followed Operation Cast Lead, more Jewish organizations jumped into the fray, including both top-down branches of existing organizations and bottom-up organizations founded at the campus level.

However much good these groups have done, the problem worsened. The year 2014 was a watershed. That summer, in response to Hamas' kidnapping of three Israeli teenagers and firing rockets at Israeli civilians, Israel counter-attacked by invading Gaza.[18] Predictably, the press focused on reporting collateral damage from Israeli attacks rather than Hamas' war crimes in attacking civilian targets while hiding[19] its personnel and military infrastructure in schools,[20] hospitals,[21] residential neighborhoods,[22] and office buildings occupied by the press.[23]

The same summer, Ferguson police shot and killed Michael Brown, sparking riots by people charging that police targeted blacks for violence. Anti-Israel activists were deeply embedded in the riots and turned them into anti-Israel protests.[24] Among other things, anti-Israel activists made anti-Israel invective part of the protests,[25] offering advice[26] to rioters and spuriously claiming that Israel promoted police violence[27] in the United States by offering police training[28] in anti-terrorism techniques. The narrative took hold.[29]

Anti-Semitic attacks spiked after this double-whammy,[30] both on[31] and off campus.[32] At both UCLA[33] and Stanford University[34] during spring 2015, the suitability of Jewish candidates for student government was challenged on the supposed grounds that they might show favoritism to Israel. Prominent figures, such as the late Jonathan Sacks, former chief rabbi of the United Kingdom, spoke openly of the return of anti-Semitism.[35] Jews warning about rising anti-Semitism were told that Israel and Jews were to blame.[36]

Sample Anti-Israel and Anti-Semitic Tactics

Israel-haters have actively promoted a narrative casting Israel in the role of villain. Professors like Columbia University's Joseph Massad have long taught their personal political views of hatred for Israel as though they were facts, and persecuted and shut down Jewish and other students questioning their opinions or expressing different views.[37] In 2018, two University of Michigan educators—associate professor John Cheney-Lippold and graduate student instructor Lucy Peterson—refused reference letters supporting study abroad for the explicit reason that the requesting students sought to study in Israel.[38]

Anti-Israel activists have frequently prevented or shut down speeches by pro-Israel speakers,[39] like Netanyahu's planned 2002 speech at Concordia, Oren's 2010 speech at UC Irvine, Jerusalem Mayor Nir Barkat's 2016 speech at San Francisco State University,[40] and 2016 and 2017 pro-Israel events at UC Irvine[41] featuring, respectively, a film about the Israel Defense Forces (IDF)[42] and a talk by IDF reservists.[43] The 2016 event at UC Irvine, in particular, featured crowds chasing attendees and putting the latter in fear of their safety.

Since 2005, BDS advocates have organized an annual campus event called "Israel Apartheid Week," designed to convince college faculty and students that Israel is a racist state that persecutes Arabs the way apartheid South Africa persecuted blacks. From its inception as a series of lectures at the University of Toronto,[44] the hate-fest has grown into an annual event at dozens of universities.[45] It features fact-free activities pushing a message that Israel is a Nazi-like, segregationist, racist, colonial, illegitimate state founded and maintained by oppressing Arabs—basically, that Israel is everything contemporary Americans and Western society loathe. These propaganda exercises have included:

- Building mock "apartheid" walls[46] (a spin on Israel's anti-terror barriers, which have sharply reduced the number of suicide bombers able to cross into Israel[47]).
- Staging mock checkpoints[48] (another basic strategy to keep terrorists out of Jewish areas) as well as "die-ins."[49]
- Posting mock eviction notices[50] on Jewish students' dormitory doors.[51]

Another tactic is pushing for passage of student BDS resolutions condemning Israel. The point isn't just to win passage. Rather, it's to raise the issue and offer opportunities to propagandize. To squelch opposition, anti-Israel advocates purposely try to schedule debates or votes on Jewish holidays,[52] when many pro-Israel students are unavailable. Passover is a particularly popular time to push what is, in effect, a modern spin on medieval blood libels.[53] Examples include:

- At Cornell University in 2014, anti-Israel activists brought a BDS resolution to the student assembly during Passover.[54]
- On April 9, 2015, which was during Passover that year,[55] a student senate committee at UC Santa Barbara approved

and passed on to the student senate a BDS resolution from SJP.[56] Two years later, the UC Santa Barbara's SJP chapter launched[57] a BDS campaign on Holocaust Remembrance Day 2017.[58] SJP insisted that "the scheduling decision was made purely for pragmatic reasons," and it "resoundingly reject[ed] the notion that this is in any way anti-Semitic."[59]

- On March 6, 2016, the University of Indianapolis' student senate conducted discussion of a BDS measure on the Jewish Sabbath.[60]

- Portland State University's student government found the Jewish holidays of Yom Kippur and Shemini Atzeret 2016 to be preferred dates to discuss a BDS resolution.[61]

- Tufts University's student senate passed a boycott resolution the day before Passover in 2017.[62]

- The University of Wisconsin's student council passed a divestment bill during Passover 2017.[63] The bill was irregularly voted on at its initial introduction,[64] and the student judiciary later voided the vote for trying to deprive interested Jewish students of their voting rights.[65]

- At Pitzer College (one of the Claremont Colleges), a BDS amendment was passed during Passover 2017.[66]

- At the University of Maryland, College Park, a boycott resolution was scheduled for the middle of Passover week 2019.[67]

Anti-Israel activists have also hijacked other movements into vehicles for castigating Israel and its supporters.[68] The entire rationale of today's BDS movement is to paint the current situation in Israel as a latter-day version of South Africa's apartheid regime. BDS supporters also tied the BLM movement to Israeli anti-terrorism police junkets, and to racism generally.[69] Black campus activists (for example, at Hamilton College[70] and Oberlin College[71]) have tied racial demands to demands for divestment from Israel.

Besides these movements, anti-Israel activists have somehow managed to convince many LGBTQ activists that Israel's positive record on gay rights, in sharp contrast to that of Palestinians and others in the Middle East,[72] is mere "pinkwashing" designed to distract from Israel's treatment of Palestinians.[73] The pinkwashing charge is essential in enabling BDS activists to finesse the abysmally anti-gay record of the Palestinian Authority and Hamas. Incredibly, anti-Israel activists have succeeded in convincing gay rights activists—who face prison or death in Arab lands—to oppose Israel (even Israeli and Jewish LGBTQ groups) and support the anti-gay Hamas and Palestinian Authority.[74]

Ditto with "anti-fascists": A 2017 anti-fascism rally at the University of Illinois Urbana-Champaign was converted into an anti-Israel rally,[75] with activists chanting, "No Zionists, no KKK, resisting fascists all the way!"[76] Activists have also tied women's groups to hatred of Israel. Women's March leadership has been explicitly tied to anti-Semitism,[77] and the International Women's Strike platform calls for "decolonization of Palestine"[78]—in other words, the destruction of Israel. Both organizations have been active on campus.[79]

Anti-Israel and Anti-Semitic Activists Largely Succeed in Neutralizing the ADL

The ADL was a particular target of 2014 activists trying to tie Israel to the BLM narrative. An *Ebony* article published ten days after Michael Brown was shot already claimed a connection between the anti-terrorism training Israel has offered to American police departments (which activists dubbed the "deadly exchange" program[80]) and the police shooting of Brown.[81] The targeting[82] of the ADL eventually led to a #DropTheADL movement to brand the ADL as racist and un-woke, a pariah with whom no woke person or organization should associate,[83] but the broad outline was already visible back in summer 2014.

A wiser organization might have concluded that the supposed fellow travelers condemning it were themselves prejudiced and dis-criminatory, but the ADL seems to have concluded that it needed to redouble its efforts to prove its heart was with the self-identified vic-tims of racial violence.

Abraham Foxman, the ADL's longtime leader, had given notice in February 2014 that he would step down in July 2015,[84] and a search for his successor was underway. One of the candidates under consideration was Jonathan Greenblatt, then director of the Obama administration's Office of Social Innovation and Civic Participation in the Domestic Policy Council.[85] As Greenblatt tells it, the ADL reached out to him rather than the reverse.[86] His background was as a tech-savvy social entrepreneur, specializing in civic engagement and impact investing, and he was a professional left-wing partisan. By November 2014, the ADL had settled on Greenblatt as Foxman's suc-cessor.[87] Why?

After taking over as ADL leader in July 2015, Greenblatt dou-bled down on ADL outreach to the left while his condemnations of anti-Semitism on campus and off campus have been mostly tepid. Under his stewardship,[88] the organization largely ignored BLM's anti-Semitism;[89] initially ignored Keith Ellison's anti-Semitism while supporting his campaign to lead the Democratic National Commit-tee;[90] allowed the anti-Semites who ran the Women's March to elbow the ADL out of participating in a Starbucks employee exercise in anti-discrimination—despite the fact that the ADL had helped to put the exercise together and that Greenblatt used to be a Starbucks vice president[91]—because the ADL was allegedly anti-Palestinian and "constantly attacking black and brown people;"[92] ignored the anti-Semitism of Obama administration officials marketing the prior Iran deal; and ignored anti-Semitic comments by Democratic Party Young Turks like Ilhan Omar, Rashida Tlaib, and Alexandria Ocasio-Cortez.

By contrast, he has turned the ADL's ire on Jews and Jewish organizations like Canary Mission, which works to expose anti-Semitism on campus.[93] During the summer of 2020, Greenblatt's ADL redefined racism to include only white racism against non-whites.[94] Given today's inclusion of Jews among "whites," the new definition appeared to deny the existence of anti-Jewish racism. (Greenblatt only tweaked the definition after Whoopi Goldberg made headlines by doing what the ADL seemed to be doing—denying that Jews were victims of racism because they're both "white.") In the fall of 2021, the ADL hired a new director of outreach (primarily to non-white Jews) with a track record of blaming Jews for black anti-Semitism and Palestinian terrorism.[95]

At the same time that the ADL has done little to oppose left-wing anti-Semitism (which is what dominates college campuses) while criticizing the Jewish community for standing up to anti-Semitism, Greenblatt has turned the organization into an active political partisan. He actively opposed the nomination of Brett Kavanaugh to the Supreme Court,[96] opposed the right of religious foster agencies to choose parents based on their religion,[97] offered to register as a Muslim for Trump's non-existent Muslim registry,[98] compared Donald Trump to Hitler,[99] and apologized for opposing the building of a mosque at Ground Zero.[100] Under Greenblatt, the ADL has promoted critical race theory.[101] It has advocated transgender accommodation for minors,[102] and keeping late-term abortions legal.[103] Essentially, Greenblatt has transformed the ADL from a non-partisan advocate for Jews confronting anti-Semitism into an advocacy organization for left-wing and culture-war causes.

Only in the summer of 2021 did Greenblatt publicly admit that "the left has an anti-Semitism problem."[104] Since then, he has mostly continued on his woke course, hiring blame-the-Jews-first outreach staff.

Still, even focusing some attention on left-wing anti-Semitism was a big step for Greenblatt, and he has taken small steps since then to grapple with that reality.[105] From July to August 2021, the ADL teamed up with Hillel to conduct an online survey of Jewish undergraduates about campus anti-Semitism. The survey was published on October 25, 2021.[106] That fall, the ADL, Hillel, and the Secure Community Network launched an online portal where college students can report anti-Semitic incidents on their campus and receive immediate support.[107] This is in addition to the ADL's later report about anti-Israelism on campus, which grudgingly allowed the fact that anti-Israel activists "occasionally" espouse anti-Semitic tropes, such as alleging that Jewish or Zionist powers control media and political affairs.[108]

Given that the ADL reached out to Greenblatt, and the coincidence of his hire months after Ferguson and the 2014 Gaza war, it seems likely that he was hired for the explicit purpose of repairing ADL ties with the left. Perhaps we should be marveling that Greenblatt reached his epiphany about left-wing anti-Semitism at all, rather than complaining that he arrived so late and has yet to confront it in a serious way.

Jews Struggle to Address Campus Anti-Israelism and Anti-Semitism

As the campus atmosphere has grown more and more intolerable, Jewish and other Israel supporters responded by forming new organizations and increasing their own activities. Their tactics have included:

- Creating new pro-Israel groups or promoting their creation and helping them to plan events.

- Exposing faculty bias and campus hostility to Israel supporters, as through the 2004 documentary film *Columbia Unbecoming*.[109]

- Encouraging pro-Israel students to involve themselves in student government, to promote a campus atmosphere friendlier (or at least, less hostile) to Jews and Israel.

- Recruiting campus influencers—including student leaders who might already favor BDS—and sending them to Israel on fact-finding tours.[110]

- Educating students and faculty about Israel and the Middle East. This can take many forms, including bringing pro-Israel speakers to campus, screening documentaries about Israel, writing opinion articles for campus newspapers, and providing students with factual research and rebuttals to false information spread about Israel.

- Employing professional political consulting firms to advise on combatting student government votes on BDS resolutions.[111]

- Rallying alumni to pressure college administrators into addressing campus anti-Israel and anti-Semitic discrimination.

Tragically, some of the ever more rabid anti-Israel voices on campus have been Jewish. Anti-Israel Jewish activists, notably the misnamed Jewish Voice for Peace, have pressured Jewish groups on campus not to oppose anti-Israel activism, and even to support it.[112] That has made it harder for campus Jewish organizations to provide full-throated support for Israel and to oppose the growing anti-Semitism concomitant with anti-Israel activism.

A Reactive Approach Is Not Working

The problem with pro-Israel Jewish campus organizations is less what they've done than what they've left undone. The actions they have taken thus far are all commendable and have been helpful in limiting damage. They're necessary, but they're not sufficient.

Currently, Jews are playing defense. By itself, that's rarely a winning strategy. The false narratives that Israel is a racist colonial enterprise and that Jews are "white oppressors" are rarely taken head on because to do so would require taking on the progressive power on campuses.

Contrast this with campus anti-Israel activists. They have been playing offense against Israel, its supporters, and Jewish students generally for many years. Groups like Students for Justice in Palestine have pursued an organized campaign of shutting down debate about Israel, imposing a narrative making outrageous claims against it (such as accusing it of Nazism and apartheid), and hounding Israel's supporters or presumed supporters into silence.

Their cause—destroying Israel and persecuting Jews—is unjust, and their tactics harmful to the very nature of the university. Nevertheless, their public relations have been wildly successful. They have controlled the narrative of converting Israel and Jews into pro-apartheid

Nazi racists, and their opponents into persecuted underdogs. Jews have responded to attacks and challenged them, but have rarely set the agenda, or tried to reframe the narrative to expose their opponents' blatant anti-Semitism and goal of annihilating the Jewish State.

Jews were not always so passive. The Soviet Jewry movement, for instance, gained much of its energy from resourceful and provocative tactics like protestors chaining themselves to a Soviet embassy fence,[113] releasing black balloons during a candlelit vigil outside the Moscow Circus,[114] picketing the Bolshoi Ballet,[115] or unfurling banners before TV cameras at the Philadelphia Flyers-Red Army exhibition hockey game. These actions may or may not have had direct political impact, but they effectively framed the issue as one of Soviet repression of Jews and kept it in the public consciousness. Activists reached out directly to Soviet Jews, visiting them and supplying them with religious materials and gifts, as well as moral support, and keeping their struggle in the public eye. They also employed more conventional tactics, such as lobbying for passage of the Jackson–Vanik amendment, which conditioned trade benefits on increased freedom of emigration from the Soviet Union.[116]

Jews could apply similar initiative to the current campus climate. For example, Jewish student activists could:

- Turn the tables on Students for Justice in Palestine and similar groups by protesting *their* events, holding up pictures of Nizar Banat[117] and journalists wrongly imprisoned and tortured by the Palestinian Authority and Hamas,[118] with captions underscoring that Students for Justice in Palestine is really not interested in "justice in Palestine," but only in castigating the Jewish state. Better yet, Jewish activists could stage mock arrests of journalists by Palestinian security services.

- Protest (through traditional means outside Students for Justice in Palestine events, or through mock trials or some other attention grabber) the oppression of homosexuals in Palestinian society. Ditto for the treatment of women. Besides potentially embarrassing pro-Palestinian groups and creating pressure to improve the lot of homosexuals and women in Palestinian society, protests like this might shame gay advocates and advocates for women into joining the protests *against* Palestinian authorities. It's one thing to claim "pinkwashing" when an Israeli quotes facts and figures, and it's another when confronted with protests against anti-gay oppression and honor killings.

- Likewise, find a way to visualize the persecution of Arab Christians by Palestinian Muslims, leading to their departure from the West Bank and Gaza. Over the past fifty years, the Palestinian Christian population has shrunk from roughly 15 percent to about 1.5 percent of the Palestinian population.[119]

- Stage a mock trial and sentencing of Isaam Akel, an American citizen sentenced to life in prison for facilitating the sale of Arab-owned land to Israeli Jews,[120] for the blatant religious and ethnic prejudice of barring land sales to Jews, and for demonstrating that what the Palestinian Authority actually wants is to make its territory *judenrein*.

- Find a way to dramatize the reality that it's the Palestinians, not Israel, holding up a peace agreement. For example, activists could demonstrate outside Students for Justice in

Palestine events with posters captioned "Palestinian Peace Proposal"—with the rest of the poster blank, as empty as Palestinian proposals.

- Demonstrate both the Jewish people's indigenous connection to Israel, and Palestinian efforts to erase same.[121] For instance, students could conduct mock archeological digs on campus "finding" ancient Jewish artifacts, bulldozing them, and throwing the artifacts into the trash.

The student-founded, grassroots organization Students Supporting Israel has begun to use more offensive tactics. During so-called Apartheid Week 2022, Students Supporting Israel tested out messaging similar to the above suggestions. That's an excellent sign. Hopefully, where they lead, others will follow.

The day before D-Day, General George S. Patton, Jr., explained his fighting philosophy to his Third Army. The gist (slightly bowdlerized) was this:

> We are not holding a damned thing. Let the Germans do that. We are advancing constantly and we are not interested in holding onto anything, except the enemy's b****. We are going to twist him and kick the living s*** out of him all of the time. Our basic plan of operation is to advance and to keep on advancing regardless of whether we have to go over, under, or through the enemy.[122]

Unfortunately, much of what pro-Israel and Jewish groups are doing today is at best trying to hold ground. The many fine things Jewish and pro-Israel groups have done to counter increasing attacks on Israel and Jews should not be confused with taking the fight to the enemy, so to speak.[123] Pro-Israel and Jewish groups today are still searching for a coherent strategy and appropriate tactics to change the anti-Israel narrative and win the battle for hearts and minds.

William A. Jacobson is a clinical professor of law at Cornell Law School, founder of the blog site Legal Insurrection, *and president of the Legal Insurrection Foundation, a non-profit devoted to free expression and academic freedom on campuses. Recently, he has created the website criticalrace.org as a resource for concerned parents to fight critical race theory in schools, and equalprotect.org to fight against racial "equity" discrimination in hiring.*

Johanna E. Markind has worked in the Justice Department, where she served on the Criminal Justice Act Panel. She has been published in the Wall Street Journal, Forward, *the* Federal Lawyer, *and at the Gatestone Institute, among other outlets.*

[1]   Sūnzǐ, *Sun Tzu on the Art of War*, trans. Lionel Giles (Atlanta, GA: Dalmatian Press Classics, 2007), p. 32.

[2]   Vijeta Uniyal, "UN: 37 Countries Withdraw From Antisemitic Durban Conference," *Legal Insurrection*, September 24, 2021. https://bit.ly/3emu7C5.

[3]   Naomi Grant, "The Sept. 2001 Hijacking of the World Conference Against Racism," *Endowment for Middle East Truth*, September 27, 2021. https://bit.ly/3rMZl8t.

[4]   See William A. Jacobson, "The REAL history of the BDS movement," *Legal Insurrection*, December 18, 2016. https://bit.ly/3RTS7u1.

[5]   Ruth R. Wisse, "Israel on Campus," *The Wall Street Journal*, December 13, 2002. https://on.wsj.com/3fOOMio.

6   Laurie Zoloth, "Where is the outrage? Pogrom at SFSU," *IndyBay*, May 20, 2002. https://bit.ly/3g22fDx. See also Mike Lumish, "Dear Professor Fred Astren, Why Does San Francisco State University Support Violence Against Jews?", *The Times of Israel*, June 26, 2014. https://bit.ly/3Mpt1Cf.

7   Tracey Madigan, "Netanyahu harsh on Canadian security after speech cancelled," *CBC News*, September 9, 2002. Archived October 1, 2002. https://bit.ly/3COAHKP. See also "Concordia quashes political speech," *CBC News*, November 15, 2002. https://bit.ly/3CKntOj.

8   "Riot at Concordia," *Aish*, May 9, 2009. https://aish.com/48884942/.

9   See "Operation Cast Lead," *Global Security*. https://bit.ly/3VhUZUr.

10 Adam Kissel, "Disruptive Protesters Face Disciplinary Consequences at UC Irvine," *The Fire*, February 10, 2010. https://bit.ly/3yxyVLU.

11 Lauren Williams, Nicole Santa Cruz, and Mike Anton, "Students guilty of disrupting speech in 'Irvine 11' case," *The Los Angeles Times*, September 24, 2011. Archived November 7, 2011. https://bit.ly/3Vig6Ga.

12 "Editorial: Suspension would be just for UCI Muslim group," *The Orange County Register*, June 22, 2010. https://bit.ly/3ervjnJ.

13 Erin Sherbert, "Jewish Woman Sues UC Berkeley Over Campus Assault by Member of Palestinian Student Group," *San Francisco Weekly*, March 7, 2011. http://bit.ly/3zIcIL6. See also Dan Pine, "Former U.C. Berkeley student files suit charges endangerment of Jewish students on campus," *JWeekly*, March 11, 2011. http://bit.ly/39FZrFF.

14 Ariella Charny, "UC Berkeley and the Israel divestment bill," *The Tufts Daily*, May 3, 2010. https://bit.ly/3ExChC6.

15 Marcy Oster, "UC San Diego student government to vote on divestment," *Jewish Telegraphic Agency*, April 28, 2010. https://bit.ly/3fZaUH8.

16 Thomas Elias, "UC campuses are hotbeds of anti-Semite vitriol," *The Mercury News*, July 13, 2010. https://bayareane.ws/3Ct5Imn.

17 Tammi Rossman-Benjamin, "Anti-Zionism and the Abuse of Academic Freedom: A Case Study at the University of California, Santa Cruz," *Jerusalem Center for Public Affairs*, No. 77, February 1, 2009. Archived June 26, 2010. https://bit.ly/3MDEwWR.

18 See Hirsch Goodman and Dore Gold, eds., *The Gaza War 2014: The War Israel Did Not Want and the Disaster It Averted* (Jerusalem: Jerusalem Center for Public Affairs, 2015). https://bit.ly/3VneKKn.

19 Terrence McCoy, "Why Hamas stores its weapons inside hospitals, mosques and schools," *The Washington Post*, July 31, 2014. Archived August 25, 2014. https://bit.ly/3rTFdRX.

20 Elad Benari, "UNRWA Finds Another Rocket Stockpile in School," *Israel National News,* July 30, 2014. https://bit.ly/3SU95tD.

21 William Booth, "While Israel held its fire, the militant group Hamas did not," *The Washington Post,* July 15, 2014. https://wapo.st/3rNVpnP.

22 Alexander Joffe and Asaf Romirowsky, "From Welfare to Warfare," *The American Interest,* August 2, 2014. https://bit.ly/3Mq38SH.

23 Alexander Ma and Sinéad Baker, "A former Associated Press editor suggested that Hamas did have offices in the agency's Gaza City building, which Israel destroyed over the weekend," *The Business Insider,* May 17, 2021. https://bit.ly/3SVVQZf. See also Matti Friedman, "What the Media Gets Wrong About Israel," *The Atlantic,* November 30, 2014. https://bit.ly/3rOyjNU.

24 Jacobson, "Intifada Missouri—Anti-Israel activists may push Ferguson over the edge," *Legal Insurrection,* October 25, 2014. https://bit.ly/3SVVnWT.

25 Jacobson, "Partners in protest: The anti-Israel, cop-bash link," *The New York Post,* December 26, 2014. https://bit.ly/3rJtFAZ.

26 Anna Isaacs, "How The Black Lives Matter and Palestinian Movements Converged," *Moment,* March 14, 2016. https://bit.ly/3STB64r.

27 "Ferguson = Gaza: Manufacturing A False Comparison," *Anti-Defamation League,* August 28, 2014. Archived December 3, 2014. http://bit.ly/3GSqrTN.

28 "The Ferguson/Palestine Connection," *Ebony,* August 19, 2014. https://bit.ly/3rPM0fu.

29 Jacobson, "New campus blood libel: Israel responsible for U.S. police shootings of blacks," *Legal Insurrection,* May 6, 2017. https://bit.ly/3emINBb.

30 "Audit: In 2014 Anti-Semitic Incidents Rose 21 Percent Across The U.S. In A 'Particularly Violent Year for Jews," *Anti-Defamation League,* March 30, 2015. https://bit.ly/3MmrVqJ.

31 Emily Babay, "Student charged in assault at Temple activities fair," *Philly.com,* September 10, 2014. Archived September 10, 2014. https://bit.ly/3RUQg8i.

32 "Three dead in shootings at Jewish facilities in Kansas City suburb," *CBS News,* April 13, 2014. https://cbsn.ws/3yuxJss.

33 Adam Nagourney, "In U.C.L.A. Debate Over Jewish Student, Echoes on Campus of Old Biases," *The New York Times,* March 5, 2015. http://nyti.ms/2LjebCc.

34 Jewish Telegraphic Agency, "Stanford student candidate questioned over her Jewish faith," *The Times of Israel,* April 14, 2015. https://bit.ly/3CRJr38.

35 Rabbi Lord Jonathan Sacks, "The Return of Anti-Semitism," *The Wall Street Journal,* January 30, 2015. https://on.wsj.com/3Ms2UdW.

36 David Bernstein, "Yale Episcopal chaplain Rev. Bruce Shipman digs deeper," *The Washington Post*, August 27, 2014. https://wapo.st/3MvJipe.

37 Charles Jacobs and Avi Goldwasser, "In Defense of The David Project," *The Columbia Spectator*, November 16, 2004. Archived December 8, 2004. https://bit.ly/3RNmPVC. See also Alan M. Dershowitz, *The Case for Peace: How the Arab-Israeli Conflict Can Be Resolved* (Hoboken, NJ: John Wiley and Sons, 2005), p. 126.

38 Jackson Richman, "A culture of discrimination? University of Michigan faces heat after educators' anti-Israel bias," *JNS*, October 10, 2018. https://bit.ly/3CQahsg.

39 "University Trustees: Educational Boycotts of Israel Threaten Academic Freedom," *The Tower*, October 3, 2017. https://bit.ly/3Ms4iNG.

40 "Jerusalem mayor shouted down during US campus speech," *Jewish Telegraphic Agency*, April 7, 2016. https://bit.ly/3SWnTaW. See also Daniel Kleo Giosuè Eisenbud, "Watch: Anti-Israel protesters crash Jerusalem mayor Barkat's speech in San Francisco," *The Jerusalem Post*, April 7, 2016. https://bit.ly/3TaWge0.

41 See Rachel Frommer, "UC-Irvine Places Students for Justice in Palestine on Two-Year Probation for Protest," *The Washington Free Beacon*, September 1, 2017. https://bit.ly/3MpSLhI.

42 Lea Speyer, "Student Group Calls for End to Intimidation, Harassment of Jewish, Zionist Students Following Violent Anti-Israel Protest at UC Irvine (VIDEO)," *The Algemeiner*, May 20, 2016. https://bit.ly/3CRgPHh.

43 Frommer, "For Second Time in a Year, University of California-Irvine Students Require Police Escort From IDF-Related Event Due to Intense Protests," *The Algemeiner*, May 12, 2017. https://bit.ly/3SMQ6kx.

44 "Toronto's 'Israel Apartheid Week' Draws Few People, but Gets Headlines," *Jewish Telegraphic Agency*, February 9, 2005. https://bit.ly/3CKE8Bl. See also Avi Weinryb, "The University of Toronto—The Institution where Israel Apartheid Week was Born," *Jerusalem Center for Public Affairs*, December 24, 2008. https://bit.ly/3RS5vyH.

45 See Anti-Defamation League, *Israeli Apartheid Week: A Year-by-Year Report* (New York, NY: Anti-Defamation League, 2012). https://bit.ly/3yyEjyl.

46 See *Ibid.*, p. 9.

47 Colonel Zohar Palti, "Israel's Security Fence: Effective in Reducing Suicide Attacks from the Northern West Bank," *The Washington Institute for Near East Policy*, July 7, 2004. https://bit.ly/3CMgIMV.

48 *Israeli Apartheid Week: A Year-by-Year Report*, p. 9.

49 Perry Chiaramonte, "Pro-Palestinian students bring hate, intimidation to campus, critics say," *Fox News*, November 21, 2015. https://fxn.ws/3g0X2ft.

50 World Zionist Organization, "Fake 'eviction notices' scare Jewish students," *The International Center for Countering Antisemitism*, October 4, 2012. http://bit.ly/35xPU1U.

51 "Emory University Mock Eviction Notices," *Anti-Defamation League,* April 4, 2019. https://bit.ly/3EDJv7J. See also "ADL Statement Regarding Mock Eviction Notices Posted on Students' Dorms at Emory University," *Anti-Defamation League*, April 5, 2019. https://bit.ly/3MoivuJ.

52 Johanna E. Markind, "Israel-Bashers Target Jews on Their Holidays," *The Tower*, August 17, 2017. https://bit.ly/3g14d78. See also Jacobson, "Passover 2017 is no different: 'in every generation they rise against us to destroy us,'" *Legal Insurrection*, April 10, 2017. https://bit.ly/3SV3T8K.

53 See "Blood Libel: A False, Incendiary Claim Against Jews," *Anti-Defamation League*, November 30, 2012. https://bit.ly/3CudM66.

54 Jacobson, "Anti-Israel BDS boycott campaign returns to Cornell," *Legal Insurrection*, February 20, 2019. https://bit.ly/3TbyWge.

55 See "Jewish Holidays in 2015," *Chabad.org*. https://bit.ly/3RNVUcc.

56 David Jackson and Peter Mounteer, "Divestment Resolution Passes to A.S. Senate," *The Daily Nexus*, April 10, 2015. https://bit.ly/3Tj5eGh.

57 UCSB Students for Justice in Palestine's Facebook page. Accessed April 24, 2017, at 1:38 A.M. https://bit.ly/3RSp36c.

58 Frommer, "UC Santa Barbara's SJP Slammed for Launching BDS Campaign on Holocaust Remembrance Day," *The Algemeiner*, April 27, 2017. https://bit.ly/3CtF78A.

59 UCSB Students for Justice in Palestine's Facebook page. Accessed April 24, 2017, at 11:10 P.M. https://bit.ly/3emYdFo.

60 Andrew Pessin, "BDS Suffers Setbacks at Vassar, Northeastern and Indianapolis in Single Week," *The Algemeiner*, March 7, 2016. https://bit.ly/3Mn95jl.

61 Ira Stoll, "'Underhanded Tactics' of BDS Movement Unnerve Jews on College Campuses Worldwide," *The Algemeiner*, December 8, 2016. https://bit.ly/3STWKFJ.

62 Jacobson, "Another sneak Passover Divestment attack, this time at Tufts University," *Legal Insurrection*, April 9, 2017. https://bit.ly/3Virsdh.

63 Nina Bertelson, "ASM divestment legislation to become financial transparency subcommittee," *The Daily Cardinal*, April 13, 2017. https://bit.ly/3yz7Qry.

[64] Alice Vagun, "Student Judiciary voids approval of bylaw change for creation of financial transparency, ethics subcommittee," *The Badger Herald*, May 10, 2017. https://bit.ly/3SV7nYV.

[65] Frommer, "University of Wisconsin Anti-Israel Bill 'Voided' by Student Judiciary; Leaders Behind Passover Vote Sanctioned," *The Algemeiner*, May 12, 2017. https://bit.ly/3SWK94H.

[66] Frommer, "Pitzer College Keeps BDS Resolution Largely Unchanged, Leaving Pro-Israel Students Disappointed," *The Algemeiner*, May 4, 2017. https://bit.ly/3Mqs5NR.

[67] "Statement on the Proposed BDS Resolution at the University of Maryland," *Alums for Campus Fairness*, April 17, 2019. https://bit.ly/3EzJzFG.

[68] Jacobson, "Anti-Israel activists attempt to hijack Women's March—again," *Legal Insurrection*, January 19, 2018. https://bit.ly/3Vmtjhe.

[69] Jacobson, "If you are surprised—#BlackLivesMatter joined war on Israel, you haven't been paying attention," *Legal Insurrection*, August 4, 2016. https://bit.ly/3CoaaCR.

[70] Jacobson, "Inflation: Hamilton College students issue 83 Demands," *Legal Insurrection*, December 2, 2015. https://bit.ly/3T08PsX.

[71] "Oberlin College Black Student Union Institutional Demands," 2015 letter to the Oberlin board of trustees. https://bit.ly/3RQ9aNr.

[72] Dr. Edy Cohen, "The Plight of the LGBT Community in the Palestinian Authority and Muslim Countries," *The Begin-Sadat Center for Strategic Studies*, September 19, 2019. https://bit.ly/3g0IhJy. See also Jack Moore, "Hamas Executes Prominent Commander After Accusations of Gay Sex," *Newsweek*, March 2, 2016. https://bit.ly/3evRIjA.

[73] Jacobson, "Another low for academia: Anti-Israel 'Homonationalism and Pinkwashing' Conference at CUNY," *Legal Insurrection*, March 29, 2012. https://bit.ly/3CNAI1E.

[74] Jacobson, "Jewish Voice for Peace helps disrupt Israeli LGBTQ group Sabbath event," *Legal Insurrection*, January 24, 2016. https://bit.ly/3yCoFll. See also Jacobson, "Psychosis-laced anti-Semitism: Anti-Israel LGBT activists ban Star of David from Chicago parade," *Legal Insurrection*, June 25, 2017. https://bit.ly/3RPf5lP.

[75] Jacobson, "Anti-Israel pro-BDS profs organizing Antifa campus network," *Legal Insurrection*, August 17, 2017. https://bit.ly/3SWH2cO.

[76] Jacobson, "Anti-Israel Rally at U. Illinois: 'No Zionists, no KKK, resisting fascists all the way,'" *Legal Insurrection*, September 6, 2017. https://bit.ly/3yCpmer.

77 Leah McSweeney and Jacob Siegel, "Is the Women's March Melting Down?", *Tablet*, December 10, 2018. https://bit.ly/3STbFzP. See also Farah Stockman, "Women's March Roiled by Accusations of Anti-Semitism," *The New York Times*, December 23, 2018. https://nyti.ms/3rNDjm1.

78 Jacobson, "March 8 International Women's Strike platform calls for destruction of Israel," *Legal Insurrection*, March 6, 2017. https://bit.ly/3STbOmR.

79 Mike LaChance, "Colleges and Universities Across the Country are Promoting the Women's March," *Legal Insurrection*, January 17, 2019. https://bit.ly/3VhKWP8.

80 Samantha Mandeles, "'Deadly Exchange' Campaign Blaming Jews and Israel For U.S. Policing Helped Drive Wave Of Antisemitic Violence," *Legal Insurrection*, May 23, 2021. https://bit.ly/3yTfr4p.

81 "The Ferguson/Palestine Connection," *Ebony*. See note 28.

82 Drop The ADL. Twitter post. March 18, 2022. 4:40 P.M. https://bit.ly/3ViXXb7.

83 "Primer: The ADL is not an ally," *Drop the ADL*. https://bit.ly/3CMq1wl. See also "Open letter to progressives: The ADL is not an ally," *Mondoweiss*, August 11, 2020. https://bit.ly/3STgyJb.

84 "ADL National Chair on Abraham H. Foxman's Retirement Announcement," *Anti-Defamation League*, February 10, 2014. https://bit.ly/3CsZYZS.

85 Uriel Heilman, "White House aide Jonathan Greenblatt to succeed Abe Foxman as ADL chief," *Jewish Telegraphic Agency*, November 6, 2014. https://bit.ly/3MmRzf4.

86 Jonathan Greenblatt, "Taking the First Step: Why I took the top job at ADL, and what we can do to secure fair treatment and justice for all," *Anti-Defamation League*, July 21, 2015. Archived September 27, 2020. https://bit.ly/3EwAr4A.

87 "ADL Succession Committee Announces Completion of Search Process," *Anti-Defamation League*, November 6, 2014. https://bit.ly/3RVFyyn.

88 Seth Mandel, "The Shame of the Anti-Defamation League," *Commentary*, November 2018. https://bit.ly/3MAL48F. See also Alex VanNess, "Jonathan Greenblatt is destroying the Anti-Defamation League," *The New York Post*, December 9, 2016. https://bit.ly/3Es6qmt.

89 Mandel, "The Revolution Inside the ADL," *Commentary*, April 2022. https://bit.ly/3yuLur8.

90 Eldad Tzioni, "The ADL has gone completely off the rails in supporting Keith Ellison as DNC chair," *24/6 Mag*, November 23, 2016. https://bit.ly/3Mr7uc9. To their credit, the ADL later denounced his nomination. See

Yair Rosenberg, "ADL Reverses on Keith Ellison, Now Opposes His DNC Leadership Bid," *Tablet*, December 1, 2016. https://bit.ly/3fXSdU4.

91 See Heilman, "White House aide Jonathan Greenblatt to succeed Abe Foxman as ADL chief."

92 Liel Leibovitz, "The ADL Kicked Out of Leading Starbucks' Diversity Training," *Tablet*, April 30, 2018. https://bit.ly/3Mnm5VW.

93 Mandel, "The Revolution Inside the ADL."

94 Markind, "Whoopi Goldberg Said What Progressives—Including ADL—Are Thinking About Racism."

95 Daniel Greenfield, "ADL Hires Director for Jewish Outreach Who Hates Jews," *FrontPage Magazine*, January 31, 2022. https://bit.ly/3RUm2C8.

96 "ADL Response to the President's Nomination of Judge Brett Kavanaugh to Serve as an Associate Justice of the United States Supreme Court," *Anti-Defamation League*, July 9, 2018. https://bit.ly/3yB0Vhv.

97 Tzvi Lev, "'ADL acting contrary to Jewish values,'" *Israel National News*, October 25, 2018. https://bit.ly/3SSXM4X.

98 Mark Hensch, "Anti-Defamation League CEO: I'll 'register as Muslim' if Trump makes database," *The Hill*, November 18, 2016. https://bit.ly/3SWx23h.

99 Adelle Nazarian, "ADL's Jonathan Greenblatt Compares Trump's Database to Holocaust," *Breitbart*, November 18, 2016. https://bit.ly/3TaWFNC.

100 Greenblatt, "ADL head: On NY Islamic center, we were wrong, plain and simple," CNN, September 5, 2021. https://cnn.it/3T9ruSE.

101 Hannah Grossman, "Anti-Defamation League launches review of education content after Fox News Digital investigation," *Fox News,* September 7, 2022. https://fxn.ws/3Mp3GrW.

102 "Anti-Transgender Legislation: Frequently Asked Questions," *Anti-Defamation League*, April 16, 2021. https://bit.ly/3fWs0Fs. The ADL has been involved in advocating transgender politics in education since at least 2015. See "Transgender Identity and Issues," *Anti-Defamation League*, March 2, 2015. https://bit.ly/3RZdoT0.

103 "ADL: Supreme Court Ruling in Dobbs v. Jackson Women's Health Organization Undermines Fundamental Rights," *Anti-Defamation League*, June 24, 2022. https://bit.ly/3SVgSY5.

104 Greenblatt, "It's Time to Admit It: The Left Has an Antisemitism Problem," *Newsweek*, July 9, 2021. https://bit.ly/3MqAPUb.

105 "'Anti-Zionism is Antisemitism,' Head of ADL Declares in Speech to Summit Combating Hate and Discrimination," *The Algemeiner,* November 9, 2021. https://bit.ly/3RU8I0K.

[106] Anti-Defamation League, *The ADL-Hillel Campus Antisemitism Survey: 2021* (New York, NY: Anti-Defamation League, 2021). Archived October 27, 2021. https://bit.ly/3CQsVAh.

[107] "Jewish groups launch online portal for college students to report anti-Semitic incidents," *JNS*, October 7, 2021. https://bit.ly/3ExqSCv.

[108] "The Anti-Israel Movement on U.S. Campuses, 2020-2021," *Anti-Defamation League*, May 3, 2022. https://bit.ly/3CSiKeG. See also "ADL Report: Inflammatory Anti-Israel Activity and BDS Calls Are Vilifying Many Jewish Students on Campus," *Anti-Defamation League*, December 7, 2021. https://bit.ly/3g3Jq3b.

[109] See apeacet. "Columbia Unbecoming (2004)." Filmed 2004. YouTube video, 37:00. Posted July 19, 2020. https://bit.ly/37te7bB. See also "Columbia Unbecoming: Video Transcript," *The David Project*. Archived February 9, 2005. https://bit.ly/2HfffVH.

[110] "Sheldon Adelson-backed pro-Israel campus initiative doubling to 80 campuses," *Jewish Telegraphic Agency*, August 30, 2018. https://bit.ly/3g2SKnB.

[111] Josh Nathan-Kazis, "A New Wave Of Hardline Anti-BDS Tactics Are Targeting Students, And No One Knows Who's Behind It," *The Forward*, August 2, 2018. https://bit.ly/3yW69or.

[112] Jacobson, "Confirmed: 'Open Hillel' an anti-Israel fraud (#OpenHillel)," *Legal Insurrection*, December 7, 2014. https://bit.ly/3Tczy5h.

[113] "17 Students Chain Themselves to Soviet Embassy to Protest Russian Treatment of Jews," *Jewish Telegraphic Agency*, April 10, 1970. https://bit.ly/3CyirnY.

[114] "Jewish Students Protest Moscow Circus," *Jewish Telegraphic Agency*, January 5, 1973. https://bit.ly/3rPdIsO.

[115] "Jewish Women Picket Bolshoi," *Jewish Telegraphic Agency*, June 11, 1974. https://bit.ly/3esxoQo.

[116] See "Jews In Former Soviet Union: The Jackson-Vanik Amendment (January 3, 1975)," *Jewish Virtual Library*. https://bit.ly/3yynl2W.

[117] Markind, "Palestinian Authority Murders Critic, Scuttles Killers' Trial," *Legal Insurrection*, October 15, 2021. https://bit.ly/3RUvNQM.

[118] Agence France-Presse, "Palestinian media rally for protection after activist's death," *Ynet News*, June 28, 2016. https://bit.ly/3CQpQAb.

[119] "Palestinian Christians," *International Christian Embassy Jerusalem*, August 20, 2013. https://bit.ly/3CtbHYo.

[120] David Rosenberg, "PA sentences American to life in prison with hard labor," *Israel National News*, December 31, 2018. https://bit.ly/3rLwBgr.

121 Markind, "New Film Beautifully Showcases Jerusalem Archaeology to Rebut Historical Revisionism," *The Algemeiner,* December 22, 2017. https://bit.ly/3CtcdFO. See also "Sifting Antiquity on the Temple Mount Sifting Project," *Biblical Archaeology Society,* September 17, 2019. https://bit.ly/3rPfpGG.

122 Quoted in Michael W. Chapman, "Patton's D-Day Speech: 'The Very Idea of Losing is Hateful to an American,'" *CNS News,* November 11, 2019. https://bit.ly/3SVqCS9.

123 See Markind, "Jews Must Organize to Face Down Anti-Semitism from All Sides," *The Tower,* January 2, 2019. https://bit.ly/3EwAVI1.

16

JEWISH LEADERSHIP FAILS
IN FAIRFAX COUNTY

REBECCA G. SCHGALLIS

Numerous reports show that public school curricula hostile to Jews and Israel are rapidly spreading into American classrooms. Jewish parents would normally assume that Jewish community leaders would be alarmed at the prospect of our children being harassed and even hated for being Jewish and supporters of Israel. One would think Jewish leaders would be on top of this. We did. We were wrong.

My informal group of Jewish parents in Fairfax County, concerned about growing anti-Semitism in Northern Virginia public schools, assumed we could count on our local Jewish leadership to help us. Instead, we found a leadership that had generally failed to educate the Jewish community about this threat and seemed to have no appreciable strategy to fight it.

While our leaders are more responsive when hatred comes from neo-Nazis and white supremacists, they still have no strategy for addressing it, and they seem utterly flummoxed and paralyzed by the more nuanced anti-Semitism arising from groups other than these.

In our case, as we became aware of multiple incidents of anti-Semitism occurring over the years in our local schools in Northern Virginia, we reached out to the Jewish Community Relations Council (JCRC), which presents itself as the authority to speak for the Jewish community. We soon found that the JCRC was conflicted in its interests, and, rather than prioritizing fighting anti-Semitism, we found it to be more interested in currying favor with elected officials and promoting a "progressive equity" agenda. The JCRC showed little interest in working with members of the Jewish community, especially grassroots organizations such as ours (we would later form United Against Antisemitism-Northern Virginia), unless we were in agreement with their agenda, and it insistently pushed back against Jewish individuals and groups who wished to take action against the growing anti-Semitism. The standard JCRC response toward concerned Jews was essentially: "We know the players. Back off and leave this to us."

The JCRC showed itself either unwilling or unable to closely evaluate friends or foes in our local community. For example, in May 2021, as Israel was defending itself from Hamas' indiscriminate shelling of Tel Aviv, we learned that Fairfax County Public School (FCPS) board member Abrar Omeish called Israel an apartheid, colonialist state, and accused Israel of killing innocents on her social media account, an account linked to her official school board webpage.[1] Individual members of the Jewish community responded by calling for the school board to censure her, but to no avail.

A few days after she made her post, the JCRC issued a statement calling her tweet a: "one-sided, inaccurate, and hateful statement that smeared Israel, defamed Israelis, and disenfranchised the thousands of Jewish families in her district." The JCRC offered her the opportunity to "amend her remarks" and tried to convince her to take down her social media post. She refused, forcing the JCRC to rescind the honor they were scheduled to present to her as a "champion of faith equity" for her work in trying to include additional days of religious observance to the FCPS school calendar.[2] Meanwhile, her post accumulated multiple anti-Semitic responses from people encouraging her, some of them calling for the destruction of Israel, some threatening Jews individually.

Now comes the truly shocking part: a cursory Google search revealed that as a college student at Yale University, Omeish was president of the Muslim Students Association,[3] an organization whose origins are associated with the Muslim Brotherhood.[4] Her father, Esam Omeish, a former president of the Muslim American Society, another organization whose origins are associated with the Muslim Brotherhood,[5] was forced to resign from a Virginia commission on immigration when videos surfaced of him advocating jihad in Israel. Her father also recommended that their mosque hire Anwar al-Awlaki as imam, which it did.[6] As recently as 2018, the elder Omeish was cited by name in congressional testimony for his ties to terrorist organizations.[7] Following in her father's footsteps, Omeish led efforts to block the courageous feminist and Islamist critic Ayaan Hirsi Ali from speaking on her campus.[8] A few weeks after her social media post, as she delivered the commencement address at a high school graduation ceremony in her official capacity as a school board member, she introduced her terrorist-linked father as a special guest in the audience.

She then told the graduating class to "remember their 'Jihad.'"[9] The JCRC staff, one assumes, is composed of competent professionals, yet all the alarm bells that we—just parents—easily found spending thirty minutes on Google, either did not sound in any JCRC office, or worse, were ignored.

We were forced to ask ourselves: Were the members of the JCRC fooled or did they willingly turn a blind eye in their desire to court an "interfaith political partner" on the school board? Did their strategy of linking with "victim groups"—and proving they were anti-Islamo-phobes—conflict with what should be their first priority: keeping the Jewish community safe? Instead of educating the Jewish community about the threat of Islamist anti-Semitism, the JCRC, patronizingly, tried to dissuade us from taking further action against Omeish.

When the school board initially ignored our calls for censuring Omeish, we became aware through multiple Jewish parents that the school district had a pattern of ignoring incidents of anti-Semitism in their schools. We naturally called on the JCRC to help us, join us—or even lead the effort in confronting the schools and protecting Jewish children from anti-Semitism. While the JCRC met with us several times, we quickly learned that it was more interested in forging political partnerships with elected officials than forcefully addressing numerous incidents of anti-Semitism in the local school district. Not only did its members not appear to have an overall strategy to address anti-Semitism in the schools, they were unaware that the few programs they had initiated to address the problem, which they boasted about to the community, were not actually getting into the classrooms, showing little understanding of how to navigate the school system's large bureaucracy. Instead, they wanted us to come to them about issues, but then at every point they discouraged us from operating on our own, effectively telling us to be quiet.

A few weeks after the Omeish incident, a Fairfax elementary school listed on its website a host of "anti-racism" resources for the community, including one called "Woke Kindergarten." Woke Kindergarten describes its mission as an "abolitionist early childhood ecosystem" promoting "black and queer and trans liberation." It advances the oppressor/oppressed binary of critical race theory. So, where are America's Jews in this framework? Well, Woke Kindergarten's website, which poses "woke wonderings" in "liberatory thought,"[10] asks: "If the United States defunded the Israeli military, how could this money be used to rebuild Palestine?"[11] On its Instagram account, Woke Kindergarten labels Israel an example of "settler colonialism" that is guilty of "geocide" and has "no… right to exist."[12] Groups like Parents Defending Education publicized these and other posts as an example of FCPS promoting a site that promoted critical race theory, and, under pressure, the school district claimed it was a mistake and removed it.

Yet, months later, after the media asserted that the Virginia gubernatorial election was, to a significant degree, about CRT, the JCRC held a two-part webinar entitled: "Beyond the Headlines: Understanding How History & Race are Taught in Our Schools," that whitewashed CRT-based curricula. The JCRC promoted the first webinar, "What is Culturally Responsive Instruction in K-12 Schools? How Does It Impact Our Children?" as intending to clarify the "complex issue and how the current debate regarding school curricula impacts American Jews."[13] While CRT was an election issue, the JCRC renamed and reframed it, giving its webinar the deceptively parve title: "Culturally Responsive Instruction in K-12 Schools." The title purposefully obfuscated the issue. CRT—a theoretical framework whose complex philosophical contentions are studied in universities—is the driving force that is changing curricula across the country. CRT ideology removes Jews from their historic position of being allies with America's minority groups, and redefines them as "adjacent whites," putting them in the "oppressor" class.

The JCRC sought to use the example of Woke Kindergarten in Fairfax schools to demonstrate how it protected Fairfax's Jews from any potential problems that CRT might present. During the webinar, the JCRC explained that the school had quickly removed Woke Kindergarten because it did not match the equity officers' vision of culturally responsive instruction. But, in fact, Woke Kindergarten was never fully removed from the school district's curriculum. Summer school lesson plans for elementary students revealed that links to Woke Kindergarten's videos were used almost daily as part of literacy instruction.[14] Our group found that this was perfectly in line with the vision of the school's equity officer, who told us in conversations: "We use critical race theory as the frame for teaching history."

Worse yet, neither of the JCRC's guest presenters were from the Commonwealth of Virginia, where this was the recent election issue. One guest was a director of equity at a Maryland school district and the other guest was a university associate director of Multicultural Affairs and Diversity Education in New York who told the audience, "Jews should embrace CRT."

Jewish leaders should tell this inconvenient truth about CRT: No matter how much their radicalized allies promote it, CRT is dangerous for Jews. It casts Jews as "white adjacents" with disproportionate and ill-gotten power, and it views the Israeli-Palestinian conflict through the lens of race, where "white" Israel becomes an apartheid state and, therefore, like all systems of oppression, must be destroyed. Instead of the JCRC explaining this to the Jewish community, and fighting it, our JCRC is telling the community we should support an ideology that inevitably leads to anti-Semitism.

The JCRC's assurances that it had anti-Semitism under control in the schools also ran counter to the many examples that parents shared of anti-Semitism that had been largely ignored by school administrators. Not only had the JCRC failed in providing much-needed clarity and leadership on nuanced and politically charged anti-Semitism, it was not even adequately addressing the more easily recognizable forms of anti-Semitism. Parents shared numerous examples of swastika graffiti which remained un-erased for years, of students performing the *Sieg heil!* salute and singing happy birthday to Hitler, and of telling deeply offensive Holocaust jokes to Jewish students, many of whom were also repeatedly subject to ethnic slurs. Administrators also refused to provide reasonable accommodations for Jewish students when school activities coincided with Jewish holidays.

Assurances by the JCRC that it was working behind the scenes to improve the situation were not reassuring. (Activists throughout the country have shared similar experiences with us about their JCRC essentially telling them to back off and let it handle the situation.) The incidents we collected had been occurring for years with no apparent improvement and no apparent larger strategy to address this ongoing issue. Even worse, when we asked the JCRC about trends in anti-Semitism in Fairfax schools, it admitted that, after all these years, it had not collected that data. Realizing the truth about the ineffectiveness of the JCRC, our group reached out to the ZOA and other Jewish organizations who agreed to officially advocate for our Jewish families by demanding that FCPS take action to address anti-Semitism in its schools.

To our astonishment, our group soon discovered that the JCRC was coordinating back-channel discussions to convince one of the Jewish organizations to rescind its support. The JCRC showed greater concern in controlling the dialogue and relationships than leading any effort to solve the problems; however, given the repeated pattern of anti-Semitic harassment ignored by school officials, the ZOA filed a Title VI complaint against the school district. Since the complaint has been filed, we have brought two more incidents of students performing the *Sieg heil!* salute and impersonating Hitler to the school district and the JCRC's attention.

Most recently, we heard from individual members of the Jewish community that the National Education Association (NEA), the largest teachers' union in the U.S., was holding a vote on three anti-Israel "New Business Items" at their upcoming annual convention. The first two items called for the NEA to allot resources to "educate members and the public about the history, culture, and struggles of Palestinians, including the detention, abuse, and displacement of children in the Occupied Palestinian Territory,"[15] and to advocate for the rights of Palestinians using one-sided and factually inaccurate sources from Amnesty International and Human Rights Watch, among others. A third New Business Item stated that the NEA will support members who engage in this work "when they are under attack."[16] While the first item failed, the second went to committee, and the third, which provides union support to members who promote a factually inaccurate narrative of the Israeli–Palestinian conflict, passed by twenty percentage points.

It came to our attention that our members were alerted to this upcoming NEA vote by the JCRC. Rather than inform the larger Jewish community and mobilize them, the JCRC decided to only share this information with those whom it considered to be concerned individuals by private email. Our organization, which had been fighting anti-Semitism in K–12 schools for over a year, did not receive an email. When we asked the JCRC if it would be making a public statement about the NEA's items, a move that would impact Jewish and non-Jewish students alike, it responded that this was being handled "nationally." Finding that answer dissatisfying, we organized Jews across the country to write letters and got media coverage of the NEA convention.

The JCRC's framing of the NEA resolutions as a national issue, and, therefore, outside its purview, seemed highly problematic given its active involvement in other national issues. At the same time the NEA issue was happening, the JCRC issued a detailed plan responding to *Dobbs v. Jackson Women's Health Organization.*[17] The JCRC coordinated with other organizations and participated in marches and appeared at events with lawmakers.[18] It had at least three webinars on abortion and reproductive rights in the month after the ruling with more planned. The JCRC also issued a statement in *Kennedy v. Bremerton.*[19] The JCRC comfortably criticized the decisions in both cases, and the Christian Right presumably behind them, for being purportedly harmful to Jews, but was unwilling to publicly criticize the leftist NEA for entertaining and supporting measures that would back teachers who engage in spreading falsehoods about Israel in Virginia's public schools.

Early in the process of our interactions with the JCRC, hoping to work together, we became aware through various news articles in

Jewish media that this situation was not unique. From Raleigh to Boston to Los Angeles, Jewish community members report a similar frustration with their local Jewish organizations, which seemingly lack a strategy for addressing growing anti-Semitism. Rather than supporting and partnering with Jewish grassroots organizations nationwide, the legacy Jewish organizations have sought to maintain their "expert" status, often dissuading and sometimes even undermining these activist groups. We reached out to the Jewish Leadership Project, which provided support to our group and others like us throughout the country who are deeply concerned about the rising tide of anti-Semitism and the lack of urgency and a cohesive strategy by organizations like the JCRC of Greater Washington.

Multiple ideological threats have left the Jewish community more vulnerable than it has been in years. Jewish leaders needs to stop promoting their social justice agenda and rethink a strategy based on the illusion that the radicalized left is our ally. They need to start prioritizing the safety of the Jewish community.

Rebecca G. Schgallis is an educator in Virginia. She was the Humanities Department chair at the nation's number-one high school, Thomas Jefferson High School for Science and Technology, teaching history, religion, and government. She holds master's degrees in both education and history, specializing in American and twentieth-century German history with her research focusing on the Holocaust and anti-Semitism. She is a co-founder of United Against Antisemitism (UAA).

Editors' Note: Just weeks before this book was published, Abrar Omeish announced that she would not seek re-election. Her reason for quitting elected politics at the end of her term was Virginia Governor Glenn Youngkin's anti-CRT stance, and specifically his administration's "stifling" investigations into her school board's racially discriminatory conduct.[20] *Despite the local Jewish establishment's refusal to confront Jew-hatred from Islamic sources, grassroots activists like Schgallis persevered regardless and succeeded in appealing to a higher, sympathetic authority. Another subsequent success was Schgallis and UAA lobbying the Virginia legislature to adopt the IHRA definition of anti-Semitism.*[21] *The lesson here is that Jews cannot depend on their communal bureaucrats to combat threats and advance Jewish interests; they can only succeed through independent initiatives which circumvent their failed establishment leadership.*

[1]   See Sayatani Nath, "Who is Abrar Omeish? Virginia school board member urges students to remember 'Jihad,'" *Media Entertainment Arts WorldWide*, June 14, 2021. https://bit.ly/3N08ioP.

[2]   "JCRC Rescinds Honor to Fairfax County School Board Member Abrar Omeish," *Jewish Community Relations Council of Greater Washington*, May 19, 2021. https://bit.ly/3Fdv1Mi.

[3]   See Ahmed Elbenni, "Q&A with Abrar Omeish '18, president of the Yale Muslim Students' Association," *The Yale Daily News*, November 23, 2016. https://bit.ly/3FdQDrM.

[4]   See Discover the Networks, "Muslim Students Association of the U.S. and Canada (MSA)," *The David Horowitz Freedom Center*. https://bit. ly/3eYN522.

[5]   See Discover the Networks, "Muslim American Society (MAS)," *The David Horowitz Freedom Center*. http://bit.ly/2QAStM7.

[6]   Luke Rosiak, "School Board Member Whose Father Led 9/11 Hijackers' Mosque Opposes Resolution Honoring Victims," *The Daily Wire*, September 10, 2021. https://bit.ly/3z7mA12.

[7]   See "MAS' Esam Omeish Seeks Virginia Office," *Investigative Project on Terrorism*, May 1, 2009. https://bit.ly/3TOQaQX.

[8]   Lauren Noble, "Hirsi Ali at Yale—A Rare Victory for Free Speech," *Minding the Campus*, September 17, 2014. https://bit.ly/3TRyLHj.

[9]   Nath, "Who is Abrar Omeish? Virginia school board member urges students to remember 'Jihad.'"

10 https://www.wokekindergarten.org.

11 "I wonder… If the United States defunded the Israeli military, how could this money be used to rebuild Palestine?", *Woke Kindergarten*. https://bit.ly/3TzPOOr.

12 Woke Kindergarten. Instagram post. May 18, 2021. https://bit.ly/3som6jx.

13 "Beyond the Headlines: Understanding How History & Race are Taught in Our Schools," *Jewish Community Relations Council of Greater Washington*. Archived November 9, 2021. https://bit.ly/3st0zpC.

14 Breccan F. Thies, "Exclusive: Radical Fairfax County 'Summer Learning Guide' Tells 2nd Graders, 'I Feel Safe When There Are No Police,'" *Breitbart*, August 5, 2021. https://bit.ly/3Dbszmy.

15 Quoted in Beth Brelje, "Teachers Leave National Education Association, Say Union Pushes Politics With Member Dues," *The Epoch Times*, October 4, 2022. https://bit.ly/3sOpmVD.

16 *RA Today*, Issue 5, July 7, 2022, p. 18. https://bit.ly/3Gx2bGs.

17 See "JCRC Condemns Supreme Court Decision Overturning Roe v. Wade," *Jewish Community Relations Council of Greater Washington*, June 24, 2022. https://bit.ly/3ziXegW.

18 See Sandy Hausman, "Jewish community leaders will fight attempts to restrict abortion in Virginia," *WVTF*, July 4, 2022. https://bit.ly/3srnOAF.

19 See "JCRC Condemns Supreme Court Decision in School Prayer Case," *Jewish Community Relations Council of Greater Washington*, June 28, 2022. https://bit.ly/3DH8gzf.

20 Angela Woolsey, "EXCLUSIVE: Abrar Omeish bows out of school board race to work with youth-focused legal nonprofit," *Fairfax Now*, April 6, 2023. http://bit.ly/43bNaDH. See also Luke Rosiak, "Extremist Virginia School Board Member To Retire, Citing Scrutiny Following Youngkin's Election," *The Daily Wire*, April 6, 2023. http://bit.ly/40PJLJ3.

21 Taneika Duhaney, "Virginia passes bill formally defining antisemitism to spark change," *The Fairfax Times*, March 10, 2023. http://bit.ly/3Muiasr.

17

BOSTON JEWISH LEADERS SUBMIT TO THE LIES OF "ETHNIC STUDIES"

KAREN D. HURVITZ

As anti-Israel curricula are spreading to public schools across Massachusetts, the Jewish community is facing a storm of institutionalized enmity. Yet Jewish leaders in the Bay State are ignorant of the basic facts and the content of the curricula, and seem incapable of an effective response.

On February 1, 2022, I described in an article for the *Jewish News Syndicate (JNS)* how state-wide guidelines on teaching the Middle East had been changed in 2018 to tilt heavily against Israel.[1] If these standards are followed, they will ensure that children across the state are taught to believe that indigenous Palestinians were driven out of their homes by the Israeli army, and that Israel is continuing this "ethnic cleansing" today. Specifically, under the new guidelines, among other directives, Massachusetts public school teachers are told to instruct their students about "Palestinian loss of land and the creation of refugees by Israeli military action," and that there had been a "diverse mix of cultures (e.g. Jews, Palestinians, and Arabs of Christian, Jewish, Muslim and Druze backgrounds) in the region in the late 20th and early 21st centuries,"[2] which has notably—and deliberately—been decreased since the nation of Israel came into existence. These lessons, in conjunction with the anti-Israel reports concerning "human rights violations" against Palestinians issued by the U.N.[3] (which is listed as a reliable informational source in the Massachusetts guidelines), can only result in significant numbers of students disapproving of the Jewish state, questioning its right to exist, and, ominously, blaming the Jews in their own community, including their classmates, for supporting "oppression" and "racism."

In their opposition to a case that I filed in 2019 to take anti-Israel bias out of the curricula in Newton, Massachusetts,[4] lawyers for the Massachusetts Teachers Union argued that the lessons are being taught pursuant to the state's 2018 standards and that, far from being discriminatory and illegal, they are actually *required* by law. It was therefore quite disconcerting to learn that when asked about how to fix these standards, Jewish leaders in Boston, in identical letters,[5] said they were not even aware of the anti-Israel changes until my article highlighted them.

It was pursuant to this state-sanctioned, agenda-driven version of history that children in a Newton high school were shown a film called *Ismail* at the school's "Middle East Day" on May 2, 2018.[6] The film's opening scene depicts Nazi-like Israeli soldiers in 1948 force-marching Palestinians, with only the belongings they could carry, to refugee camps, all the while ordering them—imitating the Nazi *"Macht schnell!"*—to move faster, mocking them, and striking them with the butts of their rifles.[7] Newton students have been taught that Jerusalem is the capital of "Palestine" and Tel Aviv the capital of Israel, that the Israeli-Palestinian conflict is definitively *not* a clash of civilizations or religions, but merely a border dispute (implying that it could easily be settled by risk-free Israeli concessions), and that the Palestinians—and not the Jews—are the true indigenous people of Israel. The Jews' ancient, historical connection to the land has been obscured, and Palestinian terrorism, as well as their leaders' repeated rejection of the Jewish state, has been obfuscated.[8] These false and deceitful lessons are the new standard in Massachusetts.

On January 17, 2022, I wrote to Massachusetts Jewish leaders—at the ADL, the Massachusetts Federation, the American Jewish Committee, and the JCRC—pleading with them to take action against this hateful indoctrination being taught under the guise of education. None of them responded. They did, however, communicate with other members of the Jewish community who read and were alarmed by my article, thanking them for "sharing their concerns," assuring them that they "consider any and all allegations of anti-Semitism in Massachusetts' curricular content with the utmost of gravity," and that they were "actively investigating."[9] Follow-up letters to these organizations asking what they are doing to investigate and what they advise the community to do, however, were ignored. It is important to note that the revised anti-Israel standards that I discovered can be verified with a click of a mouse on the Department of Elementary and Secondary Education's website, and going to page 158; anyone with access to the Internet can easily "investigate."[10]

In 2021, in order to put a halt to the rising incidents of anti-Semitism in Massachusetts and the anti-Semitic lessons being taught in Massachusetts schools, State Representative Steven Howitt (R) introduced an amendment to the budget, "Condemnation and Definition of Anti-Semitism,"[11] which would have adopted the International Holocaust Remembrance Alliance (IHRA) definition of anti-Semitism.[12] Espousal of this definition would have prohibited (1) comparing Jews to Nazis and (2) denying the Jewish right to self-determination. Claiming that the existence of the state of Israel is a racist endeavor and ahistorical, propagandistic lessons would also have been barred, but both the local ADL and JCRC refused to support the amendment, with the JCRC explaining to constituents that it would have "riled up the far left."[13] Jewish Voice for Peace, the Alliance for Water Justice in Palestine, and the Unitarian Universalists for Justice in the Middle East, among others, organized to oppose the amendment, and succeeded in getting it removed from consideration.

As if this were not enough, Massachusetts Jews are now facing yet another educational onslaught in the proposed ethnic studies bill, titled "An Act Relative to Anti-Racism, Equity and Justice in Education."[14] The preamble to the bill states that,

> Whereas the events of 2020… including… the murder of George Floyd have elucidated the emergent nature of the social, economic and health disparities caused by racial inequity, including but not limited to: police brutality, profiling and murders of Black and brown people, anti-Asian violence… [T]he insurrection of January 6, 2021 revealed the imminent danger posed by rampant disinformation and white supremacy to the safety and integrity of our nation… Whereas racial educational disparities and white-centric history have fostered lies, systemic

inequality and outright violence, it is in the best interest of the Commonwealth that education in dismantling racism be taught to all students…, that truth and reconciliation regarding slavery, genocide, land theft and systemic racism is centered, that students of color and students from immigrant and indigenous communities may find their rightful place reflected in the history they learn….[15]

This type of legislation was passed in California with very negative consequences for Jews.[16] The Committee for Accuracy in Middle East Reporting and Analysis (CAMERA) has alerted the community to the dangers this legislation presents. CAMERA's analysis shows how an ethnic studies curriculum in Massachusetts will likely have the same anti-Israel and anti-Semitic content as the one in California, and how this will put a target on the back of every Jewish child.[17] As to be expected with woke-inspired efforts, anti-Semitism and anti-Jewish violence are not mentioned in the bill's preamble. The woke movement that has captured academia has already evoked far more anti-Semitism than is being reported by the media.[18]

The JCRC, instead of fighting back, seems eager to align the Jewish community with an ideology that is inimical to Jewish interests. Relieved to have the only Jewish seat at the table of the Commission for Anti-Racism in the proposed bill, the JCRC—in testimony submitted to the Joint Committee on Education—glowingly endorsed identity pedagogy and did not comment on the problem that this approach creates for the Jewish community. It wrote only that it is "aware that research has shown that students are empowered when they see themselves and their history reflected in their school curriculum, leading to better grades and higher graduation rates."[19] (The only study on the effects of an ethnically oriented curriculum that I am aware of evaluated a pilot program in San Francisco, which improved attendance rates and grades for at-risk Hispanic students and boys.[20]) The JCRC made general procedural complaints to the Committee, writing that there are no members from the legislature or the administration on the proposed board, that the definitions in the goals section are vague, and that the board's fiscal power has no oversight. The American Jewish Committee voiced the same mild definitional concerns.[21] Boston's Jewish leaders have adopted a strategy employed by their colleagues in California: fully endorse the concepts related to identity politics, yet create "guardrails" to protect Israel and Zionism within the identity framework. This allows the left-leaning leaders to stay on the good side of their progressive allies—while hopefully eliminating the anti-Israel/anti-Semitic elements. This, as developments in California have shown, is both conceptionally and politically impossible.

The fact is that Jewish leaders and their "guardrails" in California failed to protect the community from the spread of anti-Jewish "lessons" in the public schools.[22] Yet Jewish leaders in Boston have neither explained nor discussed this approach with the community, and have not told the community of the same strategy's defeat in California. In a fit of defensiveness, Boston's JCRC castigated those in the Jewish community who simply question its strategy as people who "openly tear down other members of our community," noting that the "cause of the destruction of the [Second] Temple was the baseless hatred [*sinat chinam*] sown between Jews."[23] Its insistence on turning a blind eye to reality has interfered with crucial sober political and cultural analysis.

The most obvious peril for Jews in a mandated ethnic studies curriculum is how Jews will be portrayed. In California, the original

model—and the one that is currently being pushed—for ethnic studies cited examples of "successful" social movements fighting for change. Included in the model is the BDS movement, with a link to its website, which claims that the movement aims to end international support for Israel's "regime of settler colonialism, apartheid and occupation" and to pressure Israel to comply with international law.[24] Analysts of the BDS movement explain that its real aim is the destruction of Israel.[25] Also included as a model for a social justice movement is Black Lives Matter (BLM), whose official platform in 2016 called for an end to U.S. aid to Israel to stop its complicity "in the genocide taking place against the Palestinian people" and in Israel's practice of "apartheid."[26] Although that official platform was removed from BLM's website in 2020, BLM still supports the Palestinian "movement" and identifies with the Palestinians in their struggle for freedom from "colonial oppressors."[27] The ADL has, inconceivably, endorsed BLM.[28]

The ADL is now facing backlash to its educational wing for teaching critical race theory, which includes the "intersectional" fiction of Israel as a colonial oppressor of indigenous brown Palestinians, and American Jews as holders of white privilege.[29] CRT clearly is a permission slip for anti-Semitism.

Straddling the fence this way is also logistically impossible: although they were successful in installing some "guardrails"— namely, getting the final version approved by California authorities to omit teaching about BDS—California teachers are in fact free to use whatever model they choose, because individual school districts are autonomous, just as they are in Massachusetts. Indeed, the Council on American-Islamic Relations (CAIR) and the San Francisco-based Arab Resource and Organizing Center are brazenly promoting the original version, *not* the one approved by the education board, whose members they characterize as people "more concerned with listening to the whispers of lobbyists and the voices of the oppressors than the cries of the oppressed."[30] Authors of that version, which incorporates CRT,[31] are avidly promoting its use to school districts.[32] In that original version, which will very likely be taught in many California schools, Israel is defamed as a settler, colonialist, apartheid empire, which violates international law and should be dismantled.

If any version of the ethnic studies bill gets the nod in Massachusetts, even one that deletes the worst anti-Israel materials, radical and leftist teachers can simply follow their California comrades. Notably, Allyson Tintiangco-Cubales[33] (the California organizer responsible for producing the first version of the California bill) and Samia Shoman[34] (the author responsible for the most anti-Semitic lessons in that version) are both consulting for the Ethnic Studies Now! Organizing Committee of the Boston Teachers Union.[35] The version currently being taught in a pilot program in Boston schools looks almost identical to the original California version.[36] It is even possible that the same anti-Semitic ethnic studies curriculum that is being pushed in California, and is already being piloted in Boston schools, may become sanctioned in Massachusetts, even though Massachusetts regulations require that teachers review all educational materials for simplistic and demeaning generalizations lacking intellectual merit based on race, religion, or national origin, among others, and provide balance and context for any such stereotypes depicted in such materials.[37]

In California, the group responsible for the first version of the ethnic studies curriculum has established relationships with many California school districts, and, based on this foothold, has managed to persuade schools to use its curriculum instead of the approved one.

A school superintendent there justified his district's use of this controversial curriculum by explaining that the group has been working with his district for some time and "most districts have been working with them in some capacity in our region."[38] This development should alarm Jews in Massachusetts. Already, some curricula in Massachusetts, including a Middle East unit, is being subcontracted out to Primary Source,[39] an organization whose curriculum on the Middle East is sponsored by Qatar Foundation International,[40] an arm of the Qatari government, and has a distinctly anti-Israel point of view. Moreover, since Primary Source already has contracts with more than fifty Massachusetts school districts, if an ethnic studies bill passes here, Primary Source will likely peddle its already-prepared curriculum to schools which must teach ethnic studies.[41]

Finally, as one has come to expect, in spite of the Massachusetts guidelines' directive to teach about the "remarkable diversity of our country,"[42] there is no provision in the proposed bill on ethnic studies for the inclusion of any Jewish topics, any mention of the many Jewish men and women who have contributed to American history from 1654 onward,[43] and no mention of their being oppressed in all lands in which they lived, being expelled from many.[44] And there is no study of the remarkable achievements of Jews in spite of these impediments.[45] The creators of this identity ideology would explain that this is because Jews, who have been persecuted for millennia, have become white oppressors—in spite of the almost daily attacks against them today.[46]

Jewish leaders, even those with progressive agendas, should be protecting the Jewish community and contesting existing and proposed anti-Semitic educational curricula instead of being surprised by them and "investigating" long after the fact. Massachusetts Jewish organizations are trying to have their cake and eat it, too: embracing a left that has now turned on Jews as a whole while begging to be spared from fact-based criticism. They have kept the community in the dark about the enormity of the threat and about their strategy, which has utterly failed in California. They have painted themselves into a corner and now are as paralyzed as deer in headlights. Huddled in their private offices, they deflect questions and concerns from those they are meant to serve—and while they are hiding, the ethnic studies campaign marches on, unopposed. On March 31, 2022, the Committee on Education to which the proposed ethnic studies bill was referred for study, reported it out of committee favorably,[47] along with fourteen other "anti-racism" bills, all of which were also recommended to pass. The other bills called for legislation to develop "alternative" processes for granting educator licensure to achieve educator diversity, for the Department of Elementary and Secondary Education to implement standards and objectives on cultural studies, to establish a permanent commission on anti-racist education to develop anti-racist curricula, and similar.

Soon, if "ethnic studies" is not exposed as viciously divisive and stopped, a large proportion of the state's schoolchildren will be "learning" that the Jewish state is inherently racist and engaging in ethnic cleansing, and that the Jewish students sitting in their classroom support such evils. Jewish children will have to "learn" about the connections between the struggles of black and brown indigenous communities and the struggles of "indigenous" Palestinians against Israeli "oppressors."

Given the behavior of local Jewish leadership—their aversion to conflict, their unrequited embrace of an increasingly radicalized left, and their preference to operate behind closed doors and out of sight of the community—concerned Jews must publicize these dangers urgently and broadly, and press our "leaders" to stand up and fight for us. If they continue to ignore this obvious crisis and mislead the Jews they are charged with protecting, they must be replaced.

Karen Hurvitz is a lawyer and artist in Massachusetts. She has taught at Georgetown University Law Center, Boston University Law School, and Suffolk University Law School. Her practice is currently devoted to representing students in high school and college who object to non-historical, political propaganda in course materials. She is counsel for Education Without Indoctrination, and on the Board of LIBI, the Sandra Bornstein Holocaust Education Center, and the Massachusetts Cultural Council.

---

[1] Karen D. Hurvitz, "From Texas to Massachusetts: Will Incitement Wake up Sleeping Jewish Leaders?", *JNS*, February 1, 2022. https://bit.ly/3fLrHgv. See also "Massachusetts Learning Standards," *Massachusetts Department of Elementary and Secondary Education*. https://www.doe.mass.edu/frameworks/.

[2] Paul Sagan, *et al., History and Social Science Framework: Grades Pre-Kindergarten to 12, Massachusetts Curriculum Framework—2018* (Malden, MA: Massachusetts Department of Elementary and Secondary Education, 2018), p. 158. https://bit.ly/3TdelcQ.

[3] See "Special Rapporteur on the situation of human rights in the Occupied Palestinian Territories: Israel has imposed upon Palestine an apartheid reality in a post-apartheid world," *United Nations Human Rights Office of the High Commissioner*, March 25, 2022. https://bit.ly/3SPI8XO.

[4] See Dechter v. City of Newton School Committee, Middlesex Superior Ct. 1981-CV-00692 (MA 2019). https://bit.ly/3CQI7xo.

[5] See Jeremy Burton, Boston JCRC executive director, email, February 16, 2022, and Robert O. Trestan, New England ADL regional director, email, February 3, 2022. https://bit.ly/3rTjb22.

[6]   See Miriam F. Elman, "Newton, MA public school officials backtrack on pledge to rid curriculum of anti-Israel bias," *Legal Insurrection*, July 1, 2018. https://bit.ly/3fZEuMn.

[7]   Bumpy Road Films. "'Ismail' | Palestinian Short Film (Full)." Filmed 2013. YouTube video, 28:00. Posted October 19, 2020. https://bit.ly/3rLuLvS.

[8]   See Steven Stotsky, *Indoctrinating Our Youth: How a U.S. Public School Curriculum Skews the Arab-Israeli Conflict and Islam* (Boston, MA: Committee for Accuracy in Middle East Reporting and Analysis, 2017). https://bit.ly/3EwzlFS.

[9]   See note 5, *supra*.

[10] See note 2, *supra*.

[11] Amendment #300 to H.4000: "Condemnation and Definition of Anti-Semitism," H.4000, 191st General Court (2021). https://bit.ly/3TdAJC5.

[12] See "About the IHRA non-legally binding working definition of antisemitism," *International Holocaust Remembrance Alliance*. https://bit.ly/3CTAtT1.

[13] Burton, email, March 2, 2022. https://bit.ly/3SYPb0z.

[14] An Act Relative to Anti-Racism, Equity and Justice in Education, S.365, 192nd General Court (2022). https://bit.ly/3g2pZHM.

[15] *Ibid.*, p. 2.

[16] See Pamela Paresky and Lee Jussim, "Why No One Should Accept a 'Critical Ethnic Studies' Curriculum. Least of All, Jews," *The Jewish Journal*, January 27, 2021. https://bit.ly/3RYTGHP.

[17] Stotsky, "Proposed Ethnic Studies Curriculum in Massachusetts Sparks Controversy," *Committee for Accuracy in Middle East Reporting and Analysis*, February 8, 2022. https://bit.ly/3epepWR.

[18] "HonestReporting Research Study: Comparing US Media Coverage of Hate Crimes Against Minorities, Including Jews," *HonestReporting*, February 9, 2022. https://bit.ly/3rQuCat.

[19] Nahma Nadich, Boston JCRC deputy director, testimony to State Senator Jason M. Lewis and Representative Alice Hanlon Peisch, September 13, 2021. https://bit.ly/3rSgKwG.

[20] Thomas Dee and Emily Penner, "The Causal Effects of Cultural Relevance: Evidence from an Ethnic Studies Curriculum" (Working Paper, National Bureau of Economic Research, 2016). https://bit.ly/3TiqImI.

[21] See Sean Savage, "Ethnic-studies legislation in Massachusetts raises alarm from Jewish, watchdog groups," *JNS*, October 8, 2021. https://bit.ly/3SUTM3G.

[22] David Bernstein, "California guardrails fail to stop 'liberated' anti-Israel curriculum," *JWeekly*, March 28, 2022. https://bit.ly/3CuDF5Q. See also

"American Jewish Committee (AJC) Statement on California State Board of Education Adoption of Ethnic Studies Model Curriculum," *American Jewish Committee*, March 18, 2021. https://bit.ly/3VqUYh8.

23 Burton, "'The Good Jews,'" *Boston Jewish Community Relations Council*, August 4, 2022. https://bit.ly/3RRvlml.

24 "What is BDS?", *BDS Movement*. https://bdsmovement.net/what-is-bds.

25 Ehud Rosen, "What is the Real BDS Endgame? The Elimination of Israel," *Jerusalem Center for Public Affairs*, Vol. 14, *No. 3*, February 12, 2014. https://bit.ly/3expiWt.

26 "A Cut in US Military Expenditures and A Reallocation of those Funds to Invest in Domestic Infrastructure and Community Wellbeing," *Movement 4 Black Lives*. https://bit.ly/3TfVQ63. See p. 3.

27 Hansi Lo Wang, "The Complicated History Behind BLM's Solidarity With The Pro-Palestinian Movement," *NPR*, June 12, 2021. https://n.pr/3rQTuiw.

28 Daniel Greenfield, "ADL Signs Black Lives Matter Letter Alongside Anti-Israel Groups," *FrontPage Magazine*, September 1, 2020. https://bit.ly/3eCKM4x.

29 Jonathan S. Tobin, "The ADL's Critical Race Theory Curricula Is No Accident," *Newsweek*, September 9, 2022. https://bit.ly/3RUBSgb.

30 "California Fails Its Promise on Ethnic Studies," *CAIR California San Francisco Bay Area*, March 22, 2021. https://bit.ly/3Vr7exR. CAIR is affiliated with the Muslim Brotherhood and tied to the terrorist organization Hamas. See *United States v. Holy Land Foundation*, CR 3:04-CR-240-G (N.D. Texas 2007). Government's Memorandum in Opposition to CAIR's Motion to File Amicus Brief. https://bit.ly/3T3PyHg.

31 See "Critical Race Theory: A Pair of Eyeglass," *Liberated Ethnic Studies Model Curriculum Consortium*. https://www.liberatedethnicstudies.org/crt.html.

32 Tammi Rossman-Benjamin, "'Liberated' ethnic studies curriculum fails to liberate California schools from antisemitism," *San Diego Jewish World*, July 1, 2021. https://bit.ly/3yA6bC3.

33 See "About," *BPS-BTU Ethnic Studies Course*. https://bit.ly/3ECmQsD.

34 See "Samia Shoman," *Acosta Educational Partnership*. Archived January 29, 2022. https://bit.ly/3T1aVsK. Her professional profile notes that she is "a proud parent of boy/girl twins [named] Falestine and Jihad."

35 See "Mission of the BTU Ethnic Studies Now! Organizing Committee," *BTU Ethnic Studies Now! Organizing Committee*. https://bit.ly/3yzJ5LM.

36 See "Intro to Ethnic Studies Course," *BPS-BTU Ethnic Studies Course*. https://bit.ly/3rPWwU9.

³⁷ See "603 CMR 26.00: Access To Equal Educational Opportunity," *Massachusetts Department of Elementary and Secondary Education*. https://bit.ly/3MstvXZ.

³⁸ Quoted in Rossman-Benjamin, "New Proposal Would Force CA School Districts to Adopt 'Liberated' Curriculum if Students Want Admission to UC Schools," *The Jewish Journal*, February 23, 2022. https://bit.ly/3elL67H.

³⁹ For more information about Primary Source, see APT. "Primary Source." Filmed 2010. Vimeo video, 15:37. Posted December 29, 2011. https://vimeo.com/34351254. See also APT. "In Newton, MA: The Influence of Qatar on American High Schools—Collusion of Haters and Educators." Filmed 2019. Vimeo video, 12:34. Posted January 28, 2020. https://vimeo.com/387702619.

⁴⁰ See "Briefing: Qatar Foundation," *Middle East Forum*, March 27, 2018. https://bit.ly/3CQ1czA.

⁴¹ See "A Century of Conflict & Resolution in the Middle East: Israeli-Palestinian Conflict," *Primary Source*. https://bit.ly/3eqmXNh. Of the historical sources listed for Primary Source's Middle East unit on the Israeli-Palestinian conflict, all except one claim that Israel was founded as a colonialist enterprise and that its citizens are "occupying" the land of others. Ilan Pappé, whose book *A History of Modern Palestine* is featured, is well-known as a revisionist historian of "Palestine" and political commentator on the Israel-Palestinian conflict. He also wrote *The Ethnic Cleansing of Palestine* in which he "chronicles" how, between 1947 and 1949, over 400 Palestinian villages were deliberately destroyed, civilians massacred, and around a million men, women, and children were expelled from their homes at gunpoint. Another book, *The Arab-Israeli Reader: A Documentary History of the Middle East Conflict*, starts the history of the conflict—which has been going on since the founding of Islam—at the creation of Israel, or the "*nakbah*," the Arabic word for "catastrophe." In *Palestine*, author Joe Sacco "documents" stories of Palestinians who have suffered at the hands of Israeli soldiers, from imprisonment to torture to murder of family members. *A Little Piece of Ground* by Elizabeth Laird "helps young readers understand more about one of the worst conflicts afflicting our world today." She narrates a story which describes how, in response to a Palestinian suicide bombing in which Israelis are murdered, the Israeli military "subjects the West Bank town to a virtual siege" by imposing a curfew, which is difficult to endure by children who long to play football with their friends.

⁴² "Race, Racism, and Culturally Responsive Teaching in History and Social Science in Massachusetts: Frequently Asked Questions," *Massachusetts*

Department of Elementary and Secondary Education, August 2021. https://bit.ly/3ywiLCn.

43 See "360 Years of American Jewish Life," *American Jewish Historical Society*. Archived July 6, 2022. https://bit.ly/3yAMdXK.

44 See "Jewish Persecution | Timeline of Judaism | History of AntiSemitism," *SimpleToRemember.com*. https://bit.ly/3T46wW0. See also Paul E. Grosser and Edward G. Halperin, *Anti-Semitism: The Causes and Effects of a Prejudice* (Secaucus, NJ: Citadel Press, 1979). https://bit.ly/3CSzQJ9.

45 See "Jewish Nobel Prize Laureates (1901–2020)." *Jewish Virtual Library*. https://bit.ly/3yADzIS.

46 "HATE IN FLATBUSH: Yeshiva Bochur Assaulted by Pro-Palestinian Mob [VIDEOS OF ASSAULT]," *The Yeshiva World*, May 10, 2022. https://bit.ly/3SXZbHm.

47 An Act Relative to Educator Diversity, H.4539, 192nd General Court (2022). https://bit.ly/3CSfcZB.

18

JCPA "WOKENESS" BREEDS DIVISION

JOANNE BREGMAN

Almost every American Jewish community of a certain size has a Jewish Community Relations Council (JCRC), whose mandate it is to build bridges and foster warm relations with other communal, ethnic, and racial groups. The Jewish Council for Public Affairs (JCPA) is the national umbrella organization overseeing these local JCRCs. Few understand that rather than reflecting the values and policies of the national collective, the JCPA has come to dictate policies for every locale, policies whose ideology explains how and why everyone's JCRC seems to have become so radically left. It's time that Jews knew how their JCRCs function.

The JCRCs are either part of or affiliated with their local Jewish Federations. Sixteen other national Jewish organizations are also listed as JCPA members.

The JCPA says it represents the four main branches of American Judaism and has stylized itself as a "consensus builder" so as to navigate politically non-homogeneous Jewish communities, and at the same time claim to represent a "unified front." In reality, the JCPA has become just another "woke" progressive organization whose political activism is abetted by the self-selected members of the local JCRCs.

Founded in 1944 by the Council of Jewish Federations, the JCPA was to serve as a venue for Jewish communities and federations to discuss and organize their interests, which at one time included extensive work in the civil rights movement. And, like many of the infant communal Jewish organizations, the JCPA's formation was conceived in the ashes of the Holocaust.

Recognizing the value of working in common cause with other minority communities, in 1950, the JCPA and the NAACP cofounded the Leadership Conference on Civil Rights as a clearinghouse and coordinating body for all civil rights lobbying. According to its website, the Leadership Conference today "remains the nation's oldest, largest, and most diverse civil and human rights coalition."[1]

Since then, however, the JCPA, which remains part of the Leadership Conference, has expanded its social justice policy platform. Virtually every political matter under discussion in America, including climate change, criminal justice reform, immigration, voting rights, and LGBTQI+ issues, can be found in the JCPA's "Policy Compendium."[2] These policies are derived through a resolutions process and are intended to be *the* positions parroted by the JCRCs.

The resolutions adoption process begins with the annual plenum and is finalized by the Delegates Assembly, which is attended by one lay representative and one professional representative from each JCRC. This group is considered the "highest deliberative body" on public policy matters for the community relations network. Like the plenum, its purpose is to oversee and set new public positions and priorities for the community relations field through a resolutions process.

As part of the JCPA's network, the local JCRCs are asked to endorse JCPA resolutions and to use them to focus their local grass-roots and lobbying activities even if they do not reflect the broader community's priorities, opinions, or religious values.

JCPA resolutions forwarded to local JCRCs for endorsement in 2021 included a resolution on "voter suppression," the language of which effectively endorses the Democrats' attempted voter legislation known as H.R. 1, which weakens voter identification requirements. The federal elections takeover bill, widely known to be a top priority for Democrats in Congress (dubbed by some as the "Keep Democrats in Power Forever Act"), deliberately guts the extensive work of the bipartisan Jimmy Carter–James Baker Commission on Federal Election Reform, whose report specifically recommended *increased* voter ID requirements and other election integrity measures.[3] Keeping Democrats in power is so important to the JCPA that their version of voter suppression was retained as a 2022 federal policy priority. As intended, that same year, Nashville's JCRC staff director used her platform while speaking to a local rotary club to inappropriately cite the rise in anti-Semitism and the Holocaust as reasons to support H.R. 1.[4]

The resolution on climate change—a vast array of policy changes—failed to account for the economic, societal, or national security ramifications of this profound transformation, while the resolution to address "systemic disparities and discrimination across all aspects of our society" by "strengthening Jewish communal relations with Black communities" was designed to conceal BLM founder's and leadership's very real animus toward Israel and support for the BDS campaign.

The resolutions handed down to local JCRCs are overwhelmingly aligned with the agenda of the Democratic Party, assigning Jewish and Israeli interests to secondary status. The JCPA's leftward orientation is additionally demonstrated by its membership in a number of leftist groups including Census Counts 2020,[5] Declaration for American Democracy,[6] and the Jewish Social Justice Roundtable.[7] It should be noted that the leadership team of this last group is driven by the committed leftist Religious Action Center for Reform Judaism, and the pro-BDS groups T'ruah and Bend the Arc. These alliances among others leave little doubt that the JCPA has chosen a self-serving interpretation of "Jewish values of fairness and justice" to justify shaping the Jewish community relations field into a partisan instrument of the left while excluding a significant portion of the Jewish community.

The JCPA also pushes for legal and political action directly through established channels, such as direct lobbying for legislation and legal action in the form of filing amicus briefs with the courts, and offers its members the best practices to implement programs and issue-based advocacy toolkits. The "JCRC Playbook" and a database that includes "marketing materials" is reserved for paid JCRC staff and lay leaders.

Similar to virtually every Jewish communal organization, the JCPA's mission statement includes a specific reference to Israel, and over the years, the JCPA has addressed the BDS movement. To this end, the JCPA in conjunction with the Jewish Federations established the Israel Action Network to fight BDS and claims that "working closely with local JCRCs has helped defeat BDS at the state and municipal level and on college campuses across the nation."[8]

It's reasonable then to ask why the JCPA featured Senator Raphael Warnock (D-GA) at the April 2021 annual conference[9] after he had co-signed the 2019 National Council of Churches letter. That letter is noted for being replete with anti-Israel propaganda and statements taken from the BDS playbook with references such as the "need to preserve the option of utilizing economic pressure as a means of bringing recalcitrant dominant forces to the negotiating table," Palestinian "right of return," and comparing Israel to "oppressive regimes" like "apartheid South Africa."[10]

The incredibly tone-deaf JCPA invitation to Warnock would be laughable were it not for its hypocrisy: Warnock joined Amy Spitalnick as a speaker in a session titled "Racism, Antisemitism & Fighting Hate." That's the same Amy Spitalnick who was making the rounds with her talk "Fighting White Supremacy: From Charlottesville to Capitol Hill" and characterizing the problem as endemic to the mainstream right.

Not surprisingly, the JCPA endorsed Kristen Clarke, President Biden's nominee for Assistant Attorney General for Civil Rights, while conveniently ignoring Clarke's public support for Tamika Mallory,[11] who accused Jews of "uphold[ing] white supremacy"[12] and defended her relationship with super-anti-Semite Louis Farrakhan.[13] If you aren't convinced by the JCPA's defense of Clarke, check out Amy Spitalnick—who has accused "mainstream Republicans" of regularly trafficking in "white supremacist ideology"[14]—and her endorsement of Clarke's appointment.[15] Clarke herself, along with former State Representative Stacey Abrams (D-GA), spoke at the JCPA's 2022 national conference.[16]

JCRC membership in the JCPA is not mandatory and not all federations or JCRCS are members. Those who have wisely chosen to not throw local Jewish communal organizations directly into a partisan political fray should feel vindicated in this choice by observations made by the JCPA's former president and CEO, David Bernstein.

After leading the JCPA for five years, Bernstein, a self-described liberal, left the JCPA in mid-2021 amid the organization's increasingly extreme political advocacy. He watched as liberal and leftist Jewish voices and organizations, including the JCPA, ignored all the warning signs of the "woke cancel culture" and the "dangers this raises for Jews... [in how] it twists how some on the left talk about anti-Semitism."[17]

Generally, the JCRCs are comprised of at least one paid staff member and self-selected lay volunteers, a design that has proven unable to represent politically diverse Jewish communities. If the local JCRCs are to be authentic communal organizations—welcoming and respectful of diversity of opinion, gender identity, sexual orientation, race, ethnicity, disability, religious observance, and political affiliation—then the membership of the JCRCs and involvement with the JCPA and its political objectives should be discontinued. JCRCs would benefit from a deliberate effort to balance the political diversity of its lay volunteers and depoliticize paid staff. JCRCs should reflect the interests and issues of its Jewish community members.

JCPA directorship of the JCRCs alienates a portion of the Jewish community in which the JCRC operates—which Jewish communities can ill afford, given the efforts of a progressive movement working to elect more Ilhan Omars and Rashida Tlaibs to Congress. If the JCPA intends to be a credible leader of politically diverse Jewish communities, it needs to undergo a serious self-assessment—and re-establish Israel and Jewish interests as the first order of business.

Joanne Bregman is a Nashville attorney engaged in public policy work on a variety of issues, including advocacy for Israel and the Jewish community.

Editors' Note: Shortly after this essay was written, the JCPA broke off from the Jewish Federations of North America—the umbrella group representing all American Federations and the United Jewish Appeal—in order to form, as its press release described, a "NEW" JCPA, whose specific focus was "social justice" causes including "democracy," "disinformation," "racial justice," and abortion. As press accounts explained, this move freed the progressives within the JCPA from more "conservative" Federation donors whose concerns are more traditionally Jewish.[18] This development shows that Bregman's analysis was prescient and correct.

1   "Our History," *The Leadership Conference on Civil and Human Rights.* https://civilrights.org/about/history/.

2   See Jewish Council for Public Affairs, *2021 Policy Compendium* (New York, NY: Jewish Council for Public Affairs, 2021), pp. 16–18, 31–33, 77–82, 99–103, 132–133.https://bit.ly/3TvkSyc.

3   See "The Carter-Baker Commission: 16 Years Later," *Baker Institute for Public Policy*, October 28, 2021. https://bit.ly/3ez2cit.

4   Bill Zechman, "Rotary speaker addresses threats to democracy," *The Southern Standard*, August 15, 2021. https://bit.ly/3D41SRZ.

5   See "Census Counts 2020," *Influence Watch.* https://bit.ly/3eKhWit.

6   See "Declaration for American Democracy," *Influence Watch.* https://bit.ly/3MGhAG4.

7   See "Jewish Social Justice Roundtable," *Influence Watch.* https://bit.ly/3MF4WXV.

8   Jewish Council for Public Affairs, *Celebrating 75 of Community Relations & Advocacy (1944–2019)* [New York, NY: Jewish Council for Public Affairs, 2019], p. 10.

9   "JCPA 2021 Roundup," *Jewish Council for Public Affairs*. Archived June 24, 2021. https://bit.ly/3ez386t. The page has since been deleted from the JCPA site.

10 "Group Pilgrimage Statement on Israel and Palestine," *National Council of Churches,* March 5, 2019. Archived July 2, 2022. https://bit.ly/3TrPNM2.

11 Tobin, "The Jewish establishment thinks credible charges of anti-Semitism are a 'smear,'" *JNS*, April 14, 2021. https://bit.ly/3CE35yg.

12 Quoted in "Women's March leader says white Jews 'uphold white supremacy,'" *The Times of Israel*, December 23, 2018. https://bit.ly/3S7sp5h.

13 Tobin, "What does it mean to actually oppose anti-Semitism?", *JNS*, January 14, 2021. https://bit.ly/3g8m785.

14 Quoted in Pat Hamsa, "Nashville Jewish Community Hosts Speaker Who Says Mainstream Republicans are White Supremacists," *The Daily Roll Call*, February 9, 2021. https://bit.ly/3S8pIR1.

15 Jacob Kornbluh, "Jewish groups push back against attacks on Biden's deputy AG pick on eve of confirmation hearing," *The Forward*, April 9, 2021. https://bit.ly/3geCsIG.

16 See "JCPA 2022 National Conference," *Jewish Council for Public Affairs*. Archived April 11, 2022. https://bit.ly/3MBPyf3.

17 See Tobin, "Can liberalism be saved from cancel culture?", *JNS*, March 9, 2021. https://bit.ly/3CFCil4.

18 See Tobin, "Jews don't need another left-wing advocacy group," *JNS*, December 21, 2022. https://bit.ly/3C4pnts.

19

THE HIJACKING OF THE AMERICAN ZIONIST MOVEMENT

LAURI B. REGAN

Progressive ideologues are winning powerful leadership positions in American Jewish umbrella groups, causing great harm to the Jewish community at a time when antisemitism is surging. I was eyewitness to the left-wing takeover of the American Zionist Movement (AZM), the U.S. arm of the World Zionist Organization, an account of which will serve as a primary example of the price we pay when we allow it to happen.

In March of 2020, I wrote a column entitled "G-d Is Testing American Jews. They Are Failing," in which I argued that progressive Jewish organizations—whose *raison d'être* is to demonize Israel, harming her ability to survive—are also causing great harm to the ability of American Jews to survive.[1] I went on to suggest that American Jewish umbrella groups, whose "big tent" policy of admitting groups whose agendas involve non-stop criticism of Israel, cannot work to effectively defend the community. This is because their progressive members assist in the propagation of today's "new antisemitism," which is based on the demonization of Israel through the perpetration of lies and blood libel.

And while these progressive Jews claim to be authentic Zionists who care about Israel, they, in fact, play the role that Lenin ascribed to Western leftists—that of "useful idiots" who feed ammunition to Israel's foes as they jointly blame Israel for the conflict with the Palestinians. Their continuous and disproportionate "legitimate criticism of Israeli policy" gives a free pass to terrorist atrocities against innocent Jewish civilians, to failed and corrupt Palestinian leadership that has rejected numerous opportunities for a state of its own, and to a biased U.N., including UNRWA, which teaches Palestinian children to kill Jews. These groups—all of whom take positions aligned with Israel's and the Jewish peoples' enemies under the cover of false claims of Zionism—are further empowered by membership in pro-Israel umbrella groups, which only normalizes disproportionate Jewish criticism of Israel. It's no wonder that a 2020 Pew Research study revealed that 37 percent of Jews under the age of thirty believe that the U.S is "too supportive of Israel."[2]

Several months after my article's publication, Richard Heideman, the AZM's president at the time, asked me to help him to launch and then to chair a new AZM committee designed to fight the growing scourge of antisemitism, anti-Zionism, and Holocaust denial that was not just running rampant in countries around the globe, but was also spreading across the United States.

As the New York chapter president and advisory board member of the Endowment for Middle East Truth (and a board member of

Scholars for Peace in the Middle East), I had been speaking, writing, and working on these issues for many years, including at the U.N., on Capitol Hill, and on radio programs across the country, and I had been recognized as somewhat of an expert on these matters. I was honored that Richard asked me to launch and chair the AZM's new and important Antisemitism, Anti-Zionism, and Holocaust Denial Project (AAHDP).

Unfortunately, all my concerns about the divisiveness of leftist Jews were born out from the very first day that Richard announced the launch of the AAHDP with me as chair. Immediately, four progressive AZM coalition organizations—Ameinu, the Association of Reform Zionists of America (ARZA), Partners for a Progressive Israel, and Mercaz—all challenged the new committee and my chairmanship. Despite every effort on my part to put aside past differences and to include, whatever their ideology, every single AZM board member who wished to participate in this critically important endeavor, the AAHDP became yet one more pro-Israel project that the left—and, specifically, these four AZM organizations—wished to destroy. They ultimately succeeded.

To be clear, none of these groups challenged my abilities, experience, knowledge, passion, and credentials to chart a path of education and action against antisemitism. Furthermore, Richard and I made sure to launch the AAHDP as an apolitical committee established to educate and promote its critical mission to fight antisemitism, anti-Zionism, and Holocaust denial within the AZM community. As Richard stated, and we included at the top of our webpage:

> We find ourselves in a chess match of hatred. Fighting Antisemitism and Anti-Zionism is our communal

obligation. We must defend our people, our heritage
and our good name. We must adopt a policy of Zero
Tolerance against Antisemitism and Anti-Zionism.[3]

My committee brought together people from diverse organizations including left, right, and center, all of whom cared passionately
about working together to coordinate efforts and share ideas. And
while a few individuals from those four organizations did participate in the AAHDP, I was told that the official policy of every one of
these progressive groups was to instruct their members *not* to participate. This seemed a coordinated effort to boycott and destroy an
AZM initiative that was organized to fight antisemitism, anti-Zionism,
and Holocaust denial for partisan, political reasons. These groups
would simply not abide an unabashedly Zionist approach that did not
include labeling Israel as an oppressor, occupier, and apartheid state.

In fact, David Dormont, an AZM board member who boycotted
the AAHDP and who had a leadership role in Partners for a Progressive
Israel and J Street, appears on a video posted on the AZM website
libeling Israel with accusations of "apartheid," "oppression," and
"occupation" while speaking at an AZM-World Zionist Organization
Combatting Antisemitism Symposium in Philadelphia.[4] After dispar-
aging Israel, much to the chagrin of many in the audience (who were
berated by leadership for voicing their dissent to such libelous accusations) but also to applause of the leftists, Dormont then warned that
if Zionists do not embrace groups like J Street, the New Israel Fund,
and Breaking the Silence—all recognized by many as anti-Zionist
organizations—we will push progressive Jews further away (as if that's
even possible). In choosing the strategy of the "big tent," AZM board

members have allowed such individuals to influence, if not control, the organization's policies and direction.

It took these four groups about a year to force me out and effectively shut down the AAHDP. The AZM's elections in June 2021 resulted in an entirely new administration dominated by progressives. In one of their first personnel decisions, they summarily fired me in the middle of the COVID-19 pandemic, despite (or more likely because of) my substantial successes, which I had detailed in a lengthy report prepared for the AZM biennial.

During my tenure as chair of the AAHDP, the committee gained momentum, interest, and excitement. It's no secret that getting different groups to work together productively is no easy task, especially on emotional and ideological matters, yet we cohered and thrived. Our monthly working meetings involved coordinating plans of action, sharing what our respective organizations were working on, and planning future endeavors. We built a webpage that functioned as an educational resource for the entire Zionist community. After several very public antisemitic events, we drafted and attempted to issue statements and press releases—although the AZM bureaucracy held up most of them due to ideological differences.

For example, the AAHDP was blocked from issuing condemnations of antisemitic comments from Rashida Tlaib, NBC News, and *Saturday Night Live* because the leftists on leadership committees would not agree to them. I've since learned that the AZM was even unable to issue a statement condemning the Ben & Jerry's boycott of Israel, recognized by the vast majority of Jews across the world as antisemitic, because of pushback by some of the leftists. American Jews cannot effectively fight BDS when those in positions of power in Jewish organizations actually support some of the defamatory ideas that are anathema to Zionism.

Our committee was abuzz with pro-Israel projects. We organized and hosted monthly educational webinars aggregating thousands of viewers and participants on critically important topics. Programs included:

- Holocaust survivors discussing their lives and Zionism.
- A noted historian discussing President Franklin Roosevelt, the Holocaust, and antisemitism.
- International experts addressing the fraud perpetuated by UNRWA.
- Esteemed experts discussing antisemitism and anti-Zionism on campus.
- Distinguished academics discussing Holocaust education and its application to contemporary manifestations of antisemitism.
- International experts discussing anti-Israel bias in the media.

A number of invitations to well-respected speakers for upcoming programs were cancelled by the new AZM leadership, embarrassing themselves and me.

We had also developed specific strategies and plans for future initiatives to combat antisemitism, anti-Zionism, and Holocaust denial, all of which were laid out in my report presented to the entire AZM board and leadership committees. The committee was ready to pursue many of our ideas, including:

- Outreach to synagogues and Jewish day schools.

- Partnering with constituent organizations, non-AZM member groups, and governmental agencies to help to move legislative initiatives through Congress (such as the Antisemitism Awareness Act), as well as other governmental proposals within various agencies (including working with the State Department's Special Envoy to Monitor and Combat Antisemitism and Israeli representatives).
- Working to form alliances with Christian Zionist groups in order to bolster the effectiveness of their pro-Israel endeavors.
- Promoting the adoption of the International Holocaust Remembrance Alliance definition of antisemitism on college campuses, media platforms, and elsewhere.
- Promoting Holocaust education as well as addressing problems in K–12 curricula.
- Providing resources and organizational support to groups that use lawfare to fight BDS and other antisemitic movements and groups.

These are exactly the things that have been so lacking in Jewish self-defense—things that any Zionist would cheer, yet they were abandoned.

And so, despite—or, again, more likely, because of—a proven and successful track record, tremendous momentum, a committee of enthusiastic participants, and an agenda that included powerful upcoming events and programs, the AAHDP was initially put on hold, and, well over a year later, appears to have been permanently shut down.[5] Our plans and initiatives will not be taking place and our year of hard work was tossed aside with disdain.

Cancel culture has arrived at the AZM. I'm out. They're in. The AAHDP is now gone.

Ironically, the theme that Richard Heideman chose for the AZM's 2021 biennial meeting, which was his final act as president of the organization, was "Moving Zionism Forward." I would argue that these four boycotting organizations are moving Zionism backwards as some of their leaders are now in powerful positions within the AZM and one of their first actions was to eliminate the AAHDP.

Once inside the big tent, these four groups came dangerously close to installing J Street, a truly powerful anti-Zionist organization that blames Israel for the conflict, as one of the AZM's newest member organizations. This effort was extremely divisive and contentious. The pro-J Street faction blocked (for a time) conservative board members from being seated. Its members even filed several frivolous lawsuits with the Zionist Supreme Court embroiling the AZM in litigation. Thankfully, they failed to open the AZM tent so wide as to let J Street inside.

The destruction of the AAHDP initiative by progressive Jews and their organizations serves as a microcosm of the state of American Jewry today. Progressive Jews in general seek to minimize or deny the bias against Israel on campus, in the media, and elsewhere. They promote critiques of Israel that they characterize as "tough love," but which, in fact, are unfair, unbalanced, factually incorrect, or just plain lies that inevitably contribute to Jew-hatred. They join with Israel's foes in singling out Israel for condemnation and employing criteria for judging the Jewish state which they refuse to use when dealing with any other country. Their message: Israel is objectively committing evil, and that this—not the treatment of women, gays, democrats, atheists, and Christians in the Muslim world—must be prioritized by those who really care about human rights. As the International Holocaust Remembrance Alliance's definition of antisemitism makes clear, using double standards to hold Israel to a level of moral scrutiny not applied to other countries is a form of antisemitism.

The takeover or weakening of the AZM by Jewish leftists is a tragedy. The AZM's board allowed this to happen, demonstrating beyond any doubt that the American Jewish community lacks the strong leadership that we so desperately need in these frightening and dangerous times. Will we find it before it's too late?

Lauri B. Regan is the New York chapter president, advisory board member, and executive board member of the Endowment for Middle East Truth (EMET), and the vice president, treasurer, and board member of Scholars for Peace in the Middle East (SPME). She also served on the board of the National Women's Committee of the Republican Jewish Coalition. The opinions herein are her own and are not expressed in her professional capacities with EMET and SPME.

---

[1] See Lauri B. Regan, "G-d Is Testing American Jews. They Are Failing," *American Thinker*, March 5, 2020. https://bit.ly/3gMqrdu.

[2] "Jewish Americans in 2020," *Pew Research Center*, May 11, 2021. https://pewrsr.ch/3U2aoqe.

[3] "AZM Antisemitism, Anti-Zionism and Holocaust Denial Project," *American Zionist Movement*. Archived October 26, 2022. https://bit.ly/3SDvA56.

[4] See "Philly's AZM-WZO Anti-Zionism & Antisemitism Symposium 2019," *American Zionist Movement*. https://bit.ly/3TDAbFN. See also AZM4Israel. "AZM-WZO PHILADELPHIA ANTI-ZIONISM & ANTISEMITISM SYMPOSIUM 2019." Filmed November 18, 2019. YouTube video, 1:42:30. Posted November 26, 2019. https://bit.ly/3sAJudI.

[5] I have been told that the new administration is in the process of developing a committee that will address anti-Zionism only (inanely taking the position

that, since other groups deal with antisemitism, there is no need for it to do so as well) and they will plan on using many of the strategies that I set forth in my report and had started to initiate within the AAHDP. As of this writing, I have not seen any indication that this proposed committee is functioning on any level.

20

DEADLY EXCHANGE, DEADLY SILENCE

AMY ROSENTHAL, M.D., AND JOSH RAVITCH

It's difficult enough to fight anti-Semitism. It's that much more challenging when Jewish leaders work to silence those who want to fight, who favor creative approaches, and who think "outside the box."

"Deadly Exchange" is an anti-Semitic campaign that blames Israeli and American Jews for police assaults on American black people.[1] It promotes the false claim[2] that American police departments that take part in counter-terrorism and leadership training in Israel are actually trained to "terrorize black and brown communities" here in America.[3] Even a cursory glance at the syllabi for these training courses should put these malicious lies to rest. Yet a campaign to push city officials to boycott the Israeli training succeeded in Durham, North Carolina, when on April 16, 2018, the city council voted to ban that city's police department from participating in the Israeli programs.[4] Durham thereby became the first, and to date only, American city to acquiesce to a Deadly Exchange campaign.

Those who led the Deadly Exchange campaign were affiliated with Jewish Voice for Peace,[5] an anti-Israel, pro-BDS organization that has partnered with anti-Semites like disgraced former Women's March leader Linda Sarsour and convicted terrorist Rasmea Odeh.[6] By explicitly promoting anti-Semitism—particularly in black and brown communities—their efforts encouraged other haters to come out *en masse*, including a member of Louis Farrakhan's Nation of Islam, Rafiq Zaidi Muhammad, who called attention to the "Synagogue of Satan that's always lingering in the background" and the "inordinate [amount of] control that some Jews have over the political system in this city."[7]

The people behind the Durham victory were encouraged to bring the campaign to its sister city, Raleigh.

As co-founders of the Jewish advocacy organization North Carolina Coalition for Israel (NCCI),[8] we were appalled to learn that Raleigh was being targeted. There had been plenty of opportunity to see the damage done in Durham, both to the Jewish community and to the overall safety and security of the city. We were part of a group that met with two Durham council members to declare our case just days before their vote, and seeing the belated, appeasing response of local Jewish institutions and the damage that resulted inspired us to form the NCCI. Following approval of the Deadly Exchange resolution, Durham was inundated with vile anti-Semitism, as posters, fliers, and swastikas popped up all around town. When NCCI board member Deborah Friedman discovered a petition for a Deadly Exchange campaign in Raleigh that had more than 700 signatures, NCCI activists felt that our Jewish community had to work together to do everything we could to avoid replicating the Durham fiasco. We reached out to other community members to bring awareness of the motion and to coordinate our efforts.

What we learned was that the JCRC and at least one other local Jewish group were, in fact, aware of the Raleigh petition, but had not shared this information with the community. Several of them had met privately with two of Raleigh's seven city council members. When asked about the meetings, they told us, "If I had to guess, it's not going to pass;" however, we knew that city council members in Durham had been dishonest with us when we met, including with some of these same Jewish community leaders, providing reassurances that the council members would not be voting to approve a resolution, then promptly voting very shortly after to approve the measure. We therefore found the guessing part to be less than reassuring.

One key lesson we've learned from our experiences with combating anti-Semitism is that no single approach is a surefire solution. If dealing with reasonable people, then quietly listening to and reasoning with them may be effective; at other times, exposing the situation to the glare of the public forum is essential, especially for elected government officials; and sometimes "calling out" and shaming particularly adamant anti-Semites is effective.

One of our NCCI members, Kathryn Wolf, was an especially strong advocate for a robust, proactive response to prevent Raleigh from following in Durham's footsteps. She wanted us to speak at the Raleigh city council meeting. The NCCI board wholeheartedly agreed. We informed other local Jewish leaders of our plans to speak at the meeting to try to coordinate activities. The pressure to silence us was acute, particularly from the local JCRC and a very small local Jewish education group that have a board member in common. There were phone calls and emails almost daily, telling us not to speak, some of them angry and threatening. We were told that if Raleigh were to pass the boycott, the fault would be deliberately and publicly laid on us. We were told that the mayor was angry that NCCI planned to speak. We were told that the JCRC didn't want us to speak or be involved in any way. We were told that it was none of our business since many of our supporters don't live in Raleigh. We were told that it shouldn't look like one fringe group battling against another. We were told we would be giving Jewish Voice for Peace undeserved press.

This response from local Jewish leaders was especially intense, but otherwise not unusual; they insisted that they were the experts when it came to handling these things. We were seen as impolite loud-mouths who should stay out of "their" business. But of course, continue to send those donations!

While we appreciated that several other Jewish institutions were working behind the scenes, we believed that speaking publicly about this issue was critically important. "Why not," we argued, "get the pro-Israel narrative out first publicly so that we don't play defense as we did in Durham?" The Raleigh Deadly Exchange petitioners were running a stealth campaign, we explained, just as they did in Durham, so why let them control the rules of engagement? As exemplified by James Garfield: "Light itself is a great corrective. A thousand wrongs and abuses that are grown in darkness disappear like owls and bats before the light of day."[9]

The pressure on NCCI to be silent continued, from a variety of directions. "If you decide to speak up, all you will be doing is opening up opportunity for Jewish Voice for Peace to present their case to the media. No one knows about the issue, so why bring it up? I see nothing good that can come out of you coming to speak up. Creating a brouhaha over a non-issue is a mistake." Another of our critics cited the Torah portion of the week, the story of Korach, who led a rebellion against the leadership of Moses, in an effort to stop us, implying that speaking publicly would divide the community.

There were efforts to demoralize us. Someone with a large distribution list let people know that he had decided to lay low. Therefore, he didn't think his people would be coming to support the speeches, so NCCI should "not expect a turnout from my list."

The attacks on NCCI from so many directions were difficult to bear and took a toll. After all, there is no science to fighting defamation. Each case needs to be assessed separately. Surely there are times when not responding turns out to be the wiser path, but we were firmly convinced that in this case, given what we knew happened in Durham, we needed to be more proactive and public in our efforts. It also saddened us to realize that if these same people had put as much effort into defending our people in public as they did in attacking us, both Durham and Raleigh would be the better for it.

In the end, we pushed forward. A nice crowd came out to support NCCI at the June 15, 2021, city council meeting.[10] We all had to endure a three-hour session together. Four of us—Amy Rosenthal,[11] Deborah Friedman,[12] Josh Ravitch,[13] and Kathryn Wolf[14]—passionately and eloquently presented our case to the council. Kathryn ended her talk with George Washington's famous promise to the Jews:

> In 1790, a promise was made to us. President George Washington sent a letter to the Hebrew congregation in Rhode Island: "May the children of the stock of Abraham who dwell in this land, continue to merit and enjoy the good will of the other inhabitants and there shall be none to make him afraid."
>
> You will have a choice. You will uphold Washington's promise or you will break it. Raleigh will judge you by your decision. America will judge you by your decision, and history will judge you too.[15]

We were pleasantly surprised to learn that the chair of the JCRC had signed up after realizing that we were not to be deterred, and he, too, spoke effectively at the council meeting.[16]

Afterward, one person who had stridently opposed us graciously reached out to congratulate us. Others who had tried to intimidate us calmed down, and we renewed most of our usual relationships. The chair of the JCRC expressed the desire to work with us in the future.

As of this writing, it has been the better part of two years since NCCI went public with our concerns. The Deadly Exchange petition is stagnating online, and no police-training boycott has been proposed to the Raleigh city council. Our hope is that the old guard institutions are learning that today's formidable challenges demand more varied and vigorous approaches in defense of our Jewish people.

Jewish activists across the country must begin to challenge inadequate, misguided, and unimaginative Jewish leaders. The lesson from Durham and Raleigh is clear: Where leadership is lacking, step up and lead. Our "leaders" might follow.

Amy Rosenthal, M.D. and *Josh Ravitch* are *co-founders of the North Carolina Coalition for Israel.*

---

[1] See https://deadlyexchange.org/.

[2] Samantha Mandeles, "'Deadly Exchange' Campaign Blaming Jews and Israel For U.S. Policing Helped Drive Wave Of Antisemitic Violence," *Legal Insurrection*, May 23, 2021. https://bit.ly/3yTfr4p.

[3] See "NCCI Battles Deadly Exchange in Raleigh," *North Carolina Coalition for Israel*, June 23, 2021. https://bit.ly/3VGiQNz.

[4] Miriam F. Elman, "Demonization: Durham NC City Council bans police exchanges with Israel," *Legal Insurrection*, April 22, 2018. https://bit.ly/3MRHVRN.

5   See "Jewish Voice for Peace (JVP)," *NGO Monitor*. https://bit.ly/32lO2fG. See also Discover the Networks, "Jewish Voice for Peace (JVP)," *The David Horowitz Freedom Center*. http://bit.ly/3pLxW4k.

6   Program for JVP's 2017 National Member Meeting. "Speakers, Schedule, & Workshops," *Jewish Voice for Peace*. Archived July 6, 2017. http://bit.ly/3j9oi8V.

7   Legal Insurrection. "Open Anti-Semitism at Durham City Council Meeting." Filmed April 16, 2018. YouTube video, 2:10. Posted April 18, 2018. https://bit.ly/3sf81o9.

8   See https://nccisrael.org.

9   James Garfield, "The Ninth Census," in *The Works of James Abram Garfield: Volume 1*, ed. Burke A. Hinsdale (Boston, MA: James R. Osgood and Co., 1882), p. 455. http://bit.ly/3YOLPiD.

10 See "Raleigh City Council meeting (June 15, 2021)," *WRAL News*. Video, 3:14:09. The relevant portion begins at 2:26:56. https://bit.ly/3MOurWT.

11 See North Carolina Coalition for Israel. "Amy Rosenthal of NCCI speaks to Raleigh City Council about Deadly Exchange, June2021." Filmed June 15, 2021. YouTube video, 1:39. Posted June 30, 2021. https://bit.ly/3yVTGRk.

12 See North Carolina Coalition for Israel. "Deborah Friedman of NCCI speaks to Raleigh City Council about Deadly Exchange, June2021." Filmed June 15, 2021. YouTube video, 1:50. Posted June 30, 2021. https://bit.ly/3ySvTle.

13 See North Carolina Coalition for Israel. "Josh Ravitch of NCCI speaks to Raleigh City Council about Deadly Exchange, June202q." Filmed June 15, 2021. YouTube video, 2:14. Posted June 30, 2021. https://bit.ly/3s9McGE.

14 See North Carolina Coalition for Israel. "NCCI Kathryn speaks before Raleigh City Council June 2021." Filmed June 15, 2021. YouTube video, 3:07. Posted June 30, 2021. https://bit.ly/3CPniRt.

15 *Ibid.*

16 See "Raleigh City Council meeting (June 15, 2021)." The relevant portion begins at 2:43:46.

21

CANADA: JEWISH LEADERS
HAVE FAILED HERE, TOO

HENRY SREBRNIK

Canada's Jews, who number just under 400,000 people, making them the fourth-largest Jewish population on the planet, suffer from a failure of leadership at a momentous moment.

In their *2018 Survey of Jews in Canada*, Keith Neuman, executive director of the Environics Institute, Rhonda Lenton, president and vice chancellor of York University, and Robert Brym, professor of sociology at the University of Toronto, asserted that Canadian Jews were a model Jewish community.

"Since World War II," they wrote, "the story of the Jewish diaspora has been dominated by historical events and social processes taking place in the United States and the former Soviet Union. In both cases, community cohesiveness is on the decline. Lost in the dominant narrative is the story of Canadian exceptionalism."[1]

They provide two important reasons. First, American Jews developed a stronger national identity than Canadians did. The United States was settled earlier and has therefore had more time for a national identity to crystallize. Moreover, American national identity was forged in an anti-colonial war—always a great unifier—while Canadian national identity emerged gradually, in tandem with the peaceful evolution of independence from Great Britain.

For these reasons, when Zionism appeared on the scene at the turn of the twentieth century, it conflicted with the American patriotism of many Jews in the United States, particularly Reform Jews, who formed by far the largest religious denomination in their country. Not so in Canada, where the Reform movement was weak. Zionism was a core element of Jewish identity for the great majority of Canadian Jews by the beginning of World War I, and thus helped to keep the forces of assimilation at bay.

The second reason for Canadian-Jewish exceptionalism is that, out of political necessity, fostering the growth of ethnic institutions has been Canadian public policy since the British conquest of New France in 1760. Part of the British strategy for dominating the French population was to help the conservative Catholic Church to maintain religious, educational, and cultural control. Two centuries later, after Canada was proclaimed a bilingual and bicultural country, numerous ethnic groups asserted that they, too, deserved official recognition and funding. The era of multiculturalism had arrived. Thus, for the past half century, state support for ethnic institutions has helped Canadian Jews to ward off assimilation.

So, has there ever been a better home for Jews than Canada? Two follow-up works, the 2021 volume *No Better Home? Jews, Canada, and the Sense of Belonging*, edited by David Koffman,[2] and 2022's *Faces in the Crowd: The Jews of Canada*, by Franklin Bialystok,[3] indeed suggest that, by certain measures, Canada might be the most socially welcoming, economically secure, and religiously tolerant country for Jews in the diaspora, past or present.

This is the "official" story; behind the scenes, it's something different. One of the main changes in Canadian politics I've noticed in recent years is the strikingly diminished political role of Canadian Jews. Their influence crested in the 1960s and '70s under Liberal Prime Minister Pierre Trudeau, when many Jews were well-known cabinet ministers. Their efficacy continued into the Stephen Harper era, when Jews began voting Conservative because of his robust defense of Israel. Irwin Cotler was probably the last important Jewish political figure. The international human rights lawyer served as Canada's minister of justice and attorney general in Liberal Paul Martin's government from 2003 to 2006.

But today? Prime Minister Justin Trudeau's Liberals are a very different bunch. You'd be hard pressed to name one important Jewish politician in Canada. If anything, the community has gone back to the pre-1960s era: once again worried about anti-Semitism, which is harder to counter now since much of it comes not from old stock Canadians, but, in many, cases from "racialized" and recent arrivals— who are the mainstay of the Liberal Party's base.

In hindsight, the country's embrace of multiculturalism, something Jews supported and fought for in the 1960s as a way of breaking the British-French monopoly of power, turned out to not be an unalloyed panacea for Jewish Canadians.

In the past few decades, the country has welcomed millions of immigrants from parts of the world where respect for the memory of the Holocaust, let alone esteem for Jews, is nearly non-existent. With no serious vetting of their attitudes whatsoever, many have brought their anti-Semitism with them.

Jews remain by far the most targeted religious group for hate crimes in Canada, according to the Canadian government's annual survey of police-reported hate crimes.[4] And Jews experienced a dangerous surge in hatred during the conflict between Israel and Hamas in May 2021. People living in predominantly Jewish neighborhoods in Toronto and Montreal were verbally and physically harassed. Rocks were thrown at attendees of a peaceful pro-Israel rally in Montreal.[5]

The spike in anti-Semitism was caused by a variety of factors. The BDS movement against Israel has whipped up hatred, not just toward the Jewish state but toward Jews in general. Likewise, the rise of populism has made Jews a target both of extreme-left and extreme-right ideologies. Throw in the proliferation of anti-Semitism on social media, and the results are toxic.

Jewish Canadian leaders are found wanting on this issue. They still largely turn a blind eye to left-wing anti-Semitism, for two reasons: Much of it comes from non-whites, and some of these leaders buy into the idea that oppressed racialized communities can't be racists. They also sometimes distinguish between "anti-Zionism" and anti-Semitism, as if the actual words matter! Both are simply hatred of Jews, in other words, what could be called "Judeopathy."[6] And they are so fixated on the benefits of immigration as a positive virtue that they can't conceive of trying to limit the entry of people who hate Jews. The present leadership is so wedded to it that they would have had a hard time opposing the entry of German Nazis in the post-war period.

Prime Minister Justin Trudeau is as "woke" as they come. He has no use for ethnic groups that aren't "BIPoC" or indigenous. Multiculturalism has metastasized into this.

Two recent episodes provide readers with the way that "anti-racist" and pro-Palestinian initiatives can quickly turn into anti-Semitism—with financial and political support from Trudeau's federal government.

Particularly notorious has been the Laith Marouf affair. In 2021, an organization known as the Community Media Advocacy Center (CMAC) received $133,000 (CAD) from the federal government to build an "anti-racism strategy" for Canadian broadcasting. Housing, Diversity, and Inclusion Minister Ahmed Hussen personally and publicly endorsed the grant to allow the CMAC to instruct federally regulated broadcasters in "diversity and inclusion." The grant was channeled to the Department of Canadian Heritage. The funds enabled the CMAC to hire a senior consultant named Laith Marouf, who promised to implement the project in a "successful and responsible" manner.[7]

But it turns out the Center is nothing but the creation and vehicle of Marouf and his wife Gretchen King. And in August of 2022, it came to light that Marouf, a Syrian Arab by birth, is a particularly disgusting anti-Semite. Any screenshot of his private Twitter account provided more than ample proof.

In one tweet, he wrote, "You know all those loud mouthed bags of human feces, aka the Jewish White Supremacists; when we liberate Palestine and they have to go back to where they come from, they will return to being low voiced bitches of thier [sic] Christian/Secular White Supremacist Masters." In another tweet, he suggested that "Jewish White Supremacists" deserve "a bullet to the head."[8] Among other claims, Marouf also asserted that Zionism is a project of "white Jews who adopted Nazism."[9]

Even after another MP had alerted Hussen to Marouf's ugly habits, it took a month for the minister to acknowledge the controversy, pledging to look into the matter. Hussen finally denounced Marouf's "unacceptable behavior," saying it "clearly goes against

CHARLES JACOBS AND AVI GOLDWASSER, EDITORS

our government's values." He condemned "antisemitism and any other form of hate" and asked the Department of Canadian Heritage, the other agency involved, to "look closely at the situation."[10] Pablo Rodriguez, the Heritage minister, then also came forward to denounce the comments that had been discovered.[11] Marouf's contract was eventually cancelled, with a promise for "guidelines" to govern funding applications. This, of course, only after Marouf had been exposed.

In fact, it turned out the Marouf scandal was far worse than suspected. More than half a million dollars has been paid out by Justin Trudeau-led Canadian governments between 2016 and 2021 to the organization fronted by Laith Marouf in the name of "anti-racism."[12]

In late November of 2022 came another scandal. An all-party group of members of parliament hosted Holocaust denier and Arabic-language newspaper publisher Nazih Khatatba at a Parliament Hill reception staged by the Canada-Palestine Parliamentary Friendship Group. This event included Trudeau's Minister of Transport, Omar Alghabra, and Liberal MP Salma Zahid, who heads the "friendship" group.[13]

Khatatba's newspaper *al-Meshwar* is notorious for having printed articles alleging that the Holocaust was a Jewish plot and has referred to it as the "Holohoax." The newspaper has also published articles claiming that Jewish bankers financed the Nazi Party and praising terrorist attacks against Jews, including a bombing in Jerusalem that killed sixteen-year-old Canadian-Israeli Aryeh Schupak.[14]

Montreal's Mahmoud Khalil was also in attendance.[15] He has posted videos of himself, overlaid with dramatic music, giving a speech at a "Glory to Our Martyrs" rally in Montreal,[16] as well as reciting a poem commemorating the late Ghassan Kanafani, a spokesperson for the Popular Front for the Liberation of Palestine (PFLP).[17]

This news came just days after the Twitter account Documenting Antisemitism reported that Nabil Nassar, the head of the Fatah Movement in Canada, had also attended the reception on Parliament Hill.[18] Nassar's June 2020 appointment to lead the Canadian branch of Palestinian Authority president Mahmoud Abbas' party was noticed—widely and with alarm—in Canada's Jewish community.[19]

Only days before his appointment, Nassar was mourning the death of Ramadan Shalah, a former leader of the terror-listed Palestinian Islamic Jihad group. He has praised terrorists such as Ali Hassan Salameh, who planned the 1972 Munich Olympics massacre (Khatatba, on the other hand, has claimed that the murder of eleven Israeli athletes in Munich was an operation undertaken by the Mossad, Israel's intelligence agency[20]). Nasser has also had kind words for Dalal al-Mughrabi, one of the terrorists involved in the 1978 slaughter of thirty-seven Israelis, including twelve children. He called her the "epitome of the Palestinian woman" and "a symbol of resistance and pride."[21]

The usual condemnations of anti-Semitism, apologies, and empty excuses were offered when this came to light, among them from MP Salma Zahid, who said that it was not possible to "research the background of every guest."[22] But there they all were with *kafiyehs* and Palestinian scarves around their necks. In any case, this was a parliamentary event and invitees are regularly researched before invitations are sent.

Why, in fact, does the federal parliament have a "Friendship Group" with a jurisdiction like the Palestinian Authority? Participant Elizabeth May, leader of the federal Green Party, also an attendee, stated that "I take my marching orders from the permanent representative of

Palestine to Canada."[23] Her "marching orders" should come from her constituents and conscience, not from foreign terrorists.

This comes against the backdrop of Canada's changing position on the issue of Palestine in the U.N. Traditionally, Canada has been one of Israel's most stalwart allies on the international stage, often voting against one-sided resolutions targeting the Jewish state; however, on December 16, 2020, Canada voted in favor of a U.N. General Assembly resolution supporting Palestinian self-determination while denouncing Israel's presence in Jerusalem, characterizing it as "occupied Palestinian territory." The resolution, co-sponsored by North Korea, also condemned Israel's security barrier by claiming that it "severely impedes the right of the Palestinian people to self-determination."[24]

The vote, which passed 168 to 5 with ten abstentions,[25] followed a preliminary vote in late November at the Third Committee where Canada also voted "yes." Canada's vote went against its own principled record over two decades in opposing the annual targeting of Israel through twenty one-sided resolutions, according to the Geneva-based U.N. Watch.

Canada's diplomats, also infected with "anti-settler" ideology, don't look too kindly on the Jewish state, according to documents released in September 2022 via Access to Information legislation and obtained by Canadians for Justice and Peace in the Middle East (CJPME), a pro-Palestinian group. The released documents cover the period leading up to Canada's 2019 decision to resume its support for Palestinian self-determination at the U.N. In this report, CJPME looks at how Canadian officials really view Canada's U.N. voting record and urges Canada to support all resolutions that aim to uphold Palestinian "human rights." Many of Canada's career foreign affairs officials maintain that too-uncritical support of Israel contradicts its own values and interests, and harms its international reputation.

The released documents include a memo from Global Affairs Canada officials who recommend that Canada end its uniformly pro-Israel approach at the U.N. In that memo, officials admit that Canada has been voting against U.N. resolutions on Palestinian rights "without considering the specific merits of each resolution," and "despite their [the Palestinians'] alignment with Canadian values, interests, and standard positions." The memo identified several votes on Jerusalem, Israeli settlements, and Palestinian refugees that would likely change if Canada were to adopt a "merit-based approach" rather than automatically opposing such motions as a package. Officials also described Canada's pro-Israel voting record as a liability to its international reputation, noting that it has "has set us apart from like-minded countries" and attracts criticism from U.N. member states. Canada's representatives to the U.N. in New York, as well as officials working on U.N. Security Council issues, had been pushing for Canada to adopt an entirely "merit-based approach" to resolutions on this issue, which would have resulted in more votes in support of Palestinians.[26]

Trudeau's own cavalier attitude toward those he considers beyond the "woke" pale was summed up perfectly during the February 2022 winter "occupation" of Ottawa's downtown by truckers protesting mask and vaccine mandates during the COVID-19 pandemic. Some in the Conservative Party were sympathetic to their cause. Trudeau, however, dismissed these peaceful, grassroots protesters and those who supported them as a fringe group of "Nazi" and racist sympathizers. These supporters included Melissa Lantsman, the Conservative MP for Thornhill, north of Toronto and the most demographically Jewish constituency in the country. And she is the granddaughter of Holocaust survivors.

During a heated parliamentary exchange in which she criticized negative comments he had made concerning truck convoy supporters, Trudeau responded this way: "…Conservative Party members can stand with people who wave swastikas. They can stand with people who wave the Confederate flag." Lantsman denounced his comments: "I think the Prime Minister should think long and hard about his own history before singling out a Jewish Member of Parliament and falsely accusing me of standing with a Swastika," she tweeted. "What a disgraceful statement unbecoming of anyone in public office—he owes me an apology."[27] The prime minister refused to do so.

There was a time in Canada country when we had a national umbrella organization, the Canadian Jewish Congress (CJC), founded in 1919.[28] It was democratically elected by ordinary Jews, and so it was called the "Parliament of Canadian Jewry." It was the envy of many American Jews, who had no equivalent.

Until the rise of the federation movement in the 1970s and '80s, the CJC stood unchallenged as the community's interlocutor with government and with the non-Jewish world. But it ceased operations in 2011, essentially due to the lack of support of the "machers" who preferred to run things via the federations they control, and where the "Jew in the street" has little input.

The CJC was replaced by a top-down organization: the Center for Israel and Jewish Affairs (CIJA). But how did the CIJA react to scandals, such as a bigot like Laith Marouf becoming a legitimized mass media "anti-racism" trainer with the Trudeau government's blessing? It accepted every excuse that Diversity Minister Ahmed Hussen gave them. In fact, it said it hadn't previously heard of Marouf. If this type of radical anti-Israel instigator isn't the kind of red flag to be monitored by a Jewish community agency, then what is? Jewish Federations in Canada funnel millions of dollars from donors to the

CIJA on the premise that they act as a watchdog for Canadian Jews. Marouf alone—amongst all the other anti-Semites the government has embraced—is proof that the CIJA flunked the test. It feared the ire of the Liberal government.

Yes, there are voices raised in protest, doing good work, including B'nai Brith, Honest Reporting Canada, and others, such as the online news site TheJ.ca. But they are drowned out by those arrayed against us, those who basically control Canada's hegemonic left-wing academic, media, and political culture, up to and including, apparently, our Ottawa leaders. I myself was even called a "Zionist goon" in an op-ed published by an "anti-Zionist" in my local Prince Edward Island newspaper for writing articles defending Israel.[29]

Today, as Jews, we are experiencing an upsurge from the anti-Semites, the media, the hate-mongers, and tenured university bigots, who publicly vilify and delegitimize diaspora Jews through carefully crafted language, using Israel as their tool to inflict hate. Yet, there is deafening silence from the Canadian Jewish community's so-called leaders. They are politically adrift. The country's Jews have become the Jews of silence. Politically homeless, they have largely retreated into their own communities.

Henry Srebrnik *is a professor of political science at the University of Prince Edward Island in Canada. He is the author of* Jerusalem on the Amur: Birobidzhan and the Canadian Jewish Communist Movement, 1924–1951, *and* Dreams of Nationhood: American Jewish Communists and the Soviet Birobidzhan Project, 1924–1951, *among other works. He also co-edited the collection* A Vanished Ideology: Essays on the Jewish Communist Movement in the English-speaking World in the Twentieth Century.

1. Robert Brym, Keith Neuman, and Rhonda Lenton, *2018 Survey in Jews in Canada* (Toronto: Environics Institute, 2019), p. 5. https://bit.ly/3VWvzvr.

2. See David S. Koffman, ed., *No Better Home?: Jews, Canada, and the Sense of Belonging* (Toronto: University of Toronto Press, 2021).

3. See Franklin Bialystok, *Faces in the Crowd: The Jews of Canada* (Toronto: University of Toronto Press, 2022).

4. See "Hate crimes surge in Canada; Jews remain leading target in 2021, as per report," *JNS*, August 8, 2022. bit.ly/3Wm5HsH.

5. David Lazarus, "Canada hit with wave of antisemitic attacks sparked by Israel-Gaza conflict," *JWeekly*, May 27, 2021. https://bit.ly/3Woanyh.

6. See Alan M. Dershowitz, *Chutzpah* (Boston, MA: Little, Brown, and Company, 1991), p. 121. "...[T]he label 'anti-Semite,' invented by anti-Semites as a proud epithet, is an inherently neutral term. It simply means those who are against Jews. It does not necessarily connote the sickness and evil inherent in such bigotry. The term 'Judeopath' would seem far more fitting. It suggests a pathological hatred of Jews and clearly puts the onus on those who hate rather than on those who are hated."

7. Peter Simonjic, "Consultant Laith Marouf's comments were 'antisemitic and xenophobic,' Ahmed Hussen says," *CBC*, August 22, 2022. https://bit.ly/3Wtn1fl.

8. Quoted in Hugh Fitzgerald, "The Anti-Semitic and Racist Tweets of a Canadian Government Consultant," *FrontPage Mag*, August 29, 2022. https://bit.ly/3Vczvad.

9. Quoted in Michael Starr, "Canada ends anti-racism program with adviser who said Zionists are 'human feces,'" *The Jerusalem Post*, August 24, 2022. https://bit.ly/3G54X64.

10. Quoted in Marie Woolf, "Ottawa to probe 'disturbing' tweets by consultant on government-funded anti-racism project," *CBC*, August 19, 2022. https://bit.ly/3hAKIUn.

11. See Woolf, "Heritage Minister Pablo Rodriguez breaks silence, condemns 'disgusting' tweets," *The Province*, August 31, 2022. https://bit.ly/3HNJjEn.

12. Tristin Hopper, "FIRST READING: The Laith Marouf antisemitism affair continues to get worse," *The National Post*, August 31, 2022. https://bit.ly/3G1HoLk.

13. Darren Major, "Attendance of man accused of antisemitism at Hill event sparks outcry from MPs, Jewish groups," *CBC*, December 2, 2022. https://bit.ly/3jiL4iH.

14 "MP denounces publisher of Holocaust denialism," *The Bradford Expositor*, December 2, 2022. https://bit.ly/3FDBvCF.

15 "Man who Called for 'Auschwitz Superhero' Attended 'Friendship Group' Gathering on Parliament Hill, B'nai Brith Discovers," *B'nai Brith Canada*, December 7, 2022. https://bit.ly/3YBAt2v.

16 "FSWC calls for defunding Montreal student groups in 'Glory to Our Martyrs' rally," *JNS*, August 11, 2022. https://bit.ly/3V4uws4.

17 Brian Passifiume, "More guests at Parliament Palestinian 'solidarity' event linked to antisemitic, pro-terrorist views," *The National Post*, December 8, 2022. https://bit.ly/3jdKmU0.

18 *Ibid.*

19 "Major Canadian Jewish Group Expresses Concern After Supporter of Terrorism Appointed Secretary of Fatah Movement in Canada," *The Algemeiner*, June 21, 2020. https://bit.ly/3V9vxiD.

20 "'I take marching orders from Palestinian rep.'—Canadian politician," *The Jerusalem Post*, December 3, 2022. https://bit.ly/3BIZf71.

21 "Major Canadian Jewish Group Expresses Concern After Supporter of Terrorism Appointed Secretary of Fatah Movement in Canada," *The Algemeiner*.

22 Passifiume, "More guests at Parliament Palestinian 'solidarity' event linked to antisemitic, pro-terrorist views."

23 "'I take marching orders from Palestinian rep.'—Canadian politician," *The Jerusalem Post*.

24 Quoted in Ron Csillag, "Canada upholds UN vote on Palestinian self-determination," *The Canadian Jewish News*, December 19, 2020. https://bit.ly/3Wzcwr3.

25 See "The right of the Palestinian people to self-determination," *UN Watch*. https://bit.ly/3VcPqoZ.

26 Quoted in Alex Cosh, "Officials Warned Canada's Pro-Israel Voting Record Not Based on 'Merit': Report," *The Maple*, September 8, 2022. https://bit.ly/3FErEN2.

27 Quoted in Tim Pearce, "Trudeau Accuses Jewish Conservative MP Of Standing 'With People Who Wave Swastikas'; Parliament Erupts," *The Daily Wire*, February 16, 2022. https://bit.ly/3uXO0nE.

28 See Henry Srebrnik, *Creating the Chupah: The Zionist Movement and the Drive for Jewish Communal Unity in Canada, 1898–1921* (Brighton, MA: Academic Studies Press, 2011).

29 See Alex Rose, "Columnist quits after being called 'Zionist goon,'" *The Canadian Jewish News*, March 13, 2019. https://bit.ly/3HO5TNd.

EPILOGUE

THE FAILURE TO FIGHT BLACK
ANTI-SEMITES, AND ITS CONSEQUENCES

CHARLES JACOBS AND BEN POSER

World events move faster than books are published. In October of 2022, as we were finalizing this collection, an avalanche of hatred came crashing down upon the already beleaguered American Jewish community. Black anti-Semitism (always smoldering) caught fire, sparked by the rapper Kanye (now "Ye") West. On October 9, West, who—before his Twitter account was suspended—had more than twice the number of followers (33.2 million) than there are Jews in the world,[1] announced that he was "going death con 3 [*sic*] on JEWISH PEOPLE."[2] Louis Farrakhan seemed to have risen from the cesspools of hate. His screeds against Jews, including his lie of lies—that "the Jews" were and are black people's eternal slave masters—has found in West the mother of all force multipliers. This is uniquely dangerous. True to form, however, establishment Jewish leadership, caught unprepared, stumbled badly.

In the following days, West elaborated: The "Jewish underground media mafia" controls America;[3] Jews detest traditional family values;[4] "Jewish Zionists" corrupted his ex-wife Kim Kardashian's sexual morals;[5] and "Jewish people" have "owned the Black voice" and "milk us 'til we die."[6] Echoing Stalin, he also accused his Jewish doctor of trying to murder him.[7]

Jew-hatred suddenly became even more acceptable. White supremacists mobilized, rushing to endorse West's bipolar rants, and launched a full-throated Internet crusade in his name. Social media mobs swung into action, attacking Jews online. Neo-Nazis appeared in the flesh with a banner above the Los Angeles 405 proclaiming "Kanye is right about the Jews."[8] "Ye is right" graffiti cropped up in too many places: spray-painted on a Jewish gravestone[9] and written on the hats of passengers on a Southwest Airlines flight.[10]

Just weeks after West's delusional tirades, Kyrie Irving, the Brooklyn Nets basketball star, tweeted a link to *Hebrews to Negroes: Wake Up Black America*,[11] a Holocaust-denying film promoting the lunatic theory that American blacks are the "real" Jews, while those who call themselves Jews today are satanic, "white" imposters who contrived to steal blacks' true, honorable identity as the Children of Israel. After the Nets' owners temporarily suspended Irving—before trading him to the Dallas Mavericks—Louis Farrakhan warned "Jewish people" to leave Irving and his friend[12] "Brother Ye" alone, as they spoke the "truth."[13] Ten days later, on the occasion of Irving's first game after his suspension, hundreds of uniformed Black Hebrew Israelites, whose ideology the film propagates, marched in military fashion down to the Barclay Center chanting "Time to wake up!" and "We are the real Jews!"[14] Commonly dismissed as a minor annoyance until members murdered Orthodox Jews at both a kosher grocery store[15] and a Chanukah prayer meeting[16] in 2019, elements of the Black Hebrew Israelite cult have been preaching their message of violence[17] and racism[18] on street corners across America for decades.

Not a week after the Black Hebrews marched, former President Donald Trump—in a bizarre move for the grandfather of Jewish grandchildren—invited West for dinner at Mar-a-Lago. Kanye brought with him virulent Jew-hater Nick Fuentes, a white supremacist Internet troll and casual Holocaust denier.[19] Then, soon after praising Hitler (multiple times) on Alex Jones' *InfoWars* show,[20] West tweeted a picture of a swastika embedded within a Star of David.[21]

Yet, through it all, Jewish leaders emerged impotent, especially when it came to dealing with black anti-Semites. The Anti-Defamation League (ADL) looked like it was selling indulgences and absolution as it exchanged its "forgiveness" for a $500,000 donation from Kyrie Irving.[22] The ADL then had to reject the money after Irving refused to say he no longer believed that blacks were the real Jews.[23]

The ADL did condemn West,[24] but this could more easily be explained by West's ties to Trump than his animus against Jews. After all, the ADL does not typically campaign against people just because they are enemies of the Jews. It does not, for example, organize campaigns against Democratic politicians like Rashida Tlaib and Ilhan Omar who slander Jews and Israel,[25] nor does it condemn imams for spewing genocidal Jew-hatred from mosques across America.[26]

In fact, the ADL plainly avoids "inconvenient" Jew-hatred. It has had an unstated policy which minimizes Jew-hatred stemming from the left, from blacks, and from Muslims, though we caught a glimpse of its thinking at a 2019 congressional hearing on "hate crimes." At the hearing, the Zionist Organization of America's Mort Klein used the ADL's own worldwide polling data to explain to the House Judiciary Committee that Islamic Jew-hatred is a clear and present danger.[27] Klein cited ADL polls showing that 34 percent of American Muslims[28] and 49 percent of Muslims worldwide hate Jews,[29] and that Muslim societies around the globe are more anti-Jewish than any other. Feeling pressed to respond, the ADL's Eileen Hershenov,[30] a senior vice president for "democracy initiatives," sought to clarify her organization's policy toward different groups who hate Jews.[31] Speaking before the committee, she let the cat out of the bag:

> Um, one of the [previous] witnesses [Klein] talked about global—the global attitudes that we look at. That's non-violent—looking at attitudes—and the ADL does track that. We feel it is incumbent—vulnerable, marginalized—marginalized, ah, communities have bigotry within them.[32]

American Muslims, then—and, by extension, American blacks, whom the ADL also classes as "vulnerable" and "marginalized"— would seem to have little to fear from the ADL when they go about defaming Jews.

This policy from the ADL, the "Defense Department of the Jewish community," to tip-toe around Jew-hatred coming from these sources, has become the standard practice for nearly all other establishment Jewish organizations. It is most apparent among the Jewish Federations and JCRCs, whose long-standing relationships with local minority communities put them in an excellent position to raise and explore the problem of Jew-hatred with their supposed allies. But this is typically not done. Interestingly, the ADL doesn't seem to consider Jews a vulnerable minority.

Why ignore Jew-hatred from minority groups? In general terms, the Jewish establishment has clung to an idealized past reality which, in any case, has come undone. The classical liberalism which once included and sheltered the Jews as one minority amongst all others within an imperfect but blessed nation has been defeated in most cultural institutions by a "woke" progressivism which has flipped the game board. America is now more often seen as an inherently evil society composed of just two groups: oppressors and oppressed. Within this framework, the Jews are placed in the "oppressor" box, classed as "adjacent whites," privileged by their white skin and, often, living off ill-gotten wealth. Jews like journalist Bari Weiss and David Bernstein, president of the Jewish Institute for Liberal Values, have understood this conceptual revolution and are rallying decent liberals to fight back, but establishment Jewish leaders seem neither to have understood nor adapted to the alarming new reality.

Louis Farrakhan—also known as "Calypso Louie"—has spent the better part of seventy years trying to convince black Americans that it was primarily not white Europeans but the Jews who controlled the trans-Atlantic slave trade and, thus, are ultimately responsible for the agonies of black history. This culminated in the publication in 1991 of a *Protocols of the Elders of Zion*-type forgery called *The Secret Relationship Between Blacks and Jews*. Written by the Nation of Islam's "Historical Research Department," the book's effect on the community remained unclear for years, as far more people imbibed its contention than actually read it. Now, however, with the help of Kanye West's social media power, that calumny reaches an audience of tens of millions where it is repeated and rehearsed.

For its part, the ADL has failed to respond effectively to the potentially lethal lies of Farrakhan and other black Jew-haters. The simplest response to Farrakhan's Jewish slavers lie is to expose it as yet another in a long line of blood libels against Jews. That is precisely what Jewish scholars and their black allies did when the book first emerged: Harvard's Henry Louis Gates, Jr.,[33] and the late Simon Wiesenthal Center scholar Harold Brackman,[34] among others, did just that. They showed that every people and all major religions participated in the enslavement of human beings: Romans, Greeks, Egyptians, Christians, Muslims, Jews, and, of course, the black tribal chiefs themselves, who captured their fellow Africans and sold them to the slavers. It is true that some Jews did participate in the slave trade, but, according to the actual historical evidence, Jews as a whole played a microscopic part. This is an easily documentable truth.[35] Still, Farrakhan's book has undeniable emotional power: it provides granular detail of individual Jewish owners selling black women and children.[36] The NOI book employs the same "zoom lens" treatment that anti-Zionist propagandists use when they focus on an Israeli response to an act of Arab aggression without the surrounding context. Here, Farrakhan is proudly holding up a handful of "Jewish" sand on the vast beach of non-Jewish complicity in slavery to "prove" that "the Jews" ran the African slave trade.

Jewish leadership, therefore, needs to educate the public about the evil Farrakhan enables in Africa. This would require Jewish leaders to go on the offense, and speak a powerful truth that Farrakhan has actively worked to hide from his followers. For centuries and even today, as you read this, Arabs and Muslims capture, buy, sell, torture, and sometimes even breed blacks in at least five African nations: Algeria, Libya, Mauritania, Nigeria, and Sudan.

In Algeria and Libya, migrants *en route* to Europe, mainly fleeing poverty and violence in Niger and Nigeria, are captured by local Arabs who sell them into bondage.[37] In 2017, CNN released chilling video of a slave auction where two black men were sold for $400 apiece.[38]

Mauritania, a majority black country, is an apartheid state ruled by its 20 percent Arab-Berber minority. A 2011 CNN investigation estimated that between 340,000 and 680,000 blacks were still owned as slaves—between 10 percent and 20 percent of the entire population of 3.4 million.[39] These slaves—subjected in the past to horrific tortures when deemed "uppity"[40]—are their masters' property, passed down through his estate like the furniture. Anti-Slavery International[41] and the U.S. State Department's 2021 human rights report[42] confirm that slavery persists in Mauritania.

In Nigeria, the Islamic terrorist organization Boko Haram engages in raids on village schools in which mostly Christian children are taken for use as slaves. The girls are "married" off as concubines[43] and the boys trained as child soldiers.[44] Some of this horror came to widespread attention when Michelle Obama (briefly) championed the cause of the 276 girls kidnapped as sex slaves in 2014,[45] launching the #BringBackOurGirls Twitter hashtag.[46] More recently, an entire human rights campaign run in the U.S. by Nigerian Americans has grown up around Leah Sharibu,[47] a Christian girl kidnapped by Boko Haram in 2018 and made a "slave for life" for refusing to convert to Islam.[48]

And, in Sudan, of the estimated 200,000 black women and children captured between 1983 and 2005 in a genocidal *jihad* by the Arab Muslim north against the Christian south,[49] perhaps 35,000 remain enslaved today.[50] Forcibly converted to Islam, the little boys were made goatherds, the women and girls used as domestics and concubines.[51]

As it has in the past, educating the American public about Arabs and Muslims enslaving blacks today might stoke efforts to emancipate blacks in bondage whom history has left behind. In the 1990s, Farrakhan and the NOI passionately opposed those efforts and attacked those who helped to free black slaves.[52]

Does the ADL not understand why Farrakhan needs to hide these atrocities from American blacks? Reports about Arabs and Muslims enslaving black Africans pose a frontal challenge to Farrakhan's core message that Islamic civilization is superior, especially in racial tolerance, to American civilization. Such truths might do irreparable damage to his mission, which is to convince black Americans that Islam is the only true path to black liberation.

In addition, Farrakhan has an embarrassing financial relationship with the Arab world. In 1984, he received $5 million from the late Libyan dictator Colonel Muammar al-Qaddafi.[53] In 1996, Qaddafi pledged him another $1 billion, which the Clinton administration blocked.[54] This, even though black slavery flourished throughout Libya under Qaddafi's rule.[55]

Farrakhan is not the champion of blacks he claims to be. During the war and the slave raids in Sudan, Farrakhan met with black Sudanese leaders who were fending off Khartoum's *jihad*. One of them, Steven Wöndu, wrote that Farrakhan personally promised the South Sudanese that he would support them, his fellow blacks, over the Arabs, his fellow Muslims, but then he reneged, later urging the Sudanese Christians to surrender and convert to Islam.[56]

Farrakhan remains as vulnerable to exposure today as he was in the 1990s when he taunted the American media to prove that there is slavery in Sudan.[57] In response, *The Baltimore Sun* sent reporters to Sudan where they documented the slavery and helped to free enslaved children. The *Sun*'s Pulitzer-nominated frontpage series was presented as an answer to Farrakhan's hubristic challenge.[58] Soon after, Farrakhan mostly shut up and retreated.

Not surprisingly, the ADL is AWOL. Farrakhan's followers beat, intimidate, and harass Jews on the streets of New York.[59] Why wouldn't Jewish leaders do everything they can to diminish him and his message? Why have they refused to aggressively tell the simple truth: that it's not the Jews, but Farrakhan's Muslim friends and co-religionists, who own and have owned black slaves? Why have they refused to show that Farrakhan sold out African blacks to protect his co-religionists and his proselytizing mission?

Can it be because the ADL, in similar fashion, is selling out the Jews to protect its leftist politics? The ADL's politicized ideology is sacrificing Jewish interests in order to prioritize "progressive" causes. In a parallel fashion, the ADL refuses to present the undeniable, documented facts about today's Arab slaving as a challenge to the "intersectionalists" whose anti-Jewish concepts have become a core part of the social justice movement. "Intersectionality" has Arabs and Muslims allied with blacks as "oppressed victims" who are meant to fiercely oppose their "oppressors"—mostly whites, and now also Jews. Perhaps, just as Black Lives Matter famously demanded prospective white allies to "acknowledge" their "privilege" before joining the movement,[60] why should blacks not know that, as a condition of joining BLM, Arab and Muslim Americans must first be pressed to denounce their kin and co-religionists' enslavement of blacks?

The ADL's failure to fight black anti-Semitism is a telling and unforgivable betrayal. Its leadership, board, and major donors must be held accountable for the immense damage their actions and inactions are causing.

Charles Jacobs has, over four decades, founded, co-founded, and led several Jewish and human rights organizations, including the American Anti-Slavery Group, the David Project, Americans for Peace and Tolerance, and the Boston branch of the Committee for Accuracy in Middle East Reporting and Analysis (CAMERA). In 2000, he received Boston's Freedom Award from Coretta Scott King for his work in helping to liberate thousands of black slaves in Sudan.[61] *In 2007,* The Forward *named him as among America's top fifty Jewish leaders.*[62] *He holds a doctorate in Education from Harvard University. Today, Charles and Avi Goldwasser lead the Jewish Leadership Project.*

Ben Poser has worked as the research director for the Jewish Leadership Project and associate director of the American Anti-Slavery Group. He is now executive editor of White Rose Magazine.

---

[1] See Lee Brown, "Kanye West suspended from Twitter after swastika post," *The New York Post*, December 2, 2022. https://bit.ly/3jt94jr. See also Itamar Eichner, "On Rosh Hashanah, global Jewish population reaches 15.3 million," *Ynet News*, September 26, 2022. http://bit.ly/3hGf2wz.

[2] Quoted in Jeff Charles, "On Kanye West and Antisemitism," *RedState*, October 10, 2022. https://bit.ly/3I5qZXB. The media consensus is that West meant to write "defcon 3," a military term referring to one of five progressive levels of military alert.

[3] Quoted in Brown, "Kanye West claims 'Jewish underground media mafia' out to get him in Chris Cuomo interview," *The New York Post*, October 18, 2022. https://bit.ly/3zA5yc7.

[4] See Jonah Cohen, "The Lust Libel: Sexual Antisemitism in History and Contemporary Culture," *Fathom Journal* (November 2022). https://bit.ly/3GionEx.

[5] Quoted in Gadi Zaig, "Kanye says 'Jewish Zionists' control the media, Jews own the Black voice," *The Jerusalem Post*, October 17, 2022. https://bit.ly/3fgCSOF.

[6] Ibid.

7   "Kanye West alleges Jewish doctor might have wanted him dead," *The Jerusalem Post*, October 31, 2022. https://bit.ly/3WHVtmF.

8   "Antisemites hang banner over LA freeway declaring Kanye 'right about the Jews,'" *The Times of Israel*, October 23, 2022. http://bit.ly/3hDIjbc.

9   Brown, "Jewish cemetery in Illinois vandalized with swastikas, 'Kanye was rite' message," *The New York Post*, November 17, 2022. https://bit.ly/3jwrv6D.

10 "Antisemitism in the air: Southwest Airlines passenger dons 'Ye is right' Burger King crown," *JNS*, December 8, 2022. https://bit.ly/3jwrGij.

11 Brian Lewis and Brian Wacker, "Kyrie Irving raises eyebrows with tweet to movie filled with anti-Semitic disinformation," *The New York Post*, October 28, 2022. https://bit.ly/3WosioZ.

12 See Christine Thomasos, "Kanye West, Kim Kardashian West Meet With Minister Louis Farrakhan," *The Christian Post*, February 3, 2015. https://bit.ly/3POM4rj.

13 "The Honorable Minister Louis Farrakhan Addresses The Ye (formerly 'Kanye West') & Kyrie Irving Controversy," *The Final Call*, November 15, 2022. https://bit.ly/3PRuRNI. See also MEMRI TV Videos. "Nation of Islam Leader Louis Farrakhan on Kyrie Irving, Kanye West Antisemitism Scandals." Filmed November 10, 2022. YouTube video, 4:22. Posted November 15, 2022. https://bit.ly/3QjCiha.

14 Louise Keene, "As Black Hebrew Israelite group gathers outside arena, Kyrie Irving returns to NBA court," *The Forward*, November 20, 2022. https://bit.ly/3u98Tfj.

15 See Georgett Roberts, "Jersey City shooters attended Black Hebrew Israelite church in NYC," *The New York Post*, December 12, 2019. https://bit.ly/3WFP1fV.

16 See Patrick Dunleavy, "Monsey Attacker Praised Black Hebrew Israelite Movement," *Investigative Project on Terrorism*, December 31, 2019. http://bit.ly/3ITIOtc.

17 See David Edwards, "Man with Bible threatens to rape woman during 'Gay Day' in Michigan," *The Raw Story*, August 9, 2012. Archived August 9, 2012. https://bit.ly/3YHJbwt.

18 See James Idoine. "RACIST Street Preachers Funniest Moments." Filmed c. 2013. YouTube video, 7:02. Posted July 1, 2014. https://bit.ly/3hSrXf2.

19 See "Nicholas J. Fuentes: Five Things to Know," *Anti-Defamation League*, July 8, 2021. https://bit.ly/3YMIvG3.

20 Ariel Zilber, "Hooded Kanye West praises Nazis during Alex Jones interview: 'I see good things about Hitler,'" *The New York Post,* December 1, 2022. https://bit.ly/3WElCTX.

21 See Brown, "Kanye West suspended from Twitter after swastika post." The exact design West tweeted is commonly used by anti-Israel, pro-terrorist protesters. See Alexander Robertson, "Jeremy Corbyn in fresh anti-Semitism row as photos emerge of him at rally likening Israel to Nazi Germany with activists holding banner showing Star of David turned into a SWASTIKA," *The Daily Mail*, August 1, 2019. https://bit.ly/3WoDbHk.

22 "Kyrie Irving to donate $500,000 to anti-hate groups, admits to 'negative impact' of promoting antisemitic film," *CBS News,* November 2, 2022. https://bit.ly/3Vi6km8.

23 Jordan Dixon-Hamilton, "Anti-Defamation League Rejects Kyrie Irving's $500,000 Donation," *Breitbart*, November 4, 2022. https://bit.ly/3PVdxHW.

24 See "Ye (Kanye West): What You Need to Know," *Anti-Defamation League,* October 31, 2022. https://bit.ly/3PVYUnt.

25 See Seth Mandel, "The Jews Who Are Complicit in Jew-Hatred," *Commentary*, July–August, 2021. https://bit.ly/3GfZqJY.

26 Mohammed al-Adzee, "Antisemitism In Sermons In U.S. Mosques," *Middle East Media Research Institute*, November 8, 2021. https://bit.ly/3Lvrkm3.

27 See apeacet. "ZOA President Mort Klein Tells Congress: Islamic Jew-Hatred Threatens American Jews (April 9, 2019)." Filmed April 9, 2019. YouTube video, 7:46. Posted April 9, 2019. https://bit.ly/3PQ6wYO.

28 "In First, New ADL Poll Finds Majority of Americans Concerned About Violence Against Jews and Other Minorities, Want Administration to Act," *Anti-Defamation League*, April 5, 2017. https://bit.ly/3PPFEIl.

29 "ADL Poll of Over 100 Countries Finds More Than One-Quarter of Those Surveyed Infected With Anti-Semitic Attitudes," *Anti-Defamation League*, May 13, 2014. https://bit.ly/3FVvYaM.

30 For more information about Eileen Hershenov, see Daniel Greenfield, "Why the ADL Abandoned Antisemitism and Went Woke," *Sultan Knish*, December 20, 2022. https://bit.ly/3FSyfDu.

31 "Eileen Hershenov's Testimony before the House Judiciary Committee on Hate Crimes and the Rise of White Nationalism," *Anti-Defamation League*, April 9, 2019. https://bit.ly/3jpP4hA.

32 Quoted as said. For isolated remarks, see apeacet. "ADL Official Tries to Explain Away the ADL's Own Research (April 9, 2019)." Filmed April 9, 2019. YouTube video, 0:19. Posted November 4, 2019. https://bit.ly/3yNzQG9.

33 See Henry Louis Gates, Jr., "Black Demagogue and Pseudo-Scholars," *The New York Times*, July 20, 1992. https://nyti.ms/2XOS2iu.

34 For a complete refutation of *The Secret Relationship,* see Dr. Harold Brackman, *Ministry of Lies: The Truth Behind the Nation of Islam's "The Secret Relationship Between Blacks and Jews"* (New York, NY: Four Walls Eight Windows, 1994). https://bit.ly/3VnAEfc.

35 See, for example, Eli Faber, *Jews, Slaves, and the Slave Trade: Setting the Record Straight* (New York, NY: New York University Press, 1998).

36 See Historical Research Department of the Nation of Islam, *The Secret Relationship Between Blacks and Jews*, Volume 1 (Boston, MA: Latimer Associates, 2006), pp. 72–73, 141, 162–163. https://bit.ly/3PVTfxQ.

37 Nellie Payton, "African migrants report torture, slavery in Algeria," *Reuters*, May 30, 2018. https://reut.rs/3KIgcSq.

38 Nima Elbagir, Raja Razek, Alex Pratt, and Bryony Jones, "People for sale: Where lives are auctioned for $400," CNN, November 14, 2017. https://cnn.it/2wBu12O.

39 John D. Sutter and Edythe McNamee, "Slavery's last stronghold," CNN, March 2012. https://cnn.it/2pi1NGT.

40 See Africa Watch, *Mauritania: Slavery: Alive and Well, 10 After it was Last Abolished* (New York, NY: Human Rights Watch, June 29, 1990), pp. 14–17. https://bit.ly/3hcvfEU.

41 See "Mauritania: descent-based slavery," *Anti-Slavery International.* https://bit.ly/3FVcuCW.

42 "2021 Country Reports on Human Rights Practices: Mauritania," *United States State Department*, April 12, 2022. http://bit.ly/3q6gKbl.

43 "Marriage or slavery? For girls abducted by Boko Haram, suicide bombings an escape," *Mainichi Shinbun*, April 4, 2018. https://bit.ly/2N7CMqb.

44 Audu Bulama Bukarti, "Nigeria's Child Veterans Are Still Living a Nightmare," *Foreign Policy,* August 15, 2019. https://bit.ly/35TVxWK.

45 "Nigeria Chibok abductions: What we know," *BBC News*, May 8, 2017. https://bbc.in/2o9yZ3c.

46 First Lady–Archived (@FLOTUS44). Twitter post. May 7, 2014. 5:03 P.M. https://bit.ly/3FTtDNA.

47 See Brandon Showalter, "Leah Sharibu held captive over 1,500 days in Nigeria, but family advocates haven't lost hope," *The Christian Post,* June 2, 2022. https://bit.ly/3BdB3tX.

48 Gary Lane, "Terrorists Spare Nigerian Christian Schoolgirl Leah Sharibu, Will Instead Make Her a 'Slave for Life,'" *CBN News*, October 15, 2018. https://bit.ly/3WN8cVp.

49 "Report of the International Eminent Persons Group: Slavery, Abduction and Forced Servitude in Sudan," *United States State Department*, May 22, 2002. Archived July 31, 2016. https://bit.ly/3mkY8BV.

50 Paul Vallely, "Independent Appeal: One man's search for the lost slaves of Africa," *The Independent*, December 12, 2006. https://bit.ly/32IUcjE.

51 See "CSI in South Sudan: The Faces of Slavery," *Tumblr*. https://csi-usa. tumblr.com.

52 In the 1990s, I, Charles Jacobs, led an organization called the American Anti-Slavery Group which worked to raise awareness of modern-day black slavery in North Africa, and raise money to free the slaves. We helped the Zürich-based human rights charity Christian Solidarity International, which liberated tens of thousands of women and girls from *jihad* slave masters in Sudan, and were awarded the Boston Freedom Award by Coretta Scott King. Ironically, when the news of this atrocity broke in the black community press, Farrakhan and his minions accused us of being part of a "Jewish conspiracy" aided by—of all things—the ADL.

53 George E. Curry, "Farrakhan Reveals Loan from Libya," *The Chicago Tribune*, May 3, 1985. Archived March 8, 2021. https://bit.ly/3oyzq30.

54 Richard W. Stevenson, "Officials to Block Qaddafi Gift to Farrakhan," *The New York Times*, August 28, 1996. https://nyti.ms/2Yj3IZM.

55 Augustine Abulu Lado and Betty A. Hinds, "Where Slavery isn't History," *The Washington Post*, October 17, 1993. https://wapo.st/3fTn3Ka. See also Irene Díaz de Aguilar Hidalgo, "The Niger-Libya migration route. An odyssey shaped by Saharan connections and European fears, 2000–2017," *Instituto Español de Estudios Estratégicos*, January 15, 2018. https://bit. ly/2E4Sr74.

56 Steven K. Wöndu, "Louis Farrakhan: Tormenting the Heart of Africa," *The Sudan Democratic Gazette* (March 1998). https://bit.ly/2Z3zStI.

57 See American Anti-Slavery Group. "Louis Farrakhan Denies the Existence of Slavery in Sudan (March 14, 1996)." Filmed March 14, 1996. YouTube video, 0:15. Posted April 18, 2019. https://bit.ly/2Z4Qq4B.

58 See Gilbert A. Lewthwaite and Gregory P. Kane, "Where children live in bondage," *The Baltimore Sun*, June 16–18, 1996. https://bit.ly/3hlzGg0.

59 Snejana Farberov, "Anti-Semitic hate crimes in NYC soared 125 percent in November: NYPD," *The New York Post*, December 6, 2022. https://bit. ly/3jjkRRa. See also David Israel, "NYPD: Hate Crimes Against Jews Up 409%," *The Jewish Press*, March 9, 2022. https://bit.ly/3dpIyEO.

[60] See Kelsey Smoot, "White people say they want to be an ally to Black people. But are they ready for sacrifice?", *The Guardian*, June 29, 2020. https://bit.ly/3C1io4B.

[61] See American Anti-Slavery Group. "CBS WBZ 4 News New England: Dr. Charles Jacobs (September 24, 2000)." Filmed September 24, 2000. YouTube video, 6:55. Posted June 28, 2019. https://bit.ly/3D8VWXZ.

[62] "*Forward* 50, 2007," *The Forward*, November 2007. Archived January 8, 2009. https://bit.ly/3CLR3UA.

ABOUT THE EDITORS

Charles Jacobs has, over four decades, founded, co-founded, and led several Jewish and human rights organizations, including the American Anti-Slavery Group, the David Project, Americans for Peace and Tolerance, and the Boston branch of the Committee for Accuracy in Middle East Reporting and Analysis (CAMERA). In 2000, he received Boston's Freedom Award from Coretta Scott King for his work in helping liberate thousands of black slaves in Sudan. In 2007, the *Forward* named him as among America's top fifty Jewish leaders. He holds a doctorate in Education from Harvard University.

A vi Goldwasser is a social activist and film producer. He is a co-founder of the David Project, which was established to support Jewish students on campuses. He has served on the board of directors of several Jewish organizations including the Boston branch of the American Jewish Committee (AJC), the Boston Jewish Community Relations Council (JCRC), and Bureau of Jewish Education (BJE). Goldwasser has produced several films, including the award-winning documentary *The Forgotten Refugees* (2005), *The J Street Challenge: The Seductive Allure of Peace in Our Time* (2014), and several campus-related films including *Columbia Unbecoming* (2004) and *Hate Spaces: The Politics of Intolerance on Campus* (2016).

Made in United States
Orlando, FL
03 June 2025

61807529R00177